$ 25.00

D0442108

San Diego Christian College
2100 Greenfield Drive
El Cajon, CA 92019

Render to Caesar

270.1
B915r

Render to Caesar

*Jesus, the Early Church, and
the Roman Superpower*

CHRISTOPHER BRYAN

OXFORD
UNIVERSITY PRESS

2005

OXFORD
UNIVERSITY PRESS

Oxford University Press, Inc., publishes works that further
Oxford University's objective of excellence
in research, scholarship, and education.

Oxford   New York
Auckland   Cape Town   Dar es Salaam   Hong Kong   Karachi
Kuala Lumpur   Madrid   Melbourne   Mexico City   Nairobi
New Delhi   Shanghai   Taipei   Toronto

With offices in
Argentina   Austria   Brazil   Chile   Czech Republic   France   Greece
Guatemala   Hungary   Italy   Japan   Poland   Portugal   Singapore
South Korea   Switzerland   Thailand   Turkey   Ukraine   Vietnam

Copyright © 2005 by Oxford University Press, Inc.

Published by Oxford University Press, Inc.
198 Madison Avenue, New York, New York 10016

Oxford is a registered trademark of Oxford University Press

All rights reserved. No part of this publication may be reproduced,
stored in a retrieval system, or transmitted, in any form or by any means,
electronic, mechanical, photocopying, recording, or otherwise,
without the prior permission of Oxford University Press.

ISBN-10: 0-19-518334-7

Printed in the United States of America

Wendy
Amatissimae

Acknowledgments

From time to time I hear horror stories of academic life, of unsupportive colleagues and common room jealousies—and when I do, I think how fortunate my own experience has been. I have always found colleagues eager to assist in the scholarly enterprise, willing, whenever I brought a question to them, to lay aside whatever they were doing, and eager to share whatever they knew. I only hope that I have been as good and generous a colleague in return. In connection with the present undertaking, I am deeply aware not only of the general debt that I owe to all my teachers and mentors from the beginning but also of clear and specific debts to present friends and colleagues. I am grateful to Paul D. Hanson and Robert W. Jenson, both of whom were kind enough to read through my work at a crucial stage in the writing, and make important suggestions. I am grateful to William S. Stafford for his kindness and support. I am grateful to Mark A. Christian and William J. Danaher, Jr. for their interest in what I was doing, and for their fruitful suggestions. I am grateful to James W. Dunkly, who, as always, has supported and encouraged me from his broad and profound acquaintance with the world of theological and scholarly discourse. I am grateful to Ellen Bradshaw Aitken, who is at all times a good friend and a gracious conversation partner. I am grateful to my research assistant Kimberly L. Still for checking so many references and preparing the indices—a wearisome task, but done with grace and meticulous care. I am grateful to Shawn Horton for generally drawing my attention to what I ought to be doing, and from time to time enabling me to look a good deal more efficient than I actually am. I am grateful to Vicki Burgess, who read the page proofs and saved me from several blunders. I am grateful to Cynthia Read and all her colleagues at the Oxford University Press for their meticulous work, and especially for the fact that they do not go mad when I rewrite several chapters late in the process. I am grateful to Wendy, who continues to put up with all my nonsense, as well as leavening it with a healthy dose of her own compassion and good sense. I offer this book to her as a small sign of my love.

Christopher Bryan
Ordination of Florence Li Tim-Oi,
2005

Contents

Abbreviations

ANRW	*Aufstieg und Niedergang der Römanischen Welt*
BD	F. Blass and A. Debrunner, *A Greek Grammar of the New Testament and Other Early Christian Literature*, Robert W. Funk, trans. Chicago: University of Chicago Press, 1961
BDAG	Bauer, Walter, Frederick William Danker, William F. Arndt, and F. W. Gingrich, *A Greek-English Lexicon of the New Testament and Other Early Christian Literature*. Chicago and London: University of Chicago Press, 2000.
CBQ	*Catholic Biblical Quarterly*
HTR	*Harvard Theological Review*
ICC	International Critical Commentary
IEJ	*Israel Exploration Journal*
ILS	*Inscriptiones Latinae Selectae*, H. Dassau, ed. 3 vols. Berlin: Weidmann, 1892–1916.
JRS	*Journal of Roman Studies*
JSNTSup.	Journal for the Study of the New Testament—Supplement Series
JSOTSS	Journal for the Study of the Old Testament—Supplement Series
JSPSS	Journal for the Study of the Pseudepigrapha—Supplement Series
NIB	New Interpreters Bible

NRSV	New Revised Standard Version
NTS	*New Testament Studies*
SBT	Studies in Biblical Theology
SIG	W. Dittenberger, *Sylloge inscriptionum graecarum*, 4 vols., 3rd ed. (Leipzig: Hirzel, 1915–24; repr. Hildesheim and New York Olms, 1960)
SNTSMS	Society for New Testament Studies Monograph Series
SP	Sacra Pagina
SPCK	Society for Promoting Christian Knowledge
STR	*Sewanee Theological Review*
WBC	Word Biblical Commentary
WUNT	Wissenschaftliche Untersuchungen zum Neuen Testament
ZNW	*Zeitschrift für die neutestamentliche Wissenschaft*

Render to Caesar

Prologue

By virtue of the law, that a people which becomes a state
absorbs its neighbours who are in political infancy, and a
civilized people absorbs its neighbours who are in intellectual infancy—by virtue of this law, which is universally
valid and as much a law of nature as the law of gravity—
the Italian nation (the only one in antiquity to combine a
superior political development and a superior civilization,
though it presented the latter only in an imperfect and external manner) was entitled to reduce to subjection the
Greek states of the east which were ripe for destruction,
and to dispossess the peoples of lowest grades of culture in
the west—Libyans, Iberians, Celts, Germans—by means of
its settlers. . . . It is the imperishable glory of the Roman
democracy or monarchy—for the two coincide—to have
correctly apprehended and vigorously realized this its highest destination.
—Theodor Mommsen, *The History of Rome*[1]

Excudent alii spirantia mollius aera
(credo equidem), vivos ducent de marmore vultus,
orabunt causas melius, caelique meatus
describent radio et surgentia sidera dicent:
tu regere imperio populos, Romane, memento
(hae tibi erunt artes), pacique imponere morem,
parcere subiectis et debellare superbos.
[Others, I doubt not, shall with softer mould beat out the
breathing bronze, coax from the marble features to the life,
plead cases with greater eloquence and with a pointer trace
heaven's motions and predict the rising of the stars; you,
Roman, be sure to rule the world (be these your arts), to

crown peace with justice, to spare the vanquished and
crush the proud.]
—Virgil, *Aeneid* 6. 847–53, H. Rushton Fairclough, trans.

As I shall be using the term, "imperialism" means the
practice, the theory, and the attitudes of a dominating metropolitan center ruling a distant territory; "colonialism,"
which is almost always a consequence of imperialism, is
the implanting of settlements on distant territory. . . . In
our time, direct colonialism has been largely ended; imperialism, as we shall see, lingers where it has always been,
in a kind of general cultural sphere as well as in specific
political, ideological, economic, and social practices. Neither imperialism nor colonialism is a simple act of accu-
mulation and acquisition. Both are supported and perhaps
even impelled by impressive ideological formations that include notions that certain territories and people *require* and
beseech domination: the vocabulary of classic nineteenth
century imperial culture is plentiful with words and concepts like "inferior" or "subject races," "subordinate peoples," "dependency," "expansion," and "authority." . . . In
the expansion of the great Western Empires, profit and
hope of further profit were obviously tremendously important, as the attractions of spices, sugar, slaves, rubber, cot-
ton, opium, tin, gold, and silver over centuries amply tes-
tify. So also was inertia, the investment in already going
enterprises, tradition, and the market or institutional forces
that kept the enterprises going. But there is more than that
to imperialism and colonialism. There was a commitment
to them over and above profit, a commitment in constant
circulation and recirculation, which, on the one hand, allowed decent men and women to accept the notion that
distant territories and their native peoples *should* be subjugated, and, on the other, replenished metropolitan energies
so that these decent people could think of the *imperium* as
a protracted, almost physical obligation to rule subordinate,
inferior, or less advanced peoples. We must not forget that
there was very little domestic resistance to these empires,

although they were very frequently established and maintained under adverse and even disadvantageous conditions.
—Edward Said, *Culture and Imperialism*[2]

When I was at school, we read Virgil's *Aeneid* and Theodor Mommsen's *History
of Rome.* Of course, we knew that Rome's *imperium* ("supreme administrative
power") had its limitations and that from time to time, before Constantine the
Great, some emperors had persecuted the Christians. But still, taken all in all,
we understood that the Roman Empire had been, as Sellar and Yeatman would
have put it, "a good thing."[3] Even in relation to Christianity, therefore, we
tended to speak of Roman rule as "providential." We noted that *pax Romana*
("the Roman Peace") meant reasonably safe travel on good roads, with seas
free of pirates, and good harbors, and *that* meant that the gospel could spread.
We noted that the prevalence of Greek language and culture made communication easy. We noted that Roman officials as they appeared in the New
Testament seemed on the whole to have been rather supportive of those who
followed Jesus. All these elements we saw as "providential." "It can," said
M. A. C. Warren in a book that was published shortly before I began to study
for the priesthood, "be fairly argued that successive imperialisms have made
a significant contribution to the realization of the vision of the time when 'the
earth shall be filled with the knowledge of God as the water covers the sea.' "[4]
Not surprisingly, then, even as a theological student I was largely strengthened
in my view of the Roman Empire as having functioned "as a *preparatio* for
God's good will for the world."[5]

Needless to say, I did not at that time even conceive of the questions raised
by Edward Said. Such questions were first raised (for me, at any rate) during
the last decade of the twentieth century as a part of the kind of thinking and
critique that we have come to call "postcolonial." In the context of ending, or
at least evolving, French, British, and American imperial power in the world,
"postcolonialism" tries to reflect on the nature and meaning of that experience
(colonial and imperial, postcolonial and postimperial) for those involved in it.
Now that such thinking has arisen, however, and such questions have been
raised, we are bound to reflect again on the rise of Christianity. Was Roman
rule as "providential" for Jesus and his first followers as we thought? How did
Rome look from the viewpoint of an ordinary Galilean in the first century of
the Christian era? And what conclusions are we to draw from these considerations, not least about ourselves and our own understanding of and relationship to Jesus of Nazareth?

So various books and studies have surfaced recently that direct our thoughts in directions quite different from those with which I grew up. In *Jesus and Empire*,[6] Richard Horsley suggests that much modern Western Christianity has domesticated and "depoliticized" Jesus,[7] creating a figure who correlates with various assumptions and procedures of our own—assumptions and procedures that are, in fact, highly questionable. These include our assumption that religion must be separate from politics and economics, our individualism, and our allegedly "scientific" culture, which has influenced biblical scholarship to a point where only data about Jesus that will "pass the test of modern reasonability/rationality can be used." The net effect of all this has been to make Jesus into "a religious teacher who uttered isolated sayings and parables relevant only to individual persons."[8] As we have domesticated Jesus, so we have domesticated his background, so that we talk of "the Jews" as if they were a single entity, when in fact the society in which Jesus lived was immensely complex, involving many realities other than the religious. "The peoples of Palestine in the time of Jesus appear as a complex society full of political conflict rather than a unitary religion (Judaism)."[9] Opposition to Roman oppression regularly marked the immediate Palestinian context of Jesus' mission. "For generations before and after the ministry of Jesus, the Galilean and Judean people mounted repeated protests and revolts against the Romans and their client rulers, the Herodian kings and Jerusalem high priests."[10] Therefore, "trying to understand Jesus' speech and action without knowing how Roman imperialism determined the conditions of life in Galilee and Jerusalem" is rather like "trying to understand Martin Luther King without knowing how slavery, reconstruction, and segregation determined the lives of African-Americans in the United States."[11] We should see Jesus as a leader who "belonged in the same context with and stands shoulder to shoulder with these other leaders of movements among the Galilean and Judean people, and pursues the same general agenda in parallel paths: independence from Roman imperial rule so that the people can again be empowered to renew their traditional way of life under the rule of God."[12] Since in what follows I am somewhat critical of Horsley, let me say at once how much I admire his short, passionate book. Indeed, for better or worse I was moved to write the present volume largely as a result of reading *Jesus and Empire*. So I am in Horsley's debt, even when I disagree with him most.

Evidently, then, matters are not so clear-cut as I once believed. Yet are they quite so clear-cut as Horsley (and others) seem to suggest? Granted that the Roman Empire was not from Jesus of Nazareth's point of view simply "a good thing," are we then to understand that it was simply "a bad thing"? While we must be grateful to those who have raised postcolonial issues in relation to the biblical texts, how far should we follow them in their interpretations of those texts? Have they sufficiently considered how Israel itself reflected on and understood its experiences of empire? Was the Jewish experience of Roman rule always the same, or did it differ at different periods and under different Roman officials? Are the insights and questions of postcolonialism (a movement that already has its own history)[13] being properly understood and applied in the present connection? How far can techniques of analysis that were developed in connection with the post-Enlightenment colonial—to be precise, *post*colonial—experience of cultures formerly subject to nineteenth- and twentieth-century Western domination properly be applied to the ancient, largely Mediterranean world of the Roman Empire? And how far should these considerations affect our understanding of Jesus of Nazareth?

I do not imagine that the answers to these questions are easy, or self-evident, and answers to some of them may not be possible at all. The discussion that follows is, nonetheless, my attempt to address them.

In my opening chapters, by way of setting the New Testament within its environment, I examine Israel's traditions about empire and its attitudes toward international superpowers as it experienced them throughout its history. My first chapter looks at its witness in the scriptural and immediately post-scriptural period, from the Egyptians to the Greeks. My second considers the period from the Maccabees to the war that began in 66, with a brief look at what followed—the more immediate setting for the life of Jesus and the beginnings of the Christian movement. In my third chapter, I turn to what we may know or surmise of the teaching and ministry of Jesus and try to consider its likely significance vis-à-vis Rome. In my fourth, I attempt to do the same thing with the passion narratives, which have special problems of their own. In my fifth and sixth chapters, I turn to a selection of other early Christian witnesses, namely Paul, Luke-Acts, 1 Peter, and the Book of Revelation. In my seventh chapter, I reflect on appropriate, and possibly inappropriate, relationships between the study of first-century Israel and Rome and contemporary postcolonial insights. In a concluding "unscientific postscript," I reflect on the possible significance of all of this for our own understanding of empire and "superpower status," then and now.

Many of the questions to be addressed in the following chapters are historical and exegetical, and I try to approach them, at least in the first place, from within those disciplines. Chapters 3 and 4 in particular are largely concerned with what we usually call "the historical Jesus"—an expression that is hardly without problems of its own. To cut a long story short, by "the historical Jesus" I mean (like John P. Meier) the "Jesus" whom we can, at least in principle, recover and examine by using the ordinary tools of modern historical research.[14] In considering such questions, I prefer therefore when I can to proceed on the basis of criteria normally preferred by historical critics: multiple attestation and consistency. If, overall, I am less skeptical as to the value of the New Testament texts' historical witness than are some of my colleagues in New Testament studies (and I am), that is not because I consider the texts to be sacred (although I do) but because I believe, on the grounds of the best scholarship I can manage, that my more skeptical colleagues are mistaken.[15] As Cardinal König pointed out to the Second Vatican Council, it is not difficult to show that "the sacred books are sometimes deficient in accuracy as regards both historical and scientific matters."[16] There are, however, some in the New Testament guild who need rather to remount the horse from the other side, modestly recalling, as George Kennedy has said, that "ancient writers sometimes meant what they said and occasionally even knew what they were talking about."[17]

There are, of course, other witnesses to events of the period, and we must ask questions about them, too. We cannot proceed as if every statement in the New Testament were open to doubt but all other sources could be relied upon as "historical." When Philo criticized Pilate in his *Embassy to Gaius*, to what extent was his description of Pilate influenced by his own rhetorical objectives? Much more important—for in many matters that interest us he is our only or our main witness—how far can we trust Josephus? Are there significant differences between what he wrote in the *Jewish War* and what he wrote in the *Antiquities of the Jews* a quarter of a century later? In a still influential article published in the 1950s, Morton Smith argued for a significant change in Josephus' opinions and attitudes.[18] Smith's view of Josephus was followed by a number of scholars and historians in the ensuing decades. Recently, however, it has been challenged. Steve Mason, after a detailed analysis of relevant passages, concludes that "the theory of Rasp, Smith, Neusner and others that *Ant.* 18 dramatically improves the Pharisees' image over against *War*, or that Josephus deliberately corrects *War* (Rasp) seems to lack any basis whatsoever."[19] Personally, I have come, like Louis Feldman, to consider Josephus "more and more" to be a historian deserving our respect.[20] We need to understand, however, that he was a Hellenistic, *rhetorical* historian, who conceived it as his task not merely to narrate facts but also (like an epideictic orator) to be "laudatory or encomiastic"[21]—in other words, to be one who bestowed honor. Of course, he knew that such a historian must tell the truth. "Who does not know that the first law of history is that it should not dare to write anything false?" (Cicero, *De oratore*, 2.62). So Josephus' information is usually as reliable as his sources will allow, and his sources are often quite good. But *mere* information was not for him an end in itself, any more than it was for an epideictic orator. The facts were recited to give honor. It is worth noting that at the beginning of the *War*, Josephus criticizes others who have written on the subject *both* because they have failed to tell the truth *and* because they have thereby failed in their purpose, which was to honor Rome (*War* 1.1–3, 6–8). Quite evidently and openly, he considers both failings to be significant. To whom then does Josephus intend to give honor? To some extent, naturally, to his patrons, the Flavians, and to himself, where his own honor is involved. But much more—and it is surely to the credit of the Flavians that they must have perceived this and yet were Josephus' patrons anyway—to God and God's people Israel. That is why, quite often, Josephus writes with irony, and even (especially in his accounts of his own doings) playfulness—an irony and playfulness that subsequent readers have missed, supposing him merely tendentious, self-serving, or sycophantic but that his first hearers, including the Flavians, surely did not.[22]

Where, then, does all this lead me, and any who choose to go with me?

My conclusion, briefly, is that Jesus and the early Christians did indeed have a critique of the Roman superpower, a critique that was broadly in line with the entire biblical and prophetic tradition. Its basis is the prophetic claim "the LORD is our judge, the LORD is our ruler, the LORD is our king; he will save us" (Isa. 33.22), "the kingdom of God is at hand" (Mark 1.15). On that basis, the biblical tradition challenges all human power structures. To that extent (and I think it to be a very important "extent"), I find myself in agreement with Horsley: the privatized, depoliticized, and generally domesticated Jesuses who are at present, *mutatis mutandis*, equally characteristic of the conservative Christian right and the liberal Christian left will not do.[23] Such Jesuses are neither the Jesus of the gospels nor the "Jesus of history." One cannot worship and serve the biblical God, the God of Israel, and not be concerned about justice (including international justice) here and now. To that extent (and it is, again, a very important extent), the words and works of Jesus and his followers are both political and revolutionary.

Where I believe that Horsley and I differ is, however, in this: I think that the biblical tradition challenges human power structures not by attempting to dismantle them or replace them with other human power structures but by consistently confronting them with *the truth about their origin and purpose*. Their origin is that God permits them. Their purpose is to serve God's glory by promoting God's peace and God's justice. For so long as they attempt those things, they may do quite well. As soon as they forget them, they stand condemned, and their days are numbered, not because human wisdom or courage will put an end to them but because God will do so. To put it another way, the prophetic tradition subverts the "powers that be" by insisting at every point *that they should do their job*. This, I believe, is its burden, and this consistently emerges at every point where we examine it. Hence, to treat Jesus' political critique as a call to replace *one* human power structure with *another* ("home rule for Israel") is to miss its point. It is also to be in danger of missing the way in which, as a critique, it continues to challenge those who live under structures of government quite different from those that could or would have been envisaged by the authors of the New Testament. For if the Lord is truly king, then even twenty-first-century presidents and prime ministers elected (at least in theory) by Western processes of post-Enlightenment democracy *still* need to remember that they govern only by God's will and that the purpose of their governing is to promote God's peace and justice. Forgetting those things, they will stand condemned as surely as did any arrogant Caesar of antiquity. God is not mocked.

But I anticipate. Let us begin at the beginning.

I

Israel and Empire

From the Egyptians to the Greeks

If postcolonial studies have taught us anything, it is surely that in examining historical situations, we must listen for the voices of those who were ruled as well as for the voices of those who ruled them. Often the voices of those who were ruled are not easy to hear. They have been ignored or silenced, and so forgotten. What we call "history" tends to be written by the powerful. In his analysis of Jane Austen's *Mansfield Park*, Edward Said drew attention to the way in which Austen—surely as intelligent and compassionate a writer as ever lived—was clearly aware that what had happened in the British colony of Antigua was vastly significant for the lives and prosperity of the main characters in her story. Yet she says virtually nothing about the effect of those events on those who actually *lived* in Antigua.[1]

> All the evidence says that even the most routine aspects of holding slaves on a West Indian sugar plantation were cruel stuff. And everything we know about Austen and her values is at odds with the cruelty of slavery. Fanny Price reminds her cousin that after asking Sir Thomas about the slave trade, "There was such a dead silence" as to suggest that one world could not be connected with the other since there simply is no common language for both.[2]

A new factor was needed to change that situation, and it would come in the aftermath of empire: a *post*-colonial awareness. "In time there would no longer be dead silence when slavery was spoken of, and the subject became central to a new understanding of what Europe was."[3]

But when we have broken the silence, our difficulties are not over. In a sense, they are beginning. For then we become aware that people who were not literate could create little or no record of their thoughts and deeds, so that what the slaves on Antigua thought at the beginning of the nineteenth century is by now available to us only by way of archaeological discoveries or oral traditions that, even when we can gain access to them, may be very difficult for us to understand and evaluate. Moreover, recent research into contemporary peasant societies shows the extent to which, even where protest or resistance movements do (as we say) "rise to the surface," they often form only a small fraction of a much deeper popular resistance that remains *deliberately* hidden. In considering the communications that take place between the powerful and the subject, the anthropologist and political scientist James C. Scott distinguishes between the "public transcript of power" and the "hidden transcripts" of both rulers and ruled. The "public transcript of power" is determined largely by those who rule, and it is they who have the resources and the ability to create written resources, behind which their "hidden transcript" represents "the practices and claims of their rule that cannot be openly avowed."[4] But the "hidden transcript" of the oppressed, of those who "dare not contest the terms of their subordination openly," represents "a social space in which offstage dissent to the official transcript of power relations may be voiced."[5] Here is to be found "an entire discourse, linked to . . . culture, religion, and the experience of colonial rule."[6] That discourse is hidden, in part because those who create it do not generally have the resources to record it and in part because they *choose* to hide it from those who have power over them—and for a good reason, namely "the simple fact that most subordinate classes throughout most of history have rarely been afforded the luxury of open, organized, political activity. Or, better stated, such activity was dangerous, if not suicidal."[7]

What, then, of Israel? Israel constitutes something of an exception, for Israel created the scriptures. Through them Israel's voice, even when it spoke as subject or oppressed, has never been totally silenced. Of course, even Israel constitutes only "something" of an exception. We hear from its past only what must always have been a limited group of the literate and the articulate, and even then, in general, only from those whose voices prevailed. Throughout its history, no doubt many in Israel said and believed many things not represented in scripture, or represented only at its margins. Still—and here we are on firm historical ground—it remains that, by the first century of the Christian era, most ordinary Jews, certainly most who were in any sense believing, had come to identify the scriptures (which at this period comprised at least the Pentateuch, the prophets, and the psalms) as expressing God's word and promise to them. The first Christians continued to make that identification. In that sense, therefore, a voice that ordinary people held to be holy, true, and theirs, is still available to us. In asking, then, what they may have believed or hoped about the empire whose subjects they were, or about empire generally, it is appropriate, and indeed necessary, to begin with the scriptures.

From the viewpoint of faithful Israel, that Israel should be subject to *anyone* raises a theological problem. Israel is God's chosen, beloved and uniquely God's partner, called by God so that by it "all the communities of the earth shall find blessing." How, then, is one to understand God's purposes in relation to a foreign power that has dominion over Israel and its people? Is such dominion merely a manifestation of evil, and is acceptance of it therefore a compromise with evil? Apparently not—or, at least, the matter is more complicated than that. According to a consistent stream of biblical voices, God *chooses* that there shall be empires. Thus, Egypt (Gen. 47.7–10), Assyria (Isa. 10.5–6, 37: 26–27), Babylon (Jer. 25.9, 27.5–6; Dan. 4.17–34), and Persia (Isa. 44.24–45.7) are all, in their time and place, said (in the case of Egypt) to be blessed and to prosper, and (in the case of Assyria, Babylon, and Persia) to rule over other nations by God's mandate. Early postbiblical voices speak in a similar way of the Greeks under Ptolemy II Philadelphus (*Letter of Aristeas* 15b, 19–21). But always such power is granted within the limits of God's sovereignty. Those who exercise such power are called to obey God's command, for the Lord alone is truly king (Ps. 96:10, 117). If they flout that command, they face certain judgment (Ps. 2.10–11; Wisd. of Solomon 6.1–9). Understandably, those who speak from the midst of Israel most often present God's command as a requirement referring to the well-being of Israel itself (e.g., Isa.47.6; compare *Aristeas* 20–27), but sometimes (and very interestingly), they imply a more general command for justice and courtesy among *all* the nations (Amos 1.13, 2.1; compare, again, *Aristeas* 24, 187–90). They suggest that there is at work in the world, as Walter Brueggemann says, "a defense of human rights that is beyond the challenge or resistance of even the most powerful state. That is what it means 'to judge the world in righteousness, equity, and truth' (cf. Pss. 96:10, 13; 67:4; Isa. 2:4)."[8]

Into this mix, another factor thrusts itself. In Jeremiah's letter to the exiles in Babylon, the prophet does something that appears to be new. He not only affirms that the Babylonian sovereignty over Israel is God's will but also tells the exiles that, even though they are in a land characterized by Amos and Hosea as polluted (Hos. 9:3–4; Amos 7:17b), still God has not forsaken them (Jer. 29: 11–14). They may flourish there, and indeed have a duty to do so. Let them build, plant, and marry (29:5–6). Let them continue to pray in the expectation that God will hear them (29:7b, 12–14a). Jeremiah's letter is set in the context of his opposition to false prophesy and, indeed, expresses such opposition (Jer. 28.1–17, 29.20–32)—a striking illustration of what we observed earlier, that the voices that have been preserved for us as God's word to Israel were not the only voices in Israel, or their thoughts the only thoughts. In this case, we are given a glimpse of what may have been the "false" prophetic message that led those who heard it to "trust in a lie" (29.31). We are told about the words of Hananiah son of Azzur, words that are decidedly violent in tone: "Even so will I break the yoke of Nebuchadnezzar king of Babylon from the neck of all the nations within two years" (28.11). In opposition to this violent forecast, however, Jeremiah receives a quite different word: "Thus says the LORD of hosts, the God of Israel: I have put upon the neck of all these nations an iron yoke of servitude to Nebuchadnezzar king of Babylon, and they shall serve him, for I have given to him even the beasts of the field" (28:14). Babylonian imperial rule is, for the present, the will of God. In that context, the terms in which Jeremiah tells the exiles to flourish in Babylon—they are to build, to plant, and to marry—gain particular significance, for they are the precise terms in which God's people are granted exemption from participating in holy war (Deut. 20.5–7; compare 1 Macc. 3.56). Daniel L. Smith states the essence of the matter: "Hananiah's opposition to Jeremiah was the opposition of a Zealot, the violent revolutionary who called on Israel to draw their swords to end the yoke of Babylon. The argument between Jeremiah and Hananiah was both political and theological: how to be the people of God in a strange land."[9]

Yet Jeremiah goes even beyond that, even beyond "nonviolent resistance." For, most striking of all, the exiles are to pray *for* that land, heathen though it is, seeking the good of the city where they find themselves (Jer. 29:7). As Jeremiah makes clear, such prayer is by no means devoid of self-interest (29:7b). Even so, Walther Eichrodt's point remains: "the way in which both the personal longing for revenge and the national desire for retribution are overcome is remarkable, culminating as it does in the formation of a new fellowship with the heathen through intercession."[10] In that connection, we might reflect on Edward Said's observation that "one of imperialism's achievements was to bring the world closer together."[11] To state the matter more biblically, the very humiliation and exile of Israel serves, in the consciousness of at least one prophet, to strengthen his understanding of the greatness and universality of God and his sense of God's relationship to all peoples.

The temptation that faces those who rule empires is, however, to absolutize their power, claiming for themselves autonomy. "They divinise themselves, and then the mind of the emperor is 'changed from that of a man [and becomes] the mind of a beast' (4:16)" (O'Donovan).[12] This, according to the scriptures, is what happens at different times with Egypt (Exod. 5.2; Ezek. 29–32), Assyria (Isa. 10.7–14, 37.29a) and Babylon (Isa. 14.13–14, 47.6–8; Dan. 3.4–6, 4.29–30), and with the Greeks under Antiochus (1 Macc. 1:10, 44–53; Dan. 11:36–37).[13] Such self-absolutizing is a rebellion against God and therefore carries within it the seeds of its own destruction. So destruction comes upon Egypt (Exod. 15.4–10; Isa.19.1–20), Assyria (Isa. 10.15–19, 37.29), Babylon (Isa. 14.15, 47.9–11; Jer. 50.1–3), and the Greeks under Antiochus (1 Macc. 3:49–53, 6:5–13), for no power, not even an imperial power, can long defy God. The scriptural tradition, moreover, never attributes this falling of the great powers, this decisive break in their authority, to any cause *except* God's governance, which is partly a matter of God's own simple authority, partly a matter of God's peculiar devotion to Israel, and partly a matter of God's hatred of all injustice. Even with the Greeks, whose defeat might have been ascribed to armed rebellion on the part of Israel, still the tradition makes clear—particularly in 2 Maccabees—that Israel's deliverance is essentially God's work: "we prayed to the Lord, and our prayer was heard" (2 Macc. 1:8; compare 2:22, 3:23–40, 8:5, 18–21, 23–24, 9:4b–29, 10:29–30, 38, 15:21–29, 35).[14]

Part of God's gift to Israel is, indeed, that she should know all this:

> Daniel said: "Blessed be the name of God from age to age, for wisdom and power are his. He changes times and seasons, deposes kings and sets up kings; he gives wisdom to the wise and knowledge to those who have understanding. He reveals deep and hidden things; he knows what is in the darkness, and light dwells with him. To you, O God of my ancestors, I give thanks and praise, for you have given me wisdom and power, and have now revealed to me what we asked of you." (Dan. 2.20–23)

The knowledge that Daniel has received is a knowledge that encompasses all Nebuchadnezzar's apparent sovereignty and greatness, showing that it is, in fact, entirely subject to God's sovereignty. And such awareness inevitably has its social implications as part of a strategy for exile. As Daniel L. Smith-Christopher says, "the survival of Jews as a diaspora people partially involves the conviction of superior *knowledge* in the face of superior *strength* (cf. Prov. 16:32, 20:18, 21:22). It is precisely by *teaching*—that is, instructing the hearer of the Daniel tales about their calling and their relation to God—that these tales 'renegotiate' identity in the context of diaspora existence. That wisdom is greater than strength or money is the subversive strategy of minority cultural survival."[15]

Even that, however, is not the whole story. For, in the midst of it, a new possibility is raised. What if the imperial power were to *acknowledge* the superior knowledge and wisdom of God's people? What if the imperial power were to declare, "Truly, your God is God of gods and Lord of kings and a revealer of mysteries, for you have been able to reveal this mystery!"—which is exactly what Nebuchadezzar does say in response to Daniel's wisdom (Dan. 2.47)? What if the Emperor were then to offer Daniel and his fellow Israelites top-ranking positions in the imperial civil service—which is, again, exactly what Nebuchadnezzar does do? Then, interestingly enough, Daniel and his fellow Israelites would accept those positions, and there would be cooperation between God's people and empire—exactly, of course, as it is claimed there had been in the time of the Pharaoh who "knew" Joseph (Gen. 41.37–57).[16] Here, Jeremiah's hint at the possibility of fellowship between pagan empire and God's people moves to a entirely new level, in which pagan empire is a conscious and willing participant.

With imperial Persia, the Bible presents us with a development of this last possibility, suggesting that the experience of foreign empire may actually be positive. The Jewish scriptures in general do *not* perceive Persia as in arrogant rebellion against God. There is, as it happens, evidence other than scriptural that Persian imperial policy (no doubt on the basis of intelligent self-interest) was much more respectful of local tradition—and therefore of the religion of Israel—than was the Assyrian or Babylonian.[17] The Assyrians and, to a lesser extent, the Babylonians endeavored to establish their power by deporting local populations, particularly the upper classes, and by introducing their own religion alongside local religions. The Persians allowed and even encouraged their subjects to develop their own lives and traditions, provided they accepted Persian sovereignty. So it is that much of the Jewish Bible pictures Persia not as the enemy but as the *patron* of a renewed and restored worship at Jerusalem, which is paid for with Persian money (see Ezra 1.2–4, 6.3–5, 14; 2 Chron. 36.23).[18]

> So the elders of the Jews built and prospered, through the prophesying of the prophet Haggai and Zechariah the son of Iddo. They finished building by the command of the God of Israel and by decree of Cyrus, Darius, and King Artaxerxes of Persia. (Ezra 6.14)[19]

Evidently, then, *pace* O'Donovan, it is simply not true that "beyond making use of the moment [of ending the dominance of Babylon], Israel has nothing further to do with Cyrus." Quite the contrary! (See also Ezra 1.1–11, 5.14–6.5) Likewise, O'Donovan's more general statement—"Yhwh's world order was plurally constituted. World Empire was a beastly deformation"[20]—cannot stand unqualified as a description of the biblical attitude to empire. Of course, it represents what *may* happen, and what, alas, often *does* happen, but not, apparently, what *has* to happen. As O'Donovan himself pointed out at an earlier point in his study, "as we survey the texts which speak of Yhwh's kingship, we notice a reluctance to make direct connections with any concrete form of political order."[21] That is correct, and "World Empire" is not an exception to it.

In postbiblical tradition, *The Letter of Aristeas* offers a similar pattern. The pagan monarch Ptolemy Philadelphus is also presented as a king who is not in rebellion against God. On the contrary, he appears as philanthropic, committed to care for his people, and corresponding exactly to the Jewish sages' own model for a king that shall "keep his kingdom without offense to the end. . . . If he practice just dealing toward all, he will carry out each task well for himself, believing that every thought is manifest to God. Take the fear of God as your guiding principle, and you will not fail in anything" (187, 189). Just how far all this represents the historical reality is doubtless open to debate. As Martin Hengel points out, these stories "come from the milieu of the Jewish diaspora in Egypt, where in the second century above all a close collaboration was developed between the Ptolemeans and the Jews." So we must take them with a grain of salt.[22] What matters, nonetheless, is the continuing possibility they present of a pagan monarch who acts as God's partner and not as God's adversary. *The Letter of Aristeas* is notoriously hard to date. We should note, nonetheless, that those who date it after the anti-Jewish policies of Antiochus, when such a partnership between God and the pagan monarch would have been much harder to envisage, make its witness only the more significant.[23]

What of Israel itself, as an imperial power—for such, by its own testimony, it had once been? "Jerusalem has had mighty kings who ruled over the whole province Beyond the River, to whom tribute, custom, and toll were paid" (Ezra 4:20; cf. 1 Kings 9:21; 2 Chron. 8:8). And what is the Messianic hope, if not a hope that, under God, Israel's imperial rule will in some way be restored?

> Lo, your king comes to you . . .
> and he shall command peace to the nations;
> his dominion shall be from sea to sea,
> and from the River to the ends of the earth.
> (Zech. 9:9, 10; compare Ps. 72, especially 8–10, 15–17, 89.21–28)

Yet, kingly rule by a human being *within* Israel was from its inception as fraught with ambiguities and problems as was kingly rule by foreign nations *over* Israel. The point was made and the problem stated in a nutshell when Israel invited Gideon to be king:

> Then the Israelites said to Gideon, "Rule over us, you and your son
> and your grandson also; for you have delivered us out of the hand of

Midian." Gideon said to them, "I will not rule over you, and my son will not rule over you; the LORD will rule over you." (Judg. 8:22–23)

Precisely. The argument *for* monarchy was, however, that it was necessary. Israel must become "like other nations" so that the king could "govern us and go out before us and fight our battles for us" (1 Sam. 8:19–20). The scriptures make it clear that in this issue, too, there was more than one voice within Israel. Kingship did not come without a struggle, and even though the pro-monarchists won that struggle, in this case the voice of their opponents was not to be silenced. The prophet Samuel and the LORD are pictured as conceding monarchy reluctantly, and with warning:

These will be the ways of the king who will reign over you: he will take your sons and appoint them to his chariots and to be his horsemen, and to run before his chariots; and he will appoint for himself commanders of thousands and commanders of fifties, and some to plow his ground and to reap his harvest, and to make his implements of war and the equipment of his chariots. He will take your daughters to be perfumers and cooks and bakers. He will take the best of your fields and vineyards and olive orchards and give them to his courtiers. He will take one-tenth of your grain and of your vineyards and give it to his officers and his courtiers. He will take your male and female slaves, and the best of your young men and donkeys, and put them to his work. He will take one-tenth of your flocks, and you shall be his slaves. And in that day you will cry out because of your king, whom you have chosen for yourselves; but the LORD will not answer you in that day. (1 Sam. 8:11–18)

In short, the danger is that your king will govern for his own sake, as an autonomous potentate, and not for the sake of God's people.

Still, however, monarchy is allowed. Human kingship, with all its flaws, is accepted as a recipient of God's grace and an instrument of God's own kingship:

Now the day before Saul came, the LORD had revealed to Samuel: "Tomorrow about this time I will send to you a man from the land of Benjamin, and you shall anoint him to be prince over my people Israel. He shall save my people from the hand of the Philistines; for I have seen the affliction of my people, because their cry has come to me." (1 Sam. 9.15–16)

> I have made a covenant with my chosen one,
> I have sworn to my servant David:
> I will establish your descendants forever,
> and build your throne for all generations.
> (Ps. 89:3–4)

Here, then, is a tension, and the Old Testament insists that we live with it. As Paul D. Hanson says, "We may want to rush in where the final editor of the Bible did not dare to tread and resolve the tension by adjudicating which side was right. Are you for kings or for prophets? Declare yourselves! But that course was not the one followed by the editor [of the biblical narrative] nor by the nation [Israel]."[24]

It follows from all this that an Israelite king may no more absolutize himself or his power than may a pagan emperor. He must remember his dependence upon God, and he must keep God's commands. Oliver O'Donovan points to the political significance of the prophet's claim, "the LORD is our judge, the LORD is our ruler, the LORD is our king; he will save us" (Isa. 33.22). If that is true, then the Israelite king who reigns faithfully must seek to honor God as king and also to be God's instrument for his people in the service of God's judgment, God's law, and God's salvation.[25] This means, however, that

> If his children forsake my law
> and do not walk according to my ordinances,
> if they violate my statutes
> and do not keep my commandments,
> then I will punish their transgression with the rod
> and their iniquity with scourges.
> (Ps. 89.31–33)

So it is even with David and Solomon: when they forsake God's law and arrogate to themselves autonomous power and authority, as David did in the matters of Bathsheba and the census (2 Sam. 11:1–12:23, 24:1–25) and as Solomon did in the matter of his foreign wives (1 Kings 11:1–13), then they are held accountable. In the case of Bathsheba, in order to gain her for himself, David has lied, cheated, and arranged for the murder of one who is bound to him by ties of honor as his dependent, as faithful to him, and as a guest in his dominion. What Nathan the prophet does in response to this is virtually a paradigm of biblical prophetic address to those who abuse their power:

> But the thing that David had done displeased the LORD. And the
> LORD sent Nathan to David. He came to him, and said to him,

"There were two men in a certain city, the one rich and the other poor. The rich man had very many flocks and herds; but the poor man had nothing but one little ewe lamb, which he had bought. And he brought it up, and it grew up with him and with his children; it used to eat of his morsel, and drink from his cup, and lie in his bosom, and it was like a daughter to him. Now there came a traveler to the rich man, and he was unwilling to take one of his own flock or herd to prepare for the wayfarer who had come to him, but he took the poor man's lamb, and prepared it for the man who had come to him." Then David's anger was greatly kindled against the man; and he said to Nathan, "As the LORD lives, the man who has done this deserves to die; and he shall restore the lamb fourfold, because he did this thing, and because he had no pity." Nathan said to David, "You are the man. Thus says the LORD, the God of Israel, 'I anointed you king over Israel, and I delivered you out of the hand of Saul; and I gave you your master's house, and your master's wives into your bosom, and gave you the house of Israel and of Judah; and if this were too little, I would add to you as much more. Why have you despised the word of the LORD, to do what is evil in his sight? You have smitten Uriah the Hittite with the sword, and have taken his wife to be your wife, and have slain him with the sword of the Ammonites.'" (2 Sam. 11.27b–12.9)

Nathan's words clearly acknowledge the divine source of David's power and yet hold him utterly accountable for the misuse of it. Two other points should, moreover, be noted. First, Nathan convicts the soldier-king not on the basis of a command that might be too subtle or lofty for him to comprehend but on the basis of his own understanding of what is just. Second, Uriah *is* a foreigner: this is another of those occasions when the demand for justice in Israel is internationalized. It is not enough to be just to a fellow Jew; one must be just to all.

Solomon, for his part, was promised the glories and wealth of kingship when he sought from God not those things but wisdom to govern God's people (1 Kings 3:11–14). In the end, however, he receives a stunning rebuke:

Then the LORD was angry with Solomon, because his heart had turned away from the LORD, the God of Israel, who had appeared to him twice, and had commanded him concerning this matter, that he should not follow other gods; but he did not observe what the LORD commanded. Therefore the LORD said to Solomon, "Since this has been your mind and you have not kept my covenant and my statutes that I have commanded you, I will surely tear the kingdom from you and give it to your servant." (1 Kings 11:9–11)

So the Davidic king who flouts God is punished just as Egypt, Assyria, Babylon, and the Greeks are punished, and for the same reason. But that is not the end of the story.

> I will punish their transgression with the rod
> and their iniquity with scourges;
> but I will not remove from him my steadfast love,
> or be false to my faithfulness.
> I will not violate my covenant,
> or alter the word that went forth from my lips.
> Once and for all I have sworn by my holiness;
> I will not lie to David.
> His line shall continue forever,
> and his throne endure before me like the sun.
> (Ps. 89:32–36)

Though the house of David is unfaithful, though Israel is unfaithful, yet God remains faithful. God does not punish in order to destroy. God's faithfulness remains the basis of Israel's hope for the restoration of her empire, whether, as sometimes, it takes the form of messianic hope or whether it is stated in more general terms.

> On that day I will raise up the booth of David that is fallen,
> and repair their breaches,
> and raise up his ruins,
> and rebuild it as in the days of old;
> in order that they may possess the remnant of Edom
> and all the nations who are called by my name,
> says the LORD who does this.
> (Amos 9:11–12)

Strikingly, this divine faithfulness is also presented as the hope of Israel's enemies—of Egypt, Assyria, and Babylon. They, too, are not finally beyond hope of repentance and God's mercy. The affirmation of this hope is not central to the scriptures, but it is there. It is implicit, of course, in Jeremiah's assurance that exiles are to pray for the "good" of the heathen city (29.7), for what other "good" can there finally be, if not God's mercy? It becomes explicit in God's promise of grace to Egypt in Isaiah 19.23–25, in the picture of Nineveh's (Assyria's) repentance in Jonah, and in Nebuchadnezzar's (Babylon's) turning to

God in Daniel 4.34–37.[26] And it depends, of course, utterly and only on the faithfulness of God, who "has delivered all to disobedience, that he may have mercy on all" (Rom. 11.32).

We see, then, the same basic pattern recurring again and again throughout this material. Biblical and prophetic tradition taken as a whole is not at all interested in the forms or structures of earthly power, in the choice of one system of government over another, or even in the question as to whether those who rule are believers or pagans. It is interested only in whether those who receive such power understand that it is a gift to them from God and that it is given to them for the sake of God's people, or even for the sake of the world. The fact that empires and superpowers are seen as acting by God's command and subject to God's judgment carries with it the corollary that they exist by God's will—but also the further corollary that they exist *only* by God's will. As Brueggemann says, "Yahweh intends that there should be world powers, and that these world powers should indeed govern, but govern within the bounds of Yahweh's mandate. The mandate variously consists in special consideration for Israel and occasionally the more generic practice of human civility."[27] Any who rule in this way, whether they are pagans or members of God's household, are to be honored.

Definitive in this context are the prophecies of Deutero-Isaiah. No one is clearer than Deutero-Isaiah that the Lord God of Israel is the one Lord of all history (Isa. 45:6b–7, 46: 9–10). Yet, in the context of precisely this affirmation, the prophet speaks of God's dramatic and powerful action, which will lead to the overthrow of the Babylonian empire and the coming of Cyrus, a king who, although he is a not a member of God's covenant people, is nonetheless raised up and empowered by God as God's instrument.[28]

> Thus says the LORD, your Redeemer,
> who formed you in the womb:
> I am the LORD, who made all things,
> who alone stretched out the heavens,
> who by myself spread out the earth;
> who frustrates the omens of liars,
> and makes fools of diviners;
> who turns back the wise,
> and makes their knowledge foolish;
> who confirms the word of his servant,
> and fulfills the prediction of his messengers;
> who says of Jerusalem, "It shall be inhabited,"

and of the cities of Judah,
"They shall be rebuilt, and I will raise up their ruins,"
who says to the deep, "Be dry—I will dry up your rivers,"
who says of Cyrus, "He is my shepherd,
and he shall carry out all my purpose."
Thus says the LORD to his anointed, to Cyrus,
whose right hand I have grasped
to subdue nations before him
and strip kings of their robes,
to open doors before him,
and the gates shall not be closed:
"I will go before you
and level the mountains,
I will break in pieces the doors of bronze
and cut through the bars of iron,
I will give you the treasures of darkness
and riches hidden in secret places,
so that you may know that it is I, the LORD,
the God of Israel, who call you by your name.
For the sake of my servant Jacob,
and Israel my chosen,
I call you by your name,
I surname you, though you do not know me,
so that they may know,
from the rising of the sun and from the west,
that there is none beside me;
I am the LORD, and there is no other.
I form light and create darkness,
I make weal and create woe;
I the LORD do all these things."
(Isaiah 44:24–45:7)

"Thus says the LORD, to his annointed, to Cyrus (כֹּה־אָמַר יְהוָה לִמְשִׁיחוֹ לְכוֹרֶשׁ)":
Klaus Baltzer's comment on this passage is surely to the point:

> For Israel this designation must initially have been a tremendous
> provocation, for it was on this concept that the whole monarchical
> tradition depended. "David" was the prototype of the anointed one.
> Of course prophets and priests can also be said to be anointed in the
> OT. But in a scene that is so unequivocally linked with arguments
> about sovereignty, and in which the argument is pursued in quite

precise political or constitutional terms ("Jerusalem," "the cities of Judah"), we can assume that for listeners the declaration of the anointing established the link with the Davidic dynasty and its claim. To put it somewhat drastically: Cyrus is the new David! The dignity of the "anointed one" is transferred to a foreign ruler.[29]

Cyrus, of course, does not "know" the God of Israel (Isa. 45.5), though he may come to know him (45.3). But, in any case, as Christopher Seitz says: "God is fully able to work with Cyrus as is. The problem will be in getting Israel to accept and understand what God is doing on its behalf through Cyrus."[30] Seitz's statement is precise. Of particular importance for our present concerns is, however, this: that in the prophet's view, what God chooses to do "for the sake of my servant Israel, and Jacob my chosen" God chooses to do *through pagan emperor and pagan empire*, called and named by the same word that "made all things, who alone stretched out the heavens, who by myself spread out the earth." Moreover, this pagan emperor is called and named *as witness to the divine glory*, "so that they may know, from the rising of the sun and from the west, that there is none beside me."

2

Israel and Empire

From the Maccabees to the War against Rome

Israel and Rome

In late 63 BC, following a period of vicious inter-Jewish strife in which various parties at various points sought the aid of Rome, there was a Roman siege of the Temple Mount, in the course of which some twelve thousand Jews were said to have died. At the end of it, the Roman commander Gnaeus Pompeius found himself master of Jerusalem, and Israel again found itself subject to foreign rule. In succumbing to Rome, Israel was hardly alone. Yet Judea and Galilee are unique among Roman spheres of influence in that we have a great deal of sometimes quite detailed information as to what happened in the years that followed. This availability of information results from the fact that Rome's Jewish subjects continued to be uniquely articulate—something that is particularly interesting in view of our earlier observations about the importance, and in general the difficulty, of listening to the voices of subject as well as subjector in any imperial history. Jews of the time produced a number of documents through which they still speak, most notably Josephus' accounts of the entire period, Philo of Alexandria's comments on particular episodes in his *Embassy*,[1] and the New Testament. Even in these cases, the fact that we are hearing voices of the literate and, at least as regards Josephus and Philo, the wealthy and influential means that we are still hearing voices of privilege. Still, they are voices of a *relative* privilege. Indeed, some historians have expressed concern that no complementary accounts written from the Roman angle survive. The reason for this, of course, is that, from the Roman point of view, Galilee and Judea were not particularly significant. Nothing happened in them to attract the interest of those concerned with the empire as a whole until the rebellion of AD 66. That *did* get the empire's attention, for it provoked a war that involved four legions and two future emperors.

Still, on the basis of the sources that we do have, there are a number of assertions that we may make about the period, and about Jewish experience of it, with tolerable certainty.

First, there *was* something that we may identify as "Judaism" before AD 70, even though it was not exactly the "normative Judaism" of the later rabbis. It has become customary among some scholars to insist on talking of "Judaisms" rather than "Judaism" during the Second Temple period,[2] and there is value in that, since it reminds us of differences of form and emphasis that were clearly present. Yet academic caution must not be allowed to degenerate into another (and in this case mistaken) kind of dogmatism. Samuel Sandmel stated the issue with his usual clarity: "Insufficient awareness of the varieties can lead to untenable generalizations. But it is *Judaism* of which there are varieties, and it is necessary to understand and emphasize this point."[3] Precisely. For all its differences of form and emphasis, Judaism in the first century of the Christian era evidently did have a core, to which all our witnesses, for all their disagreements with one another, clearly point. Judaism of every kind was generally focused on belief in the one God, acceptance of Torah (the Law), and the Temple.[4] The scriptures witnessed to all three, and ordinary Jews, including the illiterate, would at least have heard those scriptures (even if, being human, they did not always pay attention to them), as they were regularly read and expounded in the synagogue. Ordinary Jews—and especially those living in Judea and Galilee—could hardly not have been aware of the great pilgrim festivals, centering on the Temple at Jerusalem. Judaism implied, moreover, a basic story, to which the scriptures served as witness—the story of God's creation, of human disobedience, of God's call to Israel, of Israel's disobedience, and of God's continuing promise and faithfulness that would lead one day to the restoration and renewal of creation, when the promise recorded in Jeremiah's letter to the exiles would be fulfilled and God would act to redeem Israel.[5] Thus, the usual meaning of the phrase "the forgiveness of sins" for a Jew of this period was "the forgiveness of *Israel's* sins" (cf. Jer. 31:31–40; Ezek. 36:24–28). When Jews talked of the coming "Kingdom of God," they meant the promised sovereignty of God when God would return to Zion to vindicate God's people and restore all things.[6] Naturally, that meant justice for God's people. By "resurrection of the dead" they meant primarily the resurrection and restoration of Israel, so that the faithful dead could share in the good time coming.[7] But the end had not happened yet. God's people were still subject to foreign dominion, still in exile.

Second, such (as we would regard them) "theological" convictions had (as we would consider them) "political" overtones. Jew and pagan would have agreed on that. The attempt to suggest a division here between the "religious" and the "political" is entirely unhistorical. What, therefore, first-century Jews did *not* mean by the kind of language we have just discussed was the end of the world, or the end of history, although they certainly sometimes used "end of the world" language to describe such events—just as we sometimes speak of a din as "earth-shattering," even though we do not really think that the sound of both our dogs suddenly barking at once in the living room where we were quietly dozing off after lunch has done any serious damage to the planet.[8] Horsley is, I think, entirely correct: "once we are more sensitive to metaphoric use of language and hyperbole, it is difficult to find any texts that attest belief in 'the end of the world' or a 'cosmic catastrophe'."[9]

Third, despite the way that 1 Maccabees 4.46 has been construed, it is evident that some in Israel during the period of the second Temple *were* looking for a prophet, and clearly there were candidates for the job. John the Baptist was one of them. Josephus comments on others in his *Jewish War* (6.285–88). These would be men who believed, or claimed to believe, that they had been called by God to lead Israel to a new stage in its history, the stage when its story would come to its climax and its exile would end. Such prophets spoke and acted in ways that evoked the history of Israel. Like other such prophets before them, they came into conflict with the authorities. Like other such prophets, they died for their pains.[10]

Fourth, Roman rule of Israel, direct and indirect, itself underwent several changes of form.[11] Following the death of Rome's client Herod the Great in 4 BC, there were two distinct phases. The first followed the deposition of Herod's son Archelaus at the request of the Jews in AD 6 and involved direct Roman rule of Judea by a series of prefects.[12] It lasted until 39. Obviously, the constitution of the new province allowed Jews to practice their religion in accordance with the same guarantees that had earlier been given for the diaspora by Julius Caesar and Augustus, and that meant that Jews were exempted from honoring the divinities of the empire. Possibly it was as a part of this arrangement that the Jews undertook to offer sacrifice on the emperor's behalf. Two lambs and a bull were to be offered daily in the Temple for the emperor's health (Philo, *Leg.* 157, 232, 317; Josephus, *War* 2.197, 409).[13] Meanwhile, during almost the whole of that time, Galilee was under Herod's son, the tetrarch Herod Antipas (referred to in the New Testament, on his coins, and by Josephus usually as

"Herod").[14] Herod Antipas was at least ostensibly an observant Jew: he went up to Jerusalem for the major festivals, he minted coins that were not offensive to Jewish sensibilities, he collected his own taxes (himself then paying his tribute direct to Rome), and he had his own army. Contrary to the pictures beloved of Hollywood, Galilee at this period was *not* full of Roman soldiers.

The second phase, from AD 44 to AD 66, involved direct rule of Galilee and Judea together by a series of procurators.

The two phases were separated by a brief period of united rule from AD 41 to AD 44 under Rome's client Agrippa I, grandson of Herod the Great, who was a personal friend of the emperor, yet also governed (apparently) with the approval of the Pharisees (*m. Bik.* 3.4, *m. Sot.* 7.8).[15] Perhaps that very alliance led to his becoming the opponent of Christianity, for Luke holds him responsible for the death of James the brother of John, and the imprisonment of Peter (see Acts 12.1–5).

Fifth, there were at various times throughout the period disturbances and protests in Judea and in Galilee. These disturbances cannot be placed in a single category. Some involved the rural poor, and some involved those who were neither poor nor rural. Some seem to have been messianic and to have made religious claims; some involved no such claims. Some were evidently violent; some were nonviolent.[16]

Sixth and finally, the period culminated in a major uprising against Rome, the "Jewish War" of 66–73.

So far, we can be reasonably sure of our facts.

The General Situation: AD 6 to AD 66

But then, we are tempted to ask, to what extent, and in what way, the sentiments of the mass of ordinary people were involved in these disturbances, and immediately we are on much slippier ground. "For generations," Horsley says, "before and after the ministry of Jesus, the Galilean and Judean people mounted repeated protests and revolts against the Romans and their client rulers, the Herodian kings and Jerusalem high priests."[17] Citing Josephus' description of how Judas the Galilean and Saddok the Pharisee incited resistance to the Roman fiscal census in Judea in AD 6, he comments,

> Once we translate from Josephus's Hellenistic philosophical terms
> back into more traditional Israelite terms, the views that they share
> with the Pharisees (*Ant.* 18.23) sound like the views of most Judeans
> and Galileans at the time. They well knew that the Romans laid sub-

ject peoples under tribute as a mark of their "slavery" and humiliation. . . . But they longed to regain their freedom, as established originally in the exodus from bondage in Egypt, which they celebrated
annually in the Passover festival. . . . Judas, Saddok, and their cohorts, motivated by their "unconquerable passion for freedom," took
direct action in the faith that God also would be acting decisively
through their action to reestablish the people's freedom.[18]

But did Judas represent the "views" of "most Judeans and Galileans at the
time"? Seán Freyne suggests a very different interpretation of his behavior:

If, as seems likely, his revolt was an attempt to restore the Hasmonean kingship, we have a clue to the background to his father also
and Herod's opposition to him. It is significant that the *Antiquities*
account says that having armed his followers, he engaged in plundering, that is, in adopting similar tactics to those of his father and
others of their ilk opposed to the Herodian aristocracy that had replaced them within the province (17.271–72, 288). Their banditry
can be described as social in that it represents the last efforts of a
dying social class to regain its former position of wealth and status
within Palestinian life. But this does not mean that they were representative of or supported by the peasantry whose social oppressors
they had once been.[19]

In Horsley's view, "in all likelihood the popular protests and movements for
which we have written accounts represent only the tip of the iceberg of popular
resistance to Roman rule. Peasants, who were not literate, of course, left no
records of their own views and actions."[20] Such evidence as we have

of resistance by both Judean scribal teachers and Galilean and Judean peasants indicates conditions of persistent political unrest and
agitation in Palestine under early Roman rule. The principal division
was clearly between the peasantry and their rulers, Herodian and high-
priestly as well as the Romans.[21]

But, again, is that the way things were? That Roman imperialism, Roman
greed, and Roman incompetence all on occasion led to resentment and hatred
of Rome and Rome's clients we need not doubt. Roman testimony itself would
be enough to assure us of that, if there were no other. "It is," said Cicero on
one occasion, "difficult to put into words, citizens, how much we are hated
among foreign nations because of those whom we have sent to govern them
throughout these years, men wanton and outrageous."[22] But as to the extent

or depth of that hatred, or the precise motivation for it among Jewish individuals and groups in the varying circumstances of Judea and Galilee during the first century—as to all that, we can for the most part only surmise. To judge from Josephus, the protests seem to have occurred with much greater frequency, and to have been much more vicious, during the second phase of Roman rule (the period of the procurators) than during the preceding phase (the period of the Judean prefects and the Galilean tetrarchy)—perhaps justifying to some extent Tacitus' claim that during the reign of Tiberius (AD 14–37) Judea was quiet (*sub Tiberio quies*) (*History* 5.9).[23] All this leads Freyne, again, to see the situation under Herod Antipas quite differently from the way in which Horsley sees it:

> Certainly there were social tensions in Galilee between rich and poor (i.e. between landowners and tenants, etc.) and between city and country, but there seems no reason for suggesting that these were any more acute than elsewhere, and there is considerable likelihood that in fact they were less pressing. At least the glimpses we get of Galilean social life in the reign of Antipas, even in the Gospels, or later from Josephus' *Life*, do not suggest a peasantry totally disaffected and ready for the millennial holy war that would overthrow the agents of repression and exploitation.[24]

To judge from Josephus, the commonest class of troublemakers throughout the period from the death of Herod to the outbreak of the war consisted of those whom he calls *lēstai*—usually translated as "brigands" or "bandits."[25] Other renderings for *lēstēs* offered by BDAG include "robber, highwayman" and "revolutionary, insurrectionist, guerilla."[26] Who, then, and what, were the *lēstai*? The variety of translations available reflects something of the variety of scholarly views. Martin Hengel sees them as essentially ideologues, "members of socially disadvantaged groups fighting, among other things, for a new system of ownership, which they regarded as God's will."[27] Richard Horsley sees them as "social bandits," which is to say that while they resist the current oppression, they are "prepolitical" and not revolutionaries (although though they can become such).[28] Freyne is doubtful of their "social banditry," pointing to the apparent willingness of *lēstai* to change sides and their readiness to be hired, on one occasion, by Sepphoris, an avowedly pro-Roman city (Josephus, *Life*, 104,111). In Freyne's view, therefore, the *lēstai* function at times virtually as mercenaries, who are willing to be used by *any* of the various parties struggling to control the situation in Galilee.[29] Seth Schwartz sees them as "violent people who had fallen through the cracks of a rickety economy," though they might "mutate into bands of armed messianists or legal rigorists."[30] These varying opinions form a part of ongoing conversations that I do not pretend to adjudicate. I would note, however, that Roman *rhetoric*, with which in this respect Josephus appears to be completely consistent, normally uses the word *lēstai* for *any* violent persons whose actions are regarded by the speaker as passing the boundaries of civilized behavior. Thus Julius Caesar and Octavian were both, at times, referred to as "bandits" by those opposed to them! This potential for persons of high social standing to be involved in what their enemies characterize as "banditry" forbids us, as Brent D. Shaw points out, from identifying "banditry" simply or invariably with "class struggle." Perhaps, then, the most we can say with certainty of Josephus' "bandits" are that they are persons of whom Josephus disapproves. The reasons for this disapproval, and the motives and social situations behind each of their "banditries" (and they do not all have to have been the same) remain to be discerned, where they can be discerned at all, by other means. Josephus' mere use of the word *"lēstai"* will not, in itself, tell us such things.[31]

The War of 66

What, then, of the situation at the outbreak of hostilities? Horsley sees the war as an explosion of the seething popular unrest that he believes characterized the entire period. Shaye J. D. Cohen, however, pictures the situation quite differently:

> In the eyes of the revolutionaries Roman rule was as oppressive and intolerable as that of Epiphanes, but many Jews disagreed with this assessment and participated in the war only in its initial chaotic stages, if at all. For every peasant willing to give up everything in order to fight the Romans, there was a peasant who did not want to suffer the inevitable disasters inflicted by war. . . . Fighting against the Romans was foolish at best and sinful at worst. God will redeem Israel by sending the messiah, but Israel can do nothing to hasten the appointed time. This point of view was advanced by Flavius Josephus in his *The Jewish War*, our major source for the history of the war and its antecedents. The same perspective is ascribed by rabbinic literature to Rabban Yohannan ben Zakkai, who is alleged to have left Jerusalem during the siege and to have hailed Vespasian as a man destined to destroy the temple and to become emperor. At his

meeting with the soon-to-be-emperor, the rabbi quoted from Isaiah (10:34): "And the Lebanon [= the Temple constructed from the cedars of Lebanon] shall fall by a majestic one [= Vespasian]."[32]

Similarly Jacob Neusner:

Large sections of the Jewish population remained at peace throughout the war. The rebellion in no sense enlisted the support of the entire Jewish population. In fact, it progressively lost whatever support it had at the outset.[33]

Neusner and Cohen are, to be sure, hardly neutral witnesses, in that both consistently present a pacific, nonrevolutionary rabbinic Judaism. So, of the passages I have quoted, one might not unreasonably say, "Well, they would say that, wouldn't they?" But then, Horsley (as he very frankly admits)[34] and those who agree with him also have their issues—notably their troubled awareness of what they see as parallels between the situation in the first century Roman Empire and the present world situtation wherein the "imperial" United States and its allies are set against oppressed peoples of the world such as the Palestinians. Both groups of scholars are certainly reading the evidence as they see it, and are doing so with intelligence, learning, and honesty. So which group (if either) is actually right? Is it possible to know? Horsley is right to point out that "peasants, who were not literate, of course, left no records of their own views and actions."[35] But that is just the problem. *They didn't*. They left some artifacts that can be discovered and (possibly) interpreted by archaeology, and some things were said about them by people like Josephus, but they left no records of their own. We have already referred to modern studies of contemporary peasant societies that show that active protests and movements of a type that, as we say, "gets into the news" (in other words, into the media, generally controlled by those who have power) represent usually only the tip of an iceberg—a much deeper and broader resistance that is deliberately covert.[36] Certainly, such considerations are relevant as we consider *possibilities* about the situation in first-century Israel. The trouble is that, unlike James C. Scott, who spent two years among his Malaysian villagers,[37] we cannot do the kind of research into the lives of first-century Judeans and Galileans that would enable us actually to *know* which of their agendas were public, and for whom, and which were hidden, and from whom.

So, for example, Josephus gives us the following account of the part played in the war by the Galilean city of Gischala:

the inhabitants were inclined to peace, being mainly agricultural labourers, whose whole attention was devoted to the prospect of the crops; but they had been afflicted by the invasion of a numerous gang of brigands, from whom some members of the community caught the contagion . . . it was through their influence that the townsfolk, who would otherwise probably have sent deputies offering to surrender, now awaited the Roman onset in an attitude of defiance. (*War* 4.84, 86)

The scenario that Josephus describes is certainly not impossible. When the revolutionaries left, apparently the townsfolk opened the gates of their own volition and surrendered the city on the second day of the siege (*War* 4.92–120). If that is correct, it scarcely suggests that they were endowed with burning martial ardor. And that many of them, or even most, should have been more interested in seeing to their olives[38] than fighting the Roman army hardly strains belief. But was that what really happened? Has Josephus correctly implied the "hidden transcript" that the townsfolk dared not reveal to the (no doubt armed and violent) revolutionaries who had appeared among them? So long as those revolutionaries were in town, did the locals "stop well short of collective defiance," limiting themselves to "the ordinary weapons of relatively powerless groups: foot dragging, dissimulation, desertion, false compliance" and so on, only to do exactly what they really wanted as soon as the revolutionaries had left?[39] Or was there in fact another "hidden transcript"—a *pro*-revolutionary "hidden transcript"—that Josephus did *not* perceive, or, at least, that he has not chosen to record? We simply do not know. We cannot do the kind of research that Scott has done with contemporary peasant societies—the kind of research that would enable to us to give answers to such questions—and we must not pretend that we can.

In considering the "seething popular unrest" theories of Horsley and others as leading up to the Jewish War of 66, we need, perhaps, also to ask one other question: do they do not, *mutatis mutandis*, fall into a trap that Scott sees as the limitation in "a great deal of recent work on the peasantry" that focuses on "large scale protest movements"? Such movements seem, "even if only momentarily," to "promise large-scale, structural change at the level of the state"—a category into which the War of 66 surely falls.[40]

What is missing from this perspective, I believe, is the simple fact that most subordinate classes throughout most of history have rarely been afforded the luxury of open, organized, political activity. Or, better stated, such activity was dangerous, if not suicidal. Even when the option did exist, it is not clear that the same objectives might not also be pursued by other stratagems. Most subordinate classes are, after all, far less interested in changing the larger structures of the state and the law than in what Hobsbawn has appropriately called "working the system . . . to their minimum disadvantage." Formal, organized political activity, even if clandestine and revolutionary, is typically the preserve of the middle class and the intelligentsia; to look for peasant politics in this realm is to look largely in vain. It is also—not incidentally—the first step to concluding that the peasantry is a political nullity unless organized and led by outsiders.[41]

Conclusions

Overall, the most that we can say with certainty is, perhaps, this: that, to a person contemplating the situation vis-à-vis Roman rule in Judea and Galilee during the period between AD 6 and 66, at least four possibilities, four options, will have been open. Certain groups at certain times appear to have followed one of them, rather than another. I would identify these options as:

1. Acceptance of and full cooperation with Roman rule. This seems to have been the option followed most of the time by Rome's clients: Herod's family and major elements of the Sadducean priestly aristocracy.

2. Acceptance of Roman rule, coupled with a willingness on occasion to question or even challenge nonviolently the justice or appropriateness of its actions. This seems to have been the option followed by those who protested to Pilate over the matter of the soldiers' standards being brought into Jerusalem (Josephus, *War*, 2.169–74), by those who protested Caligula's decision to install in the Jerusalem Temple statues of himself (2.184–203), by Herod's family on occasion, as in their protest against Pilate's erection of votive shields in the palace at Jerusalem (Philo, *Embassy*, 299–305),[42] and, of course, by Philo himself, in the mere fact of his writing his *Embassy*.

3. Nonviolent rejection of Roman rule. This, in the view of some scholars, was the option chosen by Jesus of Nazareth.[43]

4. Violent rejection of Roman rule. This, presumably, was the option chosen by, among others, Judas the Galilean, who "incited his countrymen to revolt, upbraiding them as cowards for consenting to pay tribute to the Romans and tolerating mortal masters after having God for their lord" (*War* 2.118), by the Sicarii ("dagger men") (*War* 2.254–57), and by those who started hostilities in 66.

As we consider these options, there is, on the one hand, no need to idealize any who chose any of them, or, on the other, to suppose any to have been entirely devoid of honor or piety. Those who chose the first option, full cooperation with Rome, may well have considered themselves to be following faithfully the examples of Joseph, Ezra, and Nehemiah. Those who chose the second, cooperation with Rome coupled with willingness to question or challenge it, might have looked to Queen Esther and Daniel. Both groups might have seen themselves as interpreting and applying to their own situations the principles implied by Jeremiah for those who found themselves in continuing exile. Those who chose the third option, nonviolent rejection, may have seen as their examples Eleazar and the mother with seven sons, all of whom died rather than obey Antiochus Epiphanes. Those who chose the fourth option, violent rejection, doubtless were inspired by the examples of Judith and of Judas Maccabeus and his brothers.

What Happened Afterward

So the war was fought, the Jews were defeated, and the Temple was burned. Why? Josephus says "that it owed its ruin to civil strife, and that it was the Jewish tyrants who drew down upon the holy temple the unwilling hands of the Romans and the conflagration" (*War* 1.10; compare 6.250–253). This is part of the reason why he emphasizes Titus' unwillingness to destroy the temple (*War* 1.27–28, 6.241). As Steve Mason points out, Josephus is not saying that it was the rebels rather than the Romans who destroyed the Temple. Here, rather, is a classic example of the Jewish historian's irony. "He means that the rebels' actions led the God of the Jews to destroy the temple by purging his sanctuary with fire through the agency of Roman hands. God was in control of the whole scene."[44] In other words, Rome's triumph over Israel was *not* the work of Vespasian and Titus, still less of the Roman gods, as Roman ideology claimed. It was the work of God. Rome ruled and conquered only by God's fiat. Josephus is exactly in line with the prophetic tradition, which he evidently understood very well.

Rabbinic tradition pictures Rabban Yohanan ben Zakkai, at the end of the war, standing amid the ruins of the Jerusalem Temple. What now? Was this the end of Israel? In Yohannan ben Zakkai's view, not at all.

For we have another atonement, which is like sacrifice, and what is it? Deeds of loving kindness, as it is said, "For I desire mercy and not sacrifice." (Hos. 6.6)

The work of the Sanhedrin would continue, and Israel would live on, in the academy that Yohannan ben Zakkai (with Roman permission) would found at Yavneh. The academy's program involved three things: studying Torah, practicing the Commandments, and doing good deeds. A few years later, Yohannan's successor, Gamaliel II, gained Roman approval for a semiautonomous Jewish regime, loyal to Rome, headed by Gamaliel himself and his successors at the academy and entrusted with oversight of the internal affairs of Jews in Palestine.

The academy lasted only for about sixty years, then collapsed as a result of a second disastrous Jewish war against Rome, led by the messianic pretender Bar Kochba, from 132 to 135. Even during the years when the academy flourished, it is unclear how extensive was its direct influence on the mass of Jews.[45] Archaeological evidence has suggested to some that the rabbis did not yet have much authority over ordinary Jewish life.[46] But, in any case, what they did was enough. They laid a foundation that held firm. Of that foundation we cannot speak at length here, though surely Jacob Neusner says no more of it than is its due: "When the rabbis at Yavneh affirmed their faith that the Torah remained the will of their unvanquished God, they made certain that for twenty and more centuries Judaism would endure as a living religion, and the Jews as a vital people. The founder of the Yavneh academy, Yohannan ben Zakkai, in setting out to restore the broken heart of the people, began a revolution of the spirit that has yet to run its course."[47] What we can say here—and what is of immediate relevance for our study—is that, in the decades following the war of 66–73, and even more in the years following the war of 132–135,[48] whatever the mass of Jews may have thought or believed as regards Rome, the rabbis at least maintained the second of the four options named earlier. They continued to insist that in all things that did not directly contravene their faith, the laws of the empire must be obeyed: "The law of the emperor is law" (see, for example, b. B. Qam 113a, b. B. Bathra 54b, b. Ned. 28a). That insistence on what was, in essence, still Jeremiah's view of how to live in exile, together with the rabbis' gradually increasing influence over the ensuing centuries, enabled the Jews to flourish in a situation in which they could not make decisions about society in general but could control their domestic affairs.

In turning the nation into a religious community, in eschewing force, which they did not have, in favor of faith, which they might nurture, and in lending to matters of faith—even humble details of keeping the law—a cosmic, transcendent importance, the Pharisees succeeded in reshaping the life of Jewry in a way appropriate to their new situation. . . .

The Pharisees helped the Jews reconcile themselves to their new situation, to accept what could not be changed, and to see significance in what could yet be decided. They invested powerlessness with such meaning that ordinary folk, living everyday lives, might still regard themselves as a kingdom of priests and a holy people. The ideals of Hillel and Yohannan ben Zakkai for twenty centuries illuminated the humble and, from a worldly viewpoint, unimportant affairs of a homeless, often persecuted, despised, and alien nation, dwelling alone among other nations.[49]

So much we may say, in general terms, of the history of Israel's attitudes toward empire. The question that must concern us next is where in this spectrum we should place Jesus of Nazareth? How will the Judaism of Jesus' day have perceived him? Insofar as he fitted at all into the preconceptions of his contemporaries, how and where did he fit?

3

Jesus and Empire

The Teacher and the Man of Deed

Jesus of Nazareth in Galilee

As we have already noted, Galilee during the first thirty-five years or so following the death of Herod the Great was, on the whole, stable, and, though its ruler was a client of Rome, his land was ostensibly Jewish. In other words, Jesus did not grow up in a land where Roman *imperium* faced him at every turn. As for his place in its society, Mark speaks of him as the son of an artisan, more precisely, a *tektōn* ("one who constructs") (6.3), and there seems to be no particular reason why such a tradition should have been invented.[1] In the kinship society in which he was raised,[2] he would have inherited a certain position of honor in the community in which he grew up— an honor that, no doubt, he forfeited in the eyes of some when he began what we regard as his ministry. The gospels preserve traditions of tension in his relationships with his family and his hometown that may be echoes of such forfeiture of honor (Mark 3.20–21, 31–35, 6.1–6). Still, he would not entirely have lost his status. It is noticeable that in his teaching, Jesus is remembered as speaking of "the poor" precisely as he speaks of "the rich," as groups of which he is not personally a member (Mark 14.7; Luke 6.20, 24). That, presumably, reflected social and economic reality as he experienced it. Manifestly, he and his disciples were not members of the governing elite, and no doubt they were "poor" by the standards of twenty-first-century Western Europe or North America (as is, incidentally, most of the rest of the world). But they may not have been seen in that way by contemporaries in Galilee, who would have known of many poorer—beggars, slaves, day laborers, and even tenant farmers.[3] During his ministry, Jesus appears, moreover, to have been associated with women who disposed of sufficient means to enable them to support him and his disciples in their work (Luke 8.1–3).[4] That cannot have meant poverty.

Jesus, Prophet of God's Kingdom

When Jesus began his ministry, how would he have appeared? The most obvious and immediate answer is that he would have appeared to his contemporaries as a prophet, precisely as the evangelists suggest (Mark 6.15, 8.28//; Matt. 13.57, 21.11; Luke 24.19; John 4.44, 7.40, 9.17).[5] Virtually everything we have learned or discovered in the past century—our new knowledge of the Dead Sea Scrolls, our better awareness of the pseudepigraphical literature, our wider understanding of events and persons in Palestine contemporary with Jesus, our growing understanding of both Judaism and paganism in the same period, and, perhaps above all, our growing consciousness of the gospels as first-century Jewish and Hellenistic documents—all tend to support the view that Jesus, whatever else people said or thought of him, would have been so perceived. Such a view provides us with a figure who, strange though he may seem to us, can take his place within the first-century world. Again and again, what Jesus does resembles what others did who claimed to be prophets during the period of the second Temple (Josephus, *War*, 6.285–8, 3005). He proclaims the imminent coming of God's kingdom, he calls followers, he warns of judgment to come, and he feeds his followers in the wilderness.

This is not to deny that some features characteristically associated with Jesus would also have set him apart from other prophets. Of these, the most evident was, first, his celibacy—celibacy as part of a religious calling was probably not unknown in Judaism of the period (Matt. 19.12),[6] but it was certainly unusual. Second would have been the joy that seems to have been associated with him and his ministry (Mark 2.18–22)—surely a stark contrast, as he himself implied, with John the Baptist (Matt. 11.16–19//; Luke 7.31–35), whose eschatological baptism he had nonetheless accepted. Third, there was his acceptance of unchaperoned women among the followers who accompanied him on his journeys (Mark 15.40–41; Luke 8.13)—a phenomenon that, along with his calling men to leave their families, would no doubt, as John P. Meier observes, have "raised more than a few pious eyebrows."[7]

Finally, we should note that to some people—perhaps to a good many—

certain aspects of Jesus' teaching would actually have been offensive. He offered God's forgiveness to those who came to him as if mere association with his person were sufficient to ensure it (Mark 2.1–11//, 13-17//; Luke 8.36–50, 15.1–2). He adopted a sovereign attitude to the Law and its interpretation (Mark 2.18–22//, 23–28//, 3.1–6//; Matt. 5.17–48). He pronounced God's judgment upon the Temple, seeing himself as God's agent both in prophetically enacting its destruction and, in some sense, in bringing it about (Mark 11.15–19//; Matt. 21.12–13//; Luke 19.45–48 [John 2.13-22]).[8] He seemed willing uniquely to associate himself with the fulfillment of God's purposes in the coming judgment and kingdom (Mark 9.38//, 38–41, 10.29–30//, 12.1–12//, 12.35–40, 13.31–32//, 14.3–9, 21; Luke 4.16–21; John 1.51, 5.22–23, 19.7).

Still, for good or ill, as true or false, Jesus would have appeared primarily as a prophet, and as a prophet he proclaimed the imminent coming of God's kingdom, which evidently meant, for him as for others, that God would fulfill God's promises and vindicate God's people (Mark 1.15, 9.1; Luke 11.20).[9] Naturally, such a proclamation had implications for those who held power in the present age—for masters and slave owners, for administrators and governors, for kings and emperors—since it relativized their power, declaring them accountable for their use of it. If God reigns, then God reigns over everything, "for you know that you also have a Master in heaven" (Col. 4.1). In other words, Jesus' proclamation of the kingdom involved a political challenge, a challenge connected to the social realities of this world, just as had the proclamations of other prophets before him. But precisely what kind of challenge was it? For some Jews, like Judas the Galiliean, accepting God's sovereignty meant total rejection of Roman rule, by violence if necessary. For others, such as Caiaphas,[10] Philo, and Yohannan ben Zakkai, it apparently meant nothing of the kind. What, then, did it mean for Jesus? Which, if any, of our four options did his proclamation of the kingdom imply?

Jesus and the Roman Empire

No serious scholar, so far as I know, believes that Jesus' proclamation implied option one—unquestioning acceptance of Roman rule. John Howard Yoder believes that it implied option three—nonviolent rejection: "it belongs to the nature of the new order that, though it condemns and displaces the old, it does not do so with the arms of the old."[11] Richard A Horsley is also clear that Jesus' proclamation of the kingdom involved rejection of Roman rule.[12]

By way of moving the argument forward, let me say at once that I think both Horsley and Yoder are wrong. I do not believe that Jesus rejected or counseled rejection of Roman imperial dominion—direct or indirect—in the way that they suggest. On the contrary, I agree broadly with R. S. Sugirtharajah: "What is strikingly clear is that Jesus's alternative vision did not challenge or seek to radically alter the colonial apparatus."[13] Stating the matter more positively, I believe that Jesus stood foursquare with the biblical and prophetic attitudes toward political and imperial power represented by Nathan, Jeremiah, Daniel, and Deutero-Isaiah: he would acknowledge such power, but he would also (and therefore) hold it accountable. In other words, Jesus' words and works point to the second of our four options.

An obvious place to begin this discussion, as it appears to me, is with the matter of taxes. The evangelists record frequent dealings between Jesus and tax collectors (Mark 2.15–16//; Matt. 10.3, 11.19//; Luke 15.1), and tax collection inevitably meant either Rome, or Rome's client. As is well known from Roman as well as Jewish sources, the tax system was open to abuse and was widely abused.[14] The "tax collectors" of the gospels are tax farmers who purchased concessions to gather indirect taxes (*vectigalia*), such as harbor dues. They were despised by patriots, no doubt, for being in the service of Rome or Rome's client, but perhaps above all they were despised by just about everyone because in the process they enriched themselves through extortion (compare Luke 3.13). Evidently, this led to a situation that weighed heavily and unfairly on the poor. Hence, in the gospels, tax collectors are regularly linked with "sinners" and "prostitutes" (Mark 2.15–16//; Matt. 21.31–32). All this is undeniable. Yet the striking fact is that the gospels do not contain so much as one example of a saying of Jesus that attacks the system *as a system*. He does not even speak as strongly as does the Baptist—"Collect no more than is appointed to you" (Luke 3.13). If independence from Rome and Rome's clients were Jesus' agenda, is that not strange? Sugirtharajah's remarks on the Zacchaeus story (Luke 19.1–10) are pertinent. Luke describes Zacchaeus as "rich" and calls him *architelōnēs* (19.2), a *hapax legomenon*[15] that Jerome renders *princeps publicanorum*, "chief (superintendent?) of tax collectors." Zacchaeus was presumably in charge of the Roman customs post at the Jordan crossing near Jericho, which was the first town after the border between the Roman province of Judea and Perea, which was a part of Herod Antipas' tetrarchy.[16] As Sugirtharajah says, biblical interpreters tend to see this episode

> from the perspective of a sinner being won over by Jesus. To a certain extent they are right, but what they fail to note is the apolitical nature of this encounter. Jesus did not call upon Zacchaeus to give up his profession nor did he request him to work against the system, the very system which had made him rich. Instead, Jesus be-

lieved in a person's, in this case Zacchaeus's ability to transform
things from within, beginning with his own change of heart. Jesus's
response to an oppressive structure had more to do with personalizing the issue and appealing directly to individuals to act fairly than
with calling for a radical overhaul of the system.[17]

In this general context, what, then, is to be said of the episode wherein Jesus
is asked about "taxes to the emperor," so being directly confronted with a
question about Roman rule? "Is it lawful to pay taxes to the emperor, or not?
Should we pay them, or should we not?" "Give to Caesar the things that are
Caesar's," Jesus replies, "and to God the things that are God's" (Mark 12:14–
15, 17, and //). In Horsley's view, "the Pharisees and the Herodians would
presumably have known very well that it was not lawful, according to Mosaic
covenantal law, to pay tribute to Rome . . . Jesus is clearly and simply reassert-
ing the Israelite principle that Caesar, or any other imperial ruler, has no claim
on the Israelite people, since God is their actual king and master."[18] But why
would Jesus' hearers "presumably" have "known" that? Certainly, as we have
seen, there were some who held to such a view, like Judas the Galilean, who
"incited his countrymen to revolt, upbraiding them as cowards for consenting
to pay tribute to the Romans and tolerating mortal masters after having God
for their lord" (War 2.118). But, as we have also seen, there had long been
others, including Jeremiah and Ezra, who did not "know" any such thing,
taking quite a different view of Israel and empire. Horsley himself is certainly
aware of this. In Jesus and the Spiral of Violence, he speaks of the Jewish tradition
wherein rulers—including pagan rulers—were seen "as regents instituted by
God"—and at least on occasion that meant, as Horsley is aware, Jewish high
priests acting as "imperial tax collectors."[19] "The law of the Emperor is the
law."[20] And how on earth could Herodians[21] have "known" this, since their
master, Herod Antipas, regularly paid his tribute to Caesar and yet also claimed
to be an observant Jew?[22] In short, there were, as we have observed, options
about possible Jewish attitudes to Roman rule, some for cooperation with it,
some against. And that, I take it, was the point of the Pharisees' and the Herodians' question. That being the case, it seems rather to beg that question if
we simply "presume" that Jesus' reply has to have involved choice of an anti-
Roman option rather than one of the other options, as if that were the only
choice possible for an Israelite of the period who thought himself faithful.

Herbert O'Donovan suggests an interpretation of the passage that is virtually the opposite of Horsley's. In O'Donovan's opinion, Jesus' response simply treated the question "as an irrelevant distraction from the real business of
receiving God's kingdom. If Caesar put his head upon the coin, then presum-

ably it is his: let him have what is his if he asks for it (for such transactions are not the stuff of which true government consists), but give your whole allegiance to God's rule!"[23] In other words, pay up, because it doesn't really matter! Jesus "believed that a shift in the locus of power was taking place, which made the social institutions that had prevailed to that point anachronistic."[24] This seems to involve a distinction between things spiritual and things material, a "separation of religion from the political order" that is not only quite unbiblical but also wildly anachronistic—a distinction, therefore, against which Horsley rightly warns us.[25] After all, *everything* is transitory. No doubt Caesar's (and all other human) authority *is* only for a time. (In this particular case, it was, indeed, destined to be quite a long time. Caesar's authority would, as a plain matter of historical fact, outlive Jesus' questioners, and their children, and their children's children.) Still, transitory or not, the question remained, How we are to live with it *now?* The perceived imminence of God's kingdom does not make the question as to what is "kingdom behavior" in this age *less* pressing, but more so. So—was it "kingdom behavior" to pay Caesar's head-tax, or not? However hypocritical may have been the motives of those who put the question, it was still a real question, and particularly real in the situation in which they and Jesus found themselves. The evangelist's account suggests that Jesus' reply took them by surprise, but there is nothing in it to suggest that he did not take their question seriously, or that they did not think he had.[26]

What, then, are we to make of this narrative? Only a fool would claim to be sure about the meaning of a passage that has puzzled exegetes for centuries. Still, it does appear to me that Mark's text (which in the matters that appear important is more or less repeated by Matthew and Luke) does at this point repay close attention—closer than it always receives, even from the commentators. It also repays precise translation.

The Pharisees and the Herodians ask, "Is it lawful [*exestin*] to pay [*dounai*] taxes [*kēnson*] to the emperor, or not? Should we pay [*dōmen*] them, or should we not [*mē dōmen*]?" (12.14). The *kēnsos* (Latin, "census") to which they refer is not, actually, a matter of "tax" in general but *tributum capitis*, the poll- or head-tax, a form of levy particularly offensive to Jewish sensibilities—precisely the form of taxation, indeed, to which Judas the Galilean objected.[27] When they speak of paying this tax, the Pharisees and the Herodians three times use the word *didōmi* (*didoun* [aorist infinitive], *dōmen* [aorist subjunctive]), a word that refers to "giving" in the most general terms and that can be used in a wide variety of contexts and situations, including "giving" as "an expression of generosity."[28] This, then, is their question, and it is a perfectly clear question. It is also, given their political situation, a real question. Jesus the teacher is being invited to state whether he considers it "lawful" (*exestin*—more precisely, "permitted,"[29] that is, "permitted to a faithful Israelite") to pay Caesar's head tax. If Jesus says "it is permitted," then he aligns himself with either option one or option two of the four options we mentioned in chapter 2: that is to say, he aligns himself with those who allow for at least a measure of cooperation with Rome. If Jesus says "it is *not* permitted," then he aligns himself with either option three or option four: that is, with those who refuse cooperation with Rome.

Aside from Jesus' comment on the motives of those who question him, his initial response takes the form of a request for clarification and information. "Bring me a denarius and let me see it. . . . Whose head [*eikōn*, "likeness" or "image"][30] is this, and whose title [*epigraphē*, inscription]?"[31] But, of course, the "request" is really a rhetorical trap. "The emperor's," they say.[32] Indeed, they can say nothing else. That, after all, was precisely what many of them disliked about the coin. What then? Disliked or not, the emperor's head and inscription meant that it was the emperor's coin, and according to ancient understanding a ruler's coinage was his property. The trap springs. "Give [*apodote*] to the emperor the things that are the emperor's." Jesus' statement is, actually, more forceful than his questioners required, since he has exchanged the rather general word for payment (*didōmi*) that they used for a much more precise word, *apodidōmi*—a word that speaks of payment as "a contractual or other obligation," or restoration "to an original possessor."[33] The implication is, "Pay up what you *owe*! Give *back* to the Emperor what is his!" *Pace* Horsley, I cannot see how such a response, to such a question, in the situation in which Jesus and his questioners found themselves, can possibly have been heard or intended to be heard as "subtle avoidance"[34] or anything of that kind. On the contrary, Jesus' words, once examined, appear in their context to be quite unequivocal. As Morna Hooker correctly points out, Jesus has said that, "however much the inhabitants of Judaea dislike it, they cannot escape the authority of Caesar and the obligations that entails."[35]

Had Jesus ended his answer at this point, he would simply have been aligning himself with our options one and two (cooperation with the empire), and so with the examples of Joseph, Jeremiah, Daniel, and Ezra. But Jesus does not end his answer here. He adds, "and to God, what is God's." The form of his expression evidently implies a degree of analogy.[36] We are to pay Caesar what Caesar is owed, and we are also to pay God what God is owed. In contrast to Judas the Galilean, but in conformity with the traditions of Joseph, Daniel, and Ezra, Jesus does *not*, apparently, see a contradiction here. Perhaps it is deliberately to distinguish himself from the views of revolutionaries such as

Judas that he says this. But perhaps there is more. The basis on which he has said that something is owed to Caesar is that it bears Caesar's image. What then bears *God's* image, so that it should be owed to God? No Jew, Pharisee, or even Herodian could fail to know the answer to that. *They themselves* bore God's "image" (Gen. 1.26). They owed a mere head-tax to Caesar, because the coinage was Caesar's. But they owed themselves to God, because they belonged to God. "Truly, no ransom avails for one's life, there is no price one can give to God for it" (Ps. 49.7). They have asked Jesus a question about their relation to the *polis* and he has answered it; but in doing so he has used the form of their question to challenge them with an altogether deeper and more dangerous question of his own, about their relationship to God. No wonder "they were utterly amazed at him"! (Mark 12.17).[37]

As I have said, only a fool would claim to be sure about the meaning of a text that has puzzled exegetes for centuries. The foregoing, nonetheless, appears to be the "plain sense" (blessed phrase!) of the account that Mark and the other evangelists give. It is, surely, at least a *possible* interpretation. And, for what it is worth, the attitude to Roman taxation and related issues that it implies seems perfectly in line with Jesus' general attitude to these things as we have so far discerned it.

Once during his ministry (Matt. 8:5–13//; Luke 7.1–10), Jesus is approached by a Roman centurion, who begs him to heal his servant. Surely, a clearer symbol of Roman power than a Roman centurion would be hard to conceive. Does Jesus then speak of the centurion as the agent of an alien power, exercising a dominion over God's people that ought not to be? Does Jesus in any way criticize what the centurion represents? There is not a hint of it. On the contrary, Jesus heals the man's servant, declaring that he finds in him a quality of saving faith that he has not found elsewhere, "no not in Israel" (Matt.8.10//; Luke 7.9). Moreover, the very behavior in which Jesus sees such faith is explicitly presented to him by the centurion as modeled upon his behavior *as a military agent of imperial rule*: "for I too am a person subject to authority, with soldiers subject to me. And I say to one, 'Go,' and he goes, and to another, 'Come,' and he comes" (Matt. 8.9//; Luke 7:8). Is not all this very strange, if independence from Roman rule were Jesus' agenda?

Indeed, if independence from Rome were Jesus' agenda, it is strange overall that there is not a single saying attributed to him in any gospel that unambiguously states that agenda. Certainly one accepts the distinction between "hidden transcript" and "public transcript"[38] in relating exchanges between oppressed and oppressor. The fact remains that Josephus seems not to be in the slightest doubt as to what Eleazar b. Ari, the commander of Masada, stood for: he believed that his people should "be subject neither to the Romans nor to any other person, but only to God, for only he is the true and lawful lord of men" (Josephus, *War*, 7.323). Nor are we left to work out by inference the Sicarii's conviction "that they ought not to regard the Romans as more powerful than themselves, but rather acknowledge God as the only Lord" (*War* 7.410). Certainly Jesus was remembered as having warned his followers that they must appear "before kings and governors" (Mark 13.9; Matt. 10.18; Luke 21.12); but that is *not*, as is sometimes suggested, "a prediction of persecution by kings and governors,"[39] nor does it mean that the disciples must necessarily to be in conflict with Rome. Such an interpretation ignores an important feature of Roman legal practice, namely, that prosecutions were virtually always conducted by private individuals. To "appear" before kings and governors did *not* mean, therefore, to be persecuted by them, but simply to be in a position in which they would be required to adjudicate.[40] Much of the narrative in the closing chapters of Luke-Acts is (as we shall see at a later point in this book) taken up with Luke's view of how Jesus' prediction was fulfilled, and how, moreover, when the "kings and governors" did their job, far from being the enemies of Paul and his companions, they were actually his protectors.

In my prologue to this book, I quoted Horsley's comment that "trying to understand Jesus' speech and action without knowing how Roman imperialism determined the conditions of life in Galilee and Jerusalem" is rather like "trying to understand Martin Luther King without knowing how slavery, reconstruction, and segregation determined the lives of African-Americans in the United States."[41] I agree. The comparison is valid. But for that very reason it may be pressed further. If one were to study some *other* American preacher, a contemporary of King in the southern United States, whose recorded teaching seldom even *mentioned* slavery, reconstruction, or segregation, and when it did, did so in a way that was, to say the least, ambiguous or unclear, what conclusion would one be obliged to draw from that? Surely, either that the preacher was not interested in those questions or else that he had a view of them very different from King's. And that, *mutatis mutandis*, is exactly what happens when we set the remembered teachings of Jesus alongside those of heroes of Jewish resistance to Rome such as Eleazar b. Ari, even as they appear in the pages of such a lukewarm advocate as Josephus. Moreover, the more we might incline to think that Horsley is right (over against, say, Cohen, Neusner, or Freyne) in his analysis of the *general* situation of anti-Roman unrest and resistance in first century Galilee and Judea, the weaker, in this connection, Jesus' words sound.

Jesus' Healings, Exorcisms, and Rome

Horsley sees Jesus' healings and exorcisms as particularly showing his rejection of Roman power.

> The portrayal of Jesus' exorcisms in Mark and Q indicates that at all levels Jesus was exposing and expelling, even defeating, the demonic forces (which, once exposed, were associated with Roman imperialism). . . . At the most fundamental, phenomenological level, the effects of possession by such alien forces were violent antisocial and self-destructive behavior (Mark 5:2–5, 9.18). Jesus commands power/authority over these "unclean spirits" (1:22, 27). He not only expels them but "defeats" them (1:23–26). Thus liberated from the "occupying" alien force, the person returns to a rightful state of mind and social life (5:15, 20).[42]

At the "overarching spiritual level," Jesus' exorcisms "indicated that God was finally winning the war against Satan." At the political level, since Satan/Belial and the demons were working through or were represented by the Romans, when Jesus drove out the demon whose name was "Legion," it was clear that it was really the Romans who were possessing the people.[43] So, by implication, Jesus' exorcisms were freeing the people from Roman oppression.[44]

But was that the implication? We need not dispute that the story of the Gadarene demoniac implies some association between demons who call themselves "legion" and the Roman army, although we are bound to note that this is the only time in the entire gospel tradition when such an association is made. Still, it is made here, and of course Horsley is not (and does not claim to be) the only one to have noticed this.[45] One could even go further and conceive of a scenario behind the story such as Sugirtharajah suggests: fear of recruitment into the legions. "The terror of Roman military tyranny, and the thought of expatriation" had "deranged [the demoniac's] mind, leaving him obsessed day and night with the thought of imperial service."[46] Of course, such a scenario can be no more than a guess, since the text itself tells us nothing. Still, given the narrative we have, and the reality of Roman presence and Roman recruitment practice, it is a guess that might be right.[47] What then? Even if that is the situation, the only thing that we see Jesus actually *doing* is healing the man, restoring him to "his right mind" (Mark 5.15). To argue that Jesus was thereby freeing the people from Roman rule appears to be about as logical as arguing that a doctor who cures a man who has been run over by a bus is thereby abolishing public transport. That said, one must note that Sugirtharajah's own suggestion appears equally wide of the mark. Sugirtharajah points out that "demoniac possession was a type of social mechanism developed by the colonized to face the radical pressures opposed by colonization." That may be true. What is questionable, however, is the conclusion Sugirtharajah then draws. By curing the man, he suggests, Jesus could actually be seen as "a threat to an accepted mode of open hostility towards the Roman oppressors," since he had "effectively removed one of the potential tools in the hand of the subjugated people."[48] But such trauma and its effects, however understandable, would evidently not be a "tool" against oppression at all. They would merely be ways of coping with oppression by retreating from reality—which is to say, ways of doing nothing. To remove such a mechanism would not therefore be to remove a tool for hostility. To remove it would be to set the oppressed free, free if they chose to face the facts of fear and hostility and to react to them not by retreat into nonreality, but as adults who know themselves to be children of God. Especially significant here is Jesus' counsel to the healed man. "Go home to your friends, and tell them how much the Lord has done for you, and how he has had mercy on you"(Mark 5.19). Those who honor and fear God do not need to fear the legions. "Do not fear those who kill the body but cannot kill the soul; rather fear him who can destroy both soul and body in hell" (Matt. 10.28).

In Horsley's view, others who appear in the healing stories are also "representative figures."[49] Thus,

Both the woman who had been hemorrhaging for twelve years and the nearly dead twelve-year-old girl clearly represent the people of Israel, which consisted symbolically of twelve tribes. The original hearers of the Gospel would have known tacitly and implicitly—and we can reconstruct by historical investigation—that both the individual and the social hemorrhaging and near death were the effects of the people's subjection to imperial forces. Thus as the woman's faith that special powers are working through Jesus, leading her to take the initiative in touching his garment, results in her healing, so also the people's trust that God's restorative powers are working through Jesus is leading to their recovery from the death-dealing domination by Roman imperial rule. When Jesus brings the seemingly dead twelve-year-old girl back to life just at the time she has come of age to produce children, he is mediating new life to Israel in general. In these and other episodes Jesus is healing the illnesses brought on by Roman imperialism.[50]

There are two problems with this. First, there is no evidence for it. The narratives never mention Rome, directly or indirectly. Second, such discernment of "dramatic representation," highly subjective as it is, can work in more than one way. We have already noted the role played in another healing narrative by a centurion who possessed faith not found in Israel. Surely it is just as likely that "the original hearers of the gospel" would have seen him as representative of Roman rule, as that they would have seen "the woman who had been hemorrhaging for twelve years and the nearly dead twelve-year-old girl" as "clearly" representative of "the people of Israel." And, if so, what would *that* identification have to say about "Jesus and empire"?

Conclusions

In sum, there is nothing in the narratives of Jesus' ministry that sets him apart from the general theology of empire that was adumbrated by the traditions of Nathan, Jeremiah, Daniel, Deutero-Isaiah, and Ezra and that is characteristic of the biblical tradition. The traditions of his words and works in general do not indicate the slightest interest in changing the forms or structures of temporal power, in replacing one system of government with another, or in questions as to whether those who ruled were believers or pagans. Those same traditions do, however, indicate a concern that those who have power understand it as God's gift to them, given for the sake of God's people and the world.[51] This is the attitude that Jesus consistently maintains on every occasion where he is seen dealing with those who have temporal authority.

Thus, Jesus does not question the authority of Rome's client Herod Antipas, tetrarch of Galilee, and seems as much amused as scornful at the luxury of his lifestyle (Matt. 11.8//; Luke 7.25). Still, he addresses him bluntly as "fox" and warns him that he cannot interfere in God's work (Luke 13.32).[52]

Jesus does not question the authority of Rome's collaborators the Sadducean high-priests but still warns them publicly that their failure to listen to God's prophets will lead to their fall (Mark 11.27–12.10//; Matt 21.33–46//; Luke 20.1–19). It is in this context that we should see Jesus' prophetically enacted destruction of the Temple (Mark 11.15–17//; Matt. 21.12–13//; Luke 19.45–6 [John 2.13–7]),[53] and the conversation with the "good" scribe, the upshot of which is that to concentrate on love of God and the love of neighbor is more important than the entire sacrificial system (Mark 12.28–34).

Jesus does not question the authority of the scribes who "sit on Moses' seat." On the contrary, his followers are to "do whatever they teach you and follow it" (Matt. 23.2–3). But "woe" to those Pharisees who, concerned with tithing mint, dill, and cumin, "have neglected the weightier matters of the law: justice and mercy and faith" (Matt. 23.23; compare Mark 7.1–12//; Matt. 15.1– 20; Luke 7.36–50). We have already spoken of Jesus' sovereign attitude to the Law; here we must especially beware of depoliticizing the debate. Maintenance of these traditions was, in the eyes of many, precisely what constituted Israel's identity, its separateness from "the nations" (Philo, *Special Laws*, 115–16; Josephus, *Against Apion*, 2.147, 178–98). For these traditions, its heroes and heroines had been prepared to die (see 1 Macc. 2.23–68; 2 Macc. 6.1–19). "Zeal" for the Law meant willingness to defend such traditions by violence if necessary—in other words, it meant armed resistance, in the spirit of Phinehas and Elijah (Num. 25.6–8; 1 Macc 2.25–26, 41–44). All that is what Jesus is challenging when he speaks of tithing as of minor significance in relation to the imminent kingdom. Later on, as we have seen, Yohannan ben Zakkai would propose commitment to piety and the avoidance of politics. In Jesus' situation, to treat some forms of piety as merely relative was already a political act.

Jesus does not question the authority of the pagan Caesar, within the spheres that God has allotted to him (" 'Whose likeness and inscription is this?' They said to him, 'Caesar's.' "), but still he sets that authority firmly within the sphere of God's overarching providence and power: "Render to God the things that are God's" (Mark 12.13–17; compare John 19.11). Caesar, like all who rule from Pharaoh onward, would ignore or oppose that providence and power at his peril.

Now, of course, such concerns as these had political implications—which is to say, they had implications as to how those who held political power were called to exercise it. But that did not make these concerns specifically anti-Roman any more than they were anti-Jewish or anti-Parthian or anti-anything else. In such a context, to equate the kingdom for which Jesus looked with the mere "general agenda" of "independence from Roman imperial rule"—or even with a broader agenda that God's people should be independent of foreign rule generally—is surely to trivialize it.

I would make one final point. An element that I find truly remarkable in Edward Said's work is its generosity. Despite Said's own somewhat depressing experiences of imperialism both British and American—different from each other in style, but each equally oppressive to a sensitive Palestinian boy[54]—still he was able in later years to claim that

> most of us should now regard the historical experience of empire as a common one. The task is then to describe it as pertaining to Indi-

ans *and* British, Algerians *and* French, Westerners *and* Africans, Asians, Latin Americans, and Australians, despite the horrors, the bloodshed, and the vengeful bitterness.[55]

Moreover, and perhaps most important of all, "what does need to be remembered is that narratives of emancipation and enlightenment in their strongest form were also narratives of *integration* not separation."[56] So we should take seriously our calling

> to make connections, to deal with as much of the evidence as possible . . . above all, to see complementarity and interdependence instead of an isolated, venerated, or formalized experience that excludes and forbids the hybridizing intrusions of actual human history.[57]

Such generosity of spirit is also a mark of the biblical and prophetic tradition from Jeremiah on. It was that generosity that Jesus offered in his ministry—offered it, moreover, to Jewish artisan and Roman soldier alike. He at all times insisted on a proclamation of God's kingdom that was not only "a narrative of emancipation and enlightenment" but also "a narrative of integration and not separation." If Luke is right (see Luke 4.16–30!), that very insistence made him at times seem intolerable.

So much may be said of Jesus' ministry. There remains, however, the matter of his death. In John P. Meier's opinion, "the precise reason(s) why Jesus' life ended as it did, namely at the hands of the Roman prefect on the charge of claiming to be King of the Jews, is the starkest, most disturbing, and most central of all the enigmas that Jesus posed and was."[58] To consideration of that enigma we must now turn.

APPENDIX

Jesus, Violence, and Nonviolence

I am not entirely sure whether there is a difference between Horsley and Yoder over the question of violence, on which, as it appears to me, Horsley is somewhat ambivalent. On the one hand, in his earlier book, *Jesus and the Spiral of Violence,* he expresses concern about first-world theologians telling third-world theologians not to revolt and declares with regard to texts such as Matthew 5.38–42 ("Do not resist one who is evil.... Love your enemies.") that these verses contain "nothing whatever ... pertaining to the issue of political violence."[1] In *Jesus and Empire,* moreover, he sees Jesus standing "shoulder to shoulder" with "other leaders of movements among the Galilean and Judean people" pursuing "the same general agenda in parallel paths: independence from Roman imperial rule"—which, presumably, could mean option four: violent rejection of Roman rule.[2] On the other hand, I am not entirely sure what Horsley means by "in parallel paths," and in *Jesus and Empire* he writes with obvious approval and sympathy of what he clearly sees as nonviolent popular resistance to Roman rule—in other words, of option three.[3]

Horsley's exegesis of the two closing antitheses of the Sermon on the Mount (Matt. 5.38–48) does (as he is well aware) stand apart from much—perhaps even most—scholarly opinion. We may contrast, for example, Ulrich Luz, who, while conceding that "Matthew did not think primarily and specifically in political terms of the renunciation of violence," is clear nonetheless that "one must not exclude the political realm."[4] Moreover, while we may sympathize with the concern that first-world theologians should not tell third-world theologians what to do, we must at the same time beware of a protectiveness toward them that at best may be patronizing (as if they really could not take our best shot) and at worst bids fair to become another, albeit gentler, form of oppression. I am sure that Horsley intends nothing of the kind, but, again, it appears to me to be a danger inherent in his position. As it happens, theologians of the third world have shown themselves well able to handle the concepts involved and, indeed, to find in them a source of dignity for the oppressed of which the oppressor cannot rob them. So Archbishop Desmond Tutu, perceiving human identity as "primarily defined by God's image," sees prayer as the means through which "negative abuses or negative determinations of identity are corrected" and connects this directly with the matters we have seen at issue in Matthew 5.38–48, pointing out that, in "contrast to retaliatory theologies, prayer also takes to heart the salvation of the oppressor."[5] This appears to be precisely in the spirit of Jeremiah's theology of exile. Nor is Tutu in the least fazed by "first-world" misappropriation of biblical language. On the contrary, he has declared bluntly that we "should rehabilitate the great Christian words such as reconciliation and peace which have fallen on bad days, being thoroughly devalued by those who have used them to justify evil."[6]

The only study of which I am aware that unequivocally equates Jesus' position with that of the violent revolutionaries is S. G. F. Brandon's *Jesus and the Zealots*, published in 1947.[7] Brandon argued largely on the basis of massive skepticism as to the historicity of the gospel narratives. Naturally, since for most of the matters under discussion the gospels are our only source of information, this position is hard to disprove—or, of course, to prove.[8]

4

Jesus and Empire

The Crucified

"The Romans," Horsley writes,

> of course, killed both popular messianic and popular pro-
> phetic leaders. The main conclusion we can draw from Je-
> sus' execution is based on its method. Given that crucifix-
> ion was used mainly for slaves and rebels among subject
> peoples, the Romans must have understood Jesus to be an
> insurrectionary of some sort. . . . That Jesus was crucified by
> the Roman governor stands as a vivid symbol of his histori-
> cal relationship with the Roman imperial order.[1]

But is the crucifixion really a symbol of that relationship? Or is it a
symbol of something else? Josephus recounts for us an in some
ways extraordinarily parallel affair involving one Jesus ben Hananiah, about thirty years later. According to Josephus, in the year 62,
Jesus ben Hananiah, like Jesus of Nazareth, prophesied God's coming judgment and spoke against the Temple.[2] Josephus' account of
him is part of his description of a whole series of portents and
warnings of doom for Jerusalem and the Temple that preceded the
outbreak of the war:

> Four years before the war, when the city [of Jerusalem] was
> enjoying profound peace and prosperity, there came to the
> feast at which it is the custom of all the Jews to erect taber-
> nacles to God, one Jesus ben Hananiah, a rude peasant,
> who, standing in the temple, suddenly began to cry out, "A

voice from the east, a voice from the west, a voice from the four winds; a voice against Jerusalem and the sanctuary, a voice against the bridegroom and the bride, a voice against all the people." Day and night he went about all the alleys with this cry on his lips. Some- of the leading citizens, incensed at these ill-omened words, arrested the fellow and severely chastised him. But he, without a word on his own behalf or for the private ear of those who smote him, only con- tinued his cries as before. Thereupon, the magistrates, supposing as was indeed the case, that the man was under some supernatural im- pulse, brought him before the Roman governor. There, although flayed to the bone with scourges, he neither sued for mercy nor shed a tear, but, merely introducing the most mournful variations into his ejaculation, responded to each stroke with, "Woe to Jerusa- lem!" When Albinus, the governor, asked him who and whence he was, and why he uttered these cries, he answered him never a word, but unceasingly re-iterated his dirge over the city, until Albinus pro- nounced him a maniac, and let him go. (*War* 6.300–5, H. St. J. Thackery, transl. alt.)

What this narrative indicates is that, at a time of great tension, when the general political situation was actually much more strained than in the time of Jesus, even *then* the Romans were capable of seeing a Jewish prophet who spoke against the Temple as posing no particular threat to them. Why, then, thirty years earlier, would they not have seen Jesus in that way? Well, to be sure, according to the unwavering testimony of all four evangelists, that is exactly how they *did* perceive Jesus. The passion narratives in the gospels all say, more or less, that Pilate was initially prepared to deal with Jesus of Nazareth exactly as Albinus would later deal with Jesus ben Hananiah but was then persuaded, for political reasons, to apply the death penalty where he knew it was not warranted. How far may we rely on those narratives as witnesses to what may have happened? In the opinion of a number of contemporary scholars, hardly at all. For my part, I do not share that view, although I grant that the issue is not simple.[3] In my own approach to these narratives, therefore, I continue to proceed by the normal criteria of historical judgment: treating our texts criti- cally in the light of what other evidence we have, acknowledging that many historical judgments can only be provisional, being generally more confident of conclusions that seem to meet the criteria of multiple attestation and con- sistency, and at the same time conceding, with Kennedy, the possibility that the evangelists, like other ancient writers, sometimes meant what they said and occasionally even knew what they were talking about.

The Arraignment before the Sanhedrin

According to all four gospel accounts, the Sanhedrin arraigned Jesus on a capital charge (Mark 14.63-64//; Matt. 26.65–66; Luke 22.71 [implicit]; John 19.7). Strikingly, apparent references to Jesus' execution in Jewish sources support the evangelists, to the extent that they, too, claim primary responsibility in the matter for the Jerusalem authorities: so Josephus in *Antiquities* 18.63–65 (the much discussed *testimonium Flavianum*), and the Talmudic passage *b. Sanhedrin* 43a.[4]

What may we say of a process involving the Sanhedrin that could have led to this? Here we enter other hotly debated areas. Nonetheless, we may, for our immediate purposes, file certain questions by title.

First, that there was one Sanhedrin with (subordinate to Rome) a measure of authority over Jewish affairs we do not, I think, need to doubt. It is the testimony of the New Testament, Josephus, and the later rabbinic sources. Discussions, therefore, as to the possibility of there having been two sanhedrins, what they were, and which one was involved in the arraignment and interrogation of Jesus we may leave aside.[5]

Second, we do not know under what rules the Sanhedrin would have proceeded in such an affair. It is now fairly generally agreed by Jewish and Christian scholars that the rules regarding capital charges that are recorded in the Mishnah tractate *Sanhedrin* reflect later practice and cannot usefully be applied here. We may, perhaps, surmise that the pre-70 Sanhedrin proceeded under rules that were Sadduccean. We may further surmise that those rules would have accorded with regulations set out in the books of Moses. We may then note that nothing in the accounts of Jesus' appearance before the Sanhedrin actually contradicts any Mosaic regulation.[6] But even those modest suggestions can be no more than that: suggestions. We have no actual knowledge of the rules under which the pre-70 Sanhedrin proceeded, and therefore—and this is the important point—no reason to declare, as has sometimes been done, that its proceedings in the matter of Jesus were irregular, or illegal, or anything of that kind.[7]

Third, the careful reader may have noted that in what I have written so far I have avoided the word "trial" in speaking of Jesus' appearance before the Sanhedrin, even though use of that word has become customary.[8] We are, again, not clear exactly how those who conducted such a process would have regarded it. Perhaps they would have seen it more as what we might call a preliminary interrogation, or arraignment, than as a trial. So we are on safer ground in continuing to use such generally neutral terms and avoiding "trial."

We are, however, fairly sure of one thing: that a Sanhedrin of the period between 6 and 66 was capable of handing a man over to the Romans and seeking a death penalty on the basis of what we would regard as "religious" charges—specifically, speaking against the Temple and prophesying God's coming judgment, for, as we have seen, that is apparently what happened in 62 in the case of Jesus ben Hananiah. Was that unreasonable, or wicked, of them? By our post-Enlightenment standards of toleration, of course, yes. But by their standards? Indeed, by the universal standards of the ancient world? Not at all. The ancients, Jews and pagans alike, took blasphemy with a seriousness that we modern Westerners, Jews and Christians alike, can scarcely begin to comprehend.

But would the Sanhedrin have regarded Jesus as a blasphemer? What, exactly, was "blasphemy" (blasphemein—"to abuse, to insult")? It was not only, as is sometimes claimed, a matter of cursing the divine name (Lev. 24.16) but also any matter that involved deriding, demeaning, or insulting the God of Israel. And such demeaning is implicit in the words and works of any who illicitly claim for themselves prerogatives that are God's alone (hence John 10.33: " 'It is not for a good work that we stone you but for blasphemy; because you, being a man, make yourself God' ").[9] The evangelists differ in their descriptions of the process before the Sanhedrin. Thus, Matthew stresses more than the other synoptic evangelists what he sees as the malevolence and falsehood of Jesus' accusers (Matt. 26.59). Mark writes so as to strengthen his people for persecution and stresses that Jesus goes as it is written of him. Luke, though he leaves us in no doubt as to Jesus' claim, omits direct statement of the charges against him, notably the charge of blasphemy by the high priest—a style of reticence that Luke displays elsewhere.[10] But all the evangelists more or less agree on the main issues involved, and those issues are, strikingly, precisely the issues that we have already noted in our general discussion of Jesus' ministry. Jesus spoke of God's judgment upon the Temple and, moreover, associated himself with that judgment (Mark 14.57–58//; Matt. 26.60–61; compare Mark 11.15–19//; Matt. 21.12–13//; Luke 19.45–48 [John 2.13–22]).[11] He spoke of God's purposes in the coming kingdom and judgment and again uniquely associated himself with that fulfillment (Mark 14.61–62//; Matt. 27.63–65//; Luke 22.67–71; compare Mark 8.38//, 38–41, 10.29–30//, 12.1–12//, 12.35–40, 13.31–32//, 14.3–9, 21; Luke 4.16–19; John 1.51, 5.22–23, 19.7). That said, however, we can hardly leave out of account (or suppose that the Sanhedrin could have left out of account) other well-attested aspects of Jesus' ministry to which we have also referred, most strikingly his acceptance and forgiveness of sinners, as if mere association with himself were sufficient to assure that forgiveness, and his sovereign attitude to the Law and its interpretation.

I suggested earlier that aspects of the foregoing would have been offensive to many Jews. Evidently, I was putting the matter mildly. Jesus could reasonably have been understood as calling into question precisely those three features that we have noted as the core of first-century Judaism, namely belief in the one God, acceptance of Torah (the Law), and the Temple. We have noted that Jesus would have appeared to his contemporaries in the guise of a prophet. That being so, if his claims were not true, then his blasphemy could be summed up in the charge that he was a *false* prophet, a deceiver, who was "leading the people astray" (John 7.12). The fourth evangelist's interpretation of the tradition is here exactly in line with the synoptic description of what happened before the Sanhedrin. It is as a false prophet that Jesus is reviled (Mark 14.64–65; Matt. 26.66–68; Luke 22.63–65). And false prophets are to die (Deut. 18.20). It is, incidentally, in terms of false prophecy that Jesus' condemnation is described in the *baraita* in the Babylonian Talmud: he is one who "enticed Israel to apostasy" (*b. Sanh.* 43a; also 107b).[12]

If, then, Jesus merely did and said the things, the very generally attested things, that we have mentioned, I would agree totally with Raymond Brown— "I see little reason to doubt that his opponents would have regarded him as blasphemous (i.e. arrogantly claiming prerogatives or status more properly associated with God), even as the Gospels report."[13] Indeed I would go further. I do not see how the Sanhedrin could possibly have come to any other conclusion. If the tradition is accurate, then Caiaphas, by the form of his question, actually gave Jesus the opportunity to make a messianic claim that would not have been blasphemous. Jesus, by his response, does not merely answer in the affirmative but takes the matter to a level that almost (if not quite) *invites* the charge of blasphemy (Mark 14.61–62). The traditional tag—*aut deus aut homo non bonus*—"either he was God or he was not a good man," for all it reflects the Christology of a later age, still perceives an aspect of the affair that we moderns, with our post-Enlightenment anxiety to reduce Jesus to someone whom we might understand and of whom we might approve, can easily miss. The Sanhedrin did not.[14]

The Arraignment before Pilate

So the Sanhedrin, believing that God's honor required the death of the deceiver, took Jesus before Pilate, the Roman prefect, to ratify its decision and carry out the execution. Why, if the Sanhedrin was satisfied that Jesus deserved the death penalty, did it take him before the governor? Neither the synoptic evangelists nor Josephus offers a reason. The fourth evangelist, however, does: "Pilate said to them, 'Take him yourselves and judge him by your own law.' The Jews said to him, 'It is not lawful for us to put any man to death.' This was to fulfill the word which Jesus had spoken to show by what death he was to die" (John 18.31–32). The "law" of which they speak is, of course, Roman law, not Jewish.[15] Rome, according to John, reserved the right of execution to itself. But did it? Here, again, the matter is hotly debated. My own view is that it did, and that the process described by the evangelists and implied by Josephus is more or less what had to happen.[16] But, in any case, the point made by Geza Vermes (who regards the debate as more evenly balanced than do I) remains unanswerable: even if the Sanhedrin were not *required* to hand over to the Romans every case that it regarded as capital, there can be little doubt that this is what it did, "if at any time it seemed to them expedient." Vermes refers for confirmation to the episode of Jesus ben Hananiah, to which I have already referred more than once.[17] I agree. There is, then, not the slightest reason to doubt the testimony of all our witnesses, Christian and Jewish, that this is what they did in the case of Jesus of Nazareth. In Josephus' words, "upon an indictment brought by the leading men among us, Pilate sentenced him to the cross" (*Ant.* 18.64), a description of Jesus' condemnation that, as Meier points out, "cannot stem from the four gospels—and certainly not from early Christian expansions of them."[18]

Though pagans also took seriously the matter of dishonoring the gods, they could hardly be expected to appreciate the Sanhedrin's sensitivities over someone who had blasphemed the God of Israel. So, though, again, the evangelists differ in details, they are in general agreement that the Sanhedrin's representatives chose to restate the charges against Jesus for Pilate's benefit. They presented Jesus as guilty not so much of blasphemy as of *maiestas laesa—lèse-majesté*, an offense against the state, or high treason. He calls himself "king of the Jews" (Mark 15.2; Matt. 27.11; Luke 23.2–3; John 18.33, 19.3, 14, 15). Given that God's honor demanded Jesus' death, and that Pilate's sanction would be (even if not necessary) desirable, that, too, might have seemed a reasonable, and even a proper, way of proceeding.

What, then, of Pilate? As it happens, even if Pilate were not mentioned in the gospels, he would still make it into the history books, at least as an occasional footnote. Josephus has almost nothing to say of the first four (or five) prefects who governed Judea; he appears even to be confused about how many there were (*Ant.* 18.2, 29–33, *War* 2.117).[19] But then he becomes quite expansive about Pilate and tells a number of stories about him, such as his introduction of legionary standards into Jerusalem, contrary to Jewish sensitivities (Josephus, *War*, 2.169–74), and his attempt to build an aqueduct to bring water into Jerusalem using (perhaps overusing?)[20] Temple funds (*War* 2.175–77). Philo of

Alexandria (who certainly has his own axes to grind)[21] also has things to say about Pilate. He describes him as "a man of inflexible, stubborn, and cruel disposition," whose administration was marked by "venality, violence, robbery, assault, abusive behavior, frequent executions without trial, and endless savage ferocity" (*Leg.* 301–2). Philo also tells of an episode wherein Pilate lays up gilded shields in Herod's palace in Jerusalem—again, to the fury of the people (Philo, *In Flaccum*, 299–304). Then there are the gospel portraits of Pilate. These differ among themselves. Mark presents Pilate as having no part in the Sanhedrin's desire to destroy Jesus but yet allowing himself to be pressured by them and the crowd into doing so.[22] Matthew, by contrast, while not exonerating Pilate, is especially interested in highlighting the primary responsibility of the Sanhedrin for Jesus' death.[23] Luke is interested in showing that Jesus was guilty of no crime against Roman law, so that profession of Christianity and loyalty to Rome are not incompatible. Therefore, Luke stresses Pilate's awareness of Jesus' innocence both before Rome and before Rome's client Herod Antipas so that his handing Jesus over to execution is above all an act of weakness and a *failure* to uphold Roman order.[24] John's Pilate knows that Jesus is no threat to Rome but uses the situation to mock not only the prisoner but also "the Jews." He will give them their execution, but in return they must renounce their messianic hope.[25] Still, the evangelists do all present Pilate in *essentially* the same light. He knows what he ought to do, and, for the sake of a quiet life, he does not do it.[26] Either he sees the situation involving Jesus as a threat to public order and fears a riot (Mark 15.11–15//; Matt. 27.21–24//; Luke 23.23–24), or he else fears for his reputation with the emperor (John 19.12) (the two concerns would hardly have been incompatible).

New Testament critics have come almost as a matter of course to highlight the differences between the portrait of Pilate in Philo and Josephus on the one hand and that in the gospels on the other.[27] Certainly, the Jewish and the Christian witnesses do look at Pilate from different perspectives, even as the individual evangelists differ among themselves in the way they look at him. All that granted, I rather agree with Lémonon that as historians we do better to concentrate on what the various portraits of Pilate have in common—"des phénomènes de convergence"[28]—rather than on what distinguishes them. Then we find that the various sources, and the various episodes they describe, tend to coincide as reflections of a man as weak in his understanding of those whom he was sent to govern as in his concern for their sensitivities and yet a man who cannot have been devoid of ability—he did, after all, manage to survive as governor for ten or so years (26–36), and during that time he must have arrived at some kind of *modus vivendi* with Caiaphas, who was High Priest when he arrived and remained High Priest for the whole of his tenure (18–

36).[29] Thus, whatever may have been the precise trouble over the use of Temple funds for the aqueduct, clearly such funds could not have been used at all without the High Priest's cooperation.[30] A *modus vivendi* between Pilate and the High Priest is, moreover, implicit in the kind of political accommodation to which the passion narratives, taken overall, seem to point.[31]

In terms of his reputation, Pilate had, perhaps, one piece of really bad luck. Before he returned to Rome (Josephus, *War*, 2.224) and retired from history,[32] he was unfortunate enough to be involved in the affair of Jesus of Nazareth—an affair with implications transcending anything he could possibly have imagined. The evangelists' testimony that he feared a riot may be essentially correct. If so, his evident misjudgments of local mood on previous occasions would have contributed to the delicacy of his situation. (Moreover, if, as is possible, the crucifixion took place between 30 and 32,[33] then, in the event of real trouble, it is likely that Pilate would not have been able to rely on Syria's three legions for the immediate maintenance of public order and security. He would have been totally dependent on his own troops.[34] These were all auxiliaries and amounted to no more than five infantry cohorts and one cavalry regiment—about three thousand men for the entire province.)[35] So, regardless of Pilate's personal view of the man at the center of potential trouble, he was taking the obvious route, and perhaps saving a number of lives, Jewish as well as Roman, in having him eliminated before the trouble started. In thus preferring expediency to honor and convenience to justice, and all in the name of security, Pilate would have behaved no better, but certainly no worse, than have millions of politicians and civil servants before and after him. He gave way to the will of his subjects, just as he had done on several other occasions during his governorship—over the standards, the aqueduct, and the golden shields. From his point of view, what followed was no doubt a routine execution of an alleged messianic agitator. But, notably, he appears only to have crucified the leader, not his followers. Perhaps Pilate was not so cruel as Philo suggested; or perhaps, given the volatility of the situation, he was merely being prudent. In either case, either his restraint or his common sense deserve some approval.

Conclusions

What, then, of Jesus in all this? What I find remarkable—and what is particularly relevant to our discussion—is that at no point is Jesus remembered as contesting the jurisdiction or authority of *either* of the tribunals that he faces. He who is variously portrayed as claiming authority to forgive sins, to act as lord of the Sabbath, and to set aside all other interpretations of Torah in favor of his own is *not* portrayed as having by so much as a syllable questioned the Sanhedrin's authority over him in a matter of blasphemy or the Roman prefect's authority over him in a matter of treason. When questioned, he answers (Mark 14.61–62// Matt. 26.63–64// Luke 22.67–70; Mark 15.2). When condemned, he is silent (Mark 14.64–65// Matt. 26.66–68; Mark 15.15// Matt. 27.26// Luke 23.25; John 19.16). The fourth evangelist does not record an exchange with the high priest such as is the climax of the interrogation by the Sanhedrin in the synoptics, but in his own way he goes further than they do. The Johannine Jesus explicitly denies that his "kingship" is concerned with the changing of political structures: "My kingship is not of this world; if my kingship were of this world, my servants would fight, that I might not be handed over to the Jews; but my kingship is not from the world" (John 18.36). With regard to the Roman *imperium*, he also, in good prophetic tradition, acknowledges that Pilate's authority stands within God's providence: "You would have no power over me unless it had been given you from above" (19.11). Rome is under God's judgment, but that is precisely because Rome does not rule without God's fiat.

So we return to the question with which our chapter began. Is Jesus' death a symbol of his relationship to the Roman imperial order? Of course, we cannot be sure about the precise historical realities and motivations surrounding an event that took place two thousand years ago, recorded for us by partial and often polemic witnesses whose concerns are not ours. Still, I suspect that the proper answer to that question, so far as we can frame an answer, is no. Jesus' death is no more a symbol of his relationship to the Roman imperial order than it is (as many claimed in the past) a symbol of his relationship to his own people. There is irony here, for in avoiding one form of self-serving rhetoric— "the Jews were guilty"—we are in danger of adopting another, equally self-serving—"the Romans were guilty." I sympathize with Raymond Brown's suggestion that we abandon talk of "guilt" altogether and speak simply of "responsibility."[36] But, in the end, it does not matter. For, whatever we call it, the historical probability is that Jesus' death was brought about not by bad people or evil systems but by average people—indeed, in the case of the Sanhedrin, probably rather better than average—doing the best they could under systems that were no worse than others in the ancient world, and perhaps rather better than most. Arguably, the Sanhedrin, faced with the claims that Jesus made, did the only thing that it could do: it handed him over to God. Arguably, Pilate, faced with a riot, did what he was supposed to do: he kept the peace. Now, of course, with the benefit of two thousand years' hindsight, we can see that their "best" was not good enough. But that merely sets them with the rest of us. If there is guilt here (and no doubt there is), then it is, as Paul saw, a guilt that involves us all. The death of Jesus is no more a symbol of his relationship to the Roman imperial order than it is a symbol of his relationship to the Jews. It is a symbol of his relationship to the *world*. And that means, to us.

APPENDIX A

The Gospel Passion Narratives as Historical Sources

How far may we rely on the biblical passion narratives as witnesses to what may actually have happened? The issue is not a simple one. Certainly the story of Jesus' passion was not told—or, as I would more precisely express it, proclaimed and performed[1]—for the purpose of providing historical information in the sense in which a post-Enlightenment historian looks for such information. The passion story, and indeed the entire gospel tradition as handed on by apostles and evangelists, functioned to remind the Christian community who and whose they were: it was constitutive of their identity.[2] This tradition was handed on, moreover, in a form and language that constantly echoed the form and language of Israel's Scripture, thereby establishing both Jesus' particular identity as the fulfillment of God's promises and the identity of the proclaimers as God's continuing people, the heirs of those promises.[3] Typical is the formula cited by Paul: "that Christ died for our sins (*hyper tōn hamartiōn hēmōn*) in accordance with the Scriptures" (1 Cor. 15.3). The claim that Christ died "for our sins" associates his death directly with the work of the Lord's Servant at Isaiah 53.4–6[4]; the claim that he died "for *our* sins" identifies those who proclaim the memory as the ones for whom he died; and the claim that all this is "according to the Scriptures" widens the implications of what has been said so as to refer not simply to a particular text of Scripture but to the entire tradition of the people of God.[5] So it is with the gospel passion narratives and, indeed, with the gospel narratives as a whole. I would emphasize that this was not a matter of the early Christians using Scripture for the purposes of apologetic, or of their drawing "proofs" from Scripture.[6] We are not to imagine that the community originally had a, so to speak, "pure" historical memory of Jesus, and then imported Scripture so as to explain, refine, or defend that memory. We can, I believe, make no such artificial separation. Rather, the community's memory of Jesus *always and essentially* involved articulation in the motifs, narrative patterns, and diction of Israel's story. This way of remembering was inevitable because Jesus' life and death were, in the eyes of Jesus' first followers, things that happened as a continuing and crucial part of that story. If the gospel traditions are to be trusted, that way of remembering Jesus began, essentially, with Jesus himself, when he proclaimed the fulfillment of the times and the coming of God's kingdom.

How should these considerations affect our judgment, as we consider the relationship of the passion narratives to events that may actually have happened—in other word, the kind of events that our modern, post-Enlightenment historian would normally think of as "historical"? Because Jesus' silence before his accusers is remembered and described in terms that resonate with the Suffering Servant (Mark 14.60–61, 15:44–5//; Luke 23.9, cf. Isa. 53:7), should we then assume that Jesus was *not* silent before his accusers? Such a conclusion would surely be perverse. Because the associations and beliefs of Jesus' first followers led them to select certain things to remember, and to remember those things in a certain way—different, no doubt, from our way—that gives us no grounds whatever for concluding that they had nothing to remember.[7]

But *did* they have anything to remember? Is it perhaps the case that what the evangelists tell us about the details of Christ's passion is useless as historical information, not because it was remembered in a certain way but because the first Christians did *not*, in fact, have anything to remember? "I take it for granted," writes John Dominic Crossan, "that early Christianity knew nothing about the passion beyond the fact itself."[8] But why should one "take for granted" any such thing? Can we demonstrate it? If we cannot, we do not know it; and what we do not know, we certainly must not "take for granted." Crossan suggests that the first disciples had "no available witnesses" for the details of Jesus' death.[9] But that seems intrinsically unlikely. One of the points about crucifixion was, after all, that it was *public*, and intended to be so, a vivid reminder of the power of the ruler and the weakness of the ruled. Must we then suppose that not one of those employed at that time around Pilate and/or the Sanhedrin (soldiers, secretaries, slaves, freedmen, hangers-on of every kind) took any notice of what was going on, or had any sympathy with Jesus? (I say nothing of the witness of the faithful women, who according to all evangelistic testimony did not desert Jesus at the cross—a testimony that appears extraordinarily unlikely to have been *invented*, in a patriarchal age.) Alternatively, Crossan says, the first disciples did not bother about the details of Jesus' death because "they were concerned, in any case, with more serious matters, such as whether that death negated all that Jesus had said and done . . . what followed *in one literate and highly sophisticated stream of tradition* was an intense search of the Scriptures, similar to that at Qumran."[10] In other words, we are now to envisage some among the first disciples so passionately interested in Jesus as to spend hours searching the scriptures to ascertain the meaning of his fate, yet so utterly devoid of ordinary human concern or curiosity as not to seek out those who might tell them something of what had actually happened to him. Is it actually possible, on the basis of any normally recognizable human behavior, to envisage such a group? And even if we leave aside the somewhat-hard-to-imagine emotional processes that seem to be implied by this scenario, does it not also demand that those disciples also made a very unlikely—not to say anachronistic—intellectual distinction? Would not Jesus' followers have considered that the actual manner of his dying had *a great deal* to say to them about whether his death negated (or even affirmed) what he had said and done? Was that not why the ancients commonly showed such interest in how famous people died ("exitus illustrium virorum")?[11] As Duane Reed Stuart noted some years ago, death scenes are a normal part of Greco-Roman biographical composition, precisely because such scenes are "always fraught with possibilities, dramatic and melodramatic, for portraying the character of the departed."[12] For the same reason, no doubt, "description of the death scene was a usual member of the funeral oration."[13] How you died was a good indicator as to who and what you really were—which was (according to the synoptic evangelists) exactly what the centurion at the cross observed about Jesus.

In conclusion, then, although I do not think that the passion narratives can be used without caution as sources of historical information, I regard the view that they have no historical value at all as hovering somewhere between "unlikely" and "unproven"—and at that, closer to "unlikely." As I have indicated in my main text, in approaching them I endeavor therefore to operate following the normal canons and criteria of historical judgment: treating our texts critically and cautiously in the light of what other evidence we have, acknowledging that many—perhaps most—historical judgments can only be provisional, being generally more confident of conclusions that seem to meet the criteria of multiple attestation and consistency, and at the same time conceding with Kennedy the possibility that the evangelists, like other ancient writers, sometimes meant what they said and occasionally even knew what they were talking about.

APPENDIX B

Two Jewish Witnesses to the Death of Jesus

Josephus, *Antiquities* 18

There seems now to be fairly general agreement among scholars that at *Antiquities* 18.62–64, Josephus wrote a short section about Jesus of Nazareth, to which a Christian interpolator later made several additions.[1] The section as we receive it is as follows:

> At about this time lived Jesus, a wise man [*sophos anēr*], if indeed one ought to call him a man. He performed astonishing feats [*paradoxōn*] [and was a teacher of such people as accept the truth gladly (*tōn hēdonē[i] t'alēthē dechomenōn*)]. He attracted [*epēgageto*] many Jews and many of the Greeks. He was the Messiah. Upon an indictment brought by leading members of our society, Pilate sentenced him to the cross, but those who had loved him from the very first did not cease to be attached to him. On the third day he appeared to them restored to life, for the prophets of God had prophesied there and countless other marvelous things about him. The tribe [*phulon*] of the Christians, named after him, is still in existence.[2]

With the obviously Christian interpolations removed, Geza Vermes suggests (more or less) the following "non-Christian and neutral sentences together" as Josephus' original text:

> At about this time lived Jesus, a wise man. . . . He performed astonishing feats. . . . He attracted many Jews and many of the Greeks. . . . Upon an indictment brought by the leading men among us, Pilate sentenced him to the cross, but those who had loved him from the very first did not cease to be attached to him. . . . The tribe of the Christians, named after him, is still in existence.[2]

Brown presents a broadly similar text, except that Brown considers that "a teacher of such people as gladly receive what is true" (*tōn hēdonē[i] t'alēthē dechomenōn*) may be authentic, since "Josephus is capable of deliberate ambiguity: 'They receive gladly what (they think) is true.' "[3] Meier and Crossan accept much the same text as Brown.[4]

Vermes makes an interesting additional suggestion: "we should not suppose that the interpolator merely expanded the original wording, but consider the possibility that he also omitted part of what he found in his copy of Josephus."[5] In view of what Josephus writes at *Antiquities* 18.65 ("another outrage threw the Jews into an uproar") and the material surrounding 18.63–64, Vermes suggests that what Josephus originally wrote may have contained something (presumably offensive to the Christian editor) concerning a riot. That, of course, would resonate with elements in the synoptic account (Mark 14.2//; Matt. 27.24). Nevertheless, Vermes's conclusion is that "nothing that Josephus wrote lends any support to the theory that Jesus was caught up in revolutionary, Zealotic or quasi-Zealotic activities. . . . The relatively friendly attitude of Josephus toward Jesus contrasts with his severe stricture of the Zealots and kindred activist groups among the Jews responsible for encouraging the people to defy Roman rule" (1.441).

In distinction from all the foregoing, Graham N. Stanton has suggested that Josephus' words should be understood in a negative sense: "He was a doer of strange deeds, and a deluder of the simple minded. He led astray many Jews and Greeks."[6] Such an interpretation would, indeed, lend general support to my contentions about the nature of the Sanhedrin's charges against Jesus— that he was a false prophet. Alas, as an interpretation, I do not find it persuasive. To insist on treating *paradoxōn, tōn hēdonē[i] t'alēthē dechomenōn*, and *epēgageto* all as pejorative expressions, without any indication from context, is too much of a stretch. Indeed, in the light of their proximity to *sophos anēr*, it is to interpret these expressions *against* their context; and in view of the Christian interpolator's obvious embarrassment with *sophos anēr*, that particular phrase *has* to be what Josephus wrote.

The Babylonian Talmud

The Babylonian Talmud preserves an interesting *baraita*:

> On the eve of Passover Yeshu was hanged. For forty days before the execution took place, a herald went forth and cried, "He is going forth to be stoned because he practiced sorcery and enticed Israel to apostasy.[7] Anyone who can say anything in his favor, let him come forward and plead on his behalf." But since nothing was brought

forward in his favor, he was hanged on the eve of the Passover. (*b. Sanh.* 43a)[8]

The reference to forty days of inquiry ("forty" being, in good biblical tradition, a round figure for any period of divine testing or retribution) may well be a response to Christian accusations that the Jews had not followed what we would call "due process" in their condemnation of Jesus. What is striking is that the rabbinic response to such a charge was not to deny their responsibility in the matter but, on the contrary, to claim that Jesus was condemned only after a fair hearing before God and the people. The suggestion occasionally made that the passage does not refer to Jesus of Nazareth at all is unlikely to be correct, not least in view of the discussion that follows, which refers to Yeshu's disciples, to "Mattai" (Matthew), and to the affair having involved the "government"—that is, presumably, the Romans. In other words, the fifth-century Jewish view of the *baraita* was certainly that it referred to Jesus of Nazareth.[9] Finally, it is interesting to note that the general tendency of the *baraita*—which is, as I have said, not to deny Jewish responsibility in the matter of Jesus' death but, on the contrary, to claim that he was condemned only after a fair hearing before God and the people—lives on in later Jewish traditions as represented, for example, by the various *Toledoth Jeshu.*[10] This is a fact that might lead us to caution over the modern critical tendency to assume that claiming some Jewish responsibility for the death of Jesus is evidence of hostility toward Judaism. As William Horbury pointed out some years ago, "Many passages from Jewish texts would, if found in Christian sources, certainly be ascribed to anti-Jewish sentiment."[11]

APPENDIX C

Did the Sanhedrin in the Time of Jesus Have Authority to Execute the Death Penalty?

A number of influential discussions, including that by E. Mary Smallwood, have argued (more or less) that, while the Roman governor retained to himself power of life and death "in the case of political offenses," the Sanhedrin retained the right to carry out executions, at least as regards "religious offenses, which were of no intrinsic concern to the Romans, and in any event beyond their ability to assess."[1] Therefore, if the Sanhedrin had wished to execute Jesus, it could have done so. The conclusions that follow from this are important. Evidently, the evangelist's accounts of the Sanhedrin's requiring Roman ratification for Jesus' execution must be inaccurate.[2] But, in that case, since the Romans did execute Jesus, using the form of execution prescribed for rebels, clearly it must have been their initiative that led to the execution. Why would the Romans have done that? Presumably for the same reason that they executed other rebels, because Jesus was opposed to Roman rule. He was executed as a rebel.[3] But how do we know that at this period the Sanhedrin had authority to carry out executions? The evidence most commonly appealed to is, first, that the Jews were allowed to execute summarily any foreigner found within the temple (*War* 6.126; *Ant.* 15.417; Philo, *Ad Gaium*, 31, #212);[4] second, that they executed Stephen (Acts 7.54–8.1); and, third, that they executed James, the brother of Jesus (*Ant.* 20.197–203). As a final point, Smallwood notes that "the Jews were privileged in other respects, and the grant of a further privilege in AD 6, strictly limited to matters of religion, would have been in line with established Roman policy towards them."[5]

The last point is telling, but I remain doubtful. To begin with—and this alone may be fatal to Smallwood's theory—this analysis involves Rome's having made a division between "political" and "religious" matters, which, as we have repeatedly noticed and shall notice again, is a division that in a matter such as blasphemy would not have come naturally either to Jew or Roman. As regards the issue of Roman law, it is certainly true that there was no universal Roman criminal code for provincial trials *extra ordinem* ("outside the normal system"). It is equally clear, however, what general Roman practice was in the provinces. While a certain degree of autonomy could be allowed to local authorities such as the Sanhedrin, that did *not* extend to the imposition of the death penalty (for either Roman citizens or the local population), which had to be pronounced by the Roman governor.[6] Especially relevant here are the edicts of the senatorial province of Cyrene, dating from the time of Augustus. In these, the governor's authority in capital matters is clearly regarded not as something to be established but as something normal and taken for granted.[7] Also relevant, though from a somewhat later period, are an edict of Antoninus Pius (*Digest* 48.3.6) relating to Asia and the explicit statement of Ulpian (dating from the time of Severus) regarding general Roman practice (*Digest* 1.18). All point in the same direction. Rabbinical tradition also witnesses to the fact that under Roman rule the Sanhedrin was deprived of power to execute on a capital charge (for example, the *baraita* preserved in *j. Sanh.* 18a, 24b).[8] In other words, all the evidence we have, Roman and Jewish, suggests that the accounts given by the evangelists, though indicating no particular expertise in principles of Roman law, are nonetheless broadly correct in their descriptions of what happened within its jurisdiction.

What, then, of the three reasons for supposing an exception in the case of the Sanhedrin at this period?

With regard to the right of putting to death foreigners who transgress the Temple, this is clearly presented by Josephus as such an extraordinary concession on the part of Rome as in itself to militate *against* the notion that the Jews possessed such a right in any other context (*War* 6.124–28). If the Sanhedrin already had authority to impose the death penalty, what would be so significant about the Jews being allowed to execute those who violated the sanctity of the Temple? (Even when that much has been granted, one's impression is that at most this "right" meant little more than the willingness of the Roman authorities on occasion to turn a blind eye; the events around Paul's near-lynching described in Acts 21 suggest that they were not always prepared to do even that.)

What of the deaths of Stephen (at some time during the mid-30s)[9] and of James (in 32)? The latter is an apparent exception to the rule that, again, on investigation serves rather to confirm it. Josephus makes perfectly clear that Ananias the high priest took advantage of the fact that the previous Roman governor, Porcius Festus, was dead and the new governor, Albinus, had not yet arrived. Albinus, on hearing what had happened, was furious and promptly arranged for the high priest to be replaced. Clearly, Josephus' view is that Ananias had exceeded his authority (*Ant.* 20.197–203). Hence, his account of the death of James, taken as a whole, is actually evidence that the Sanhedrin under

Roman administration did *not* have authority to impose the death penalty, rather than evidence that it did.[10]

With regard to the death of Stephen, the evidence is, on any view, confusing. Luke tells the story in such a way that we are reminded (and are clearly meant to be reminded) of the arraignment and death of Jesus (Acts 7.56 cf. Luke 22.69; Acts 7.59 cf. Luke 23.46; Acts 7.60 cf. Luke 23.34). At the same time, Luke does not hide some obvious differences between the two processes. In Stephen's trial, we do not gain the impression of a formally completed procedure—in marked contrast to the gospel's account of what happened to Jesus. The description begins with a solemn gathering of people, elders, and scribes, but then, as Bond says, "the proceedings descend into chaos: there is no verdict, no sentence; Stephen's death resembles a mob lynching rather than an official execution."[11] One might be forgiven, therefore, for suggesting that the death of Stephen is useless as evidence for what was actually *legal*, one way or another. It was simply an example of lynch law. Marta Sordi, however, offers a quite different view: the proceedings against Stephen "did have something of a legitimate trial about them. They began with the Sanhedrin hearing the charges brought against him by witnesses, went on with the accused gaining permission from the Chief Priest to speak in his own defence (Acts 6:11 ff.) and ended with the Sanhedrin's unanimous verdict in favour of the death sentence (Acts 7:57), which was then carried out by the witnesses themselves, in accordance with the ancient Hebrew law against blasphemers."[12] So was this a formal trial or not? It is impossible, on the evidence we have, to be certain: both Bond's and Sordi's interpretations of the text are possible, for the text itself does not provide enough information to exclude one or the other.

Whatever it was, just *how* did it happen? Was it, as Bond and Sordi both suggest, after Pilate had left office, during a power vacuum such as the one that occurred between the death of Porcius Festus and the arrival of Albinus?[13] Or was Pilate (who lasted through most of 36, probably leaving in December) still in office, as Jeremias asserts?[14] If the latter case, did Pilate *connive* at Stephen's death? And was that connivance a factor in Pilate's departure? It is, again, in the state of our knowledge, impossible to answer any of these questions.

According to Josephus, L. Vitellius, the legate of Syria, on a generally placatory visit to Jerusalem in AD 36 or 37, in the course of which a number of benefits were bestowed upon the city, removed the high priest Caiaphas from his office (*Ant.* 18.90–95).[15] But Josephus does not say why. Was it that Caiaphas had become unpopular?[16] Or was it, as Bond suggests, that Caiaphas had taken "advantage of the power vacuum in Judaea [following Pilate's departure]," grown "too assertive," and become "too powerful for his own good"?[17] If the latter, then in what way had this overassertiveness manifested itself? Bond's own suggestion—essentially, that Caiaphas' very success in negotiating with the Romans was the cause of his undoing—seems unlikely.[18] Why should a shrewd Roman administrator such as Vitellius remove from office someone with whom he could do business? Was it, then, that Caiaphas (with or without Pilate's connivance) had exceeded his authority in the execution of Stephen, exactly as Ananias was to do in 62?[19] Incidental confirmation of that might be implied by Luke, who notes that following the meeting of Peter and Paul, perhaps in the same year as the deposition of Caiaphas,[20] "the church through-out all Judea and Galilee and Samaria had peace" (Acts 9.31). And Judea, Gal-ilee, and Samaria were precisely the areas under Roman control (direct or indirect) at that time, as opposed to Damascus, under the control of Aretas the enemy of Rome, where Christians were being persecuted (Acts 9.19b–25, 2 Cor. 11.32).[21] But, again, though such a scenario is possible, there is no way that we can arrive at even reasonable certainty about it.

So much, then, for the three "reasons" to dismiss the fourth evangelist's claim that the Sanhedrin had no authority to impose the death penalty. Two of them, on investigation, turn out to require precisely the opposite explanation: they are actually evidence that the evangelist was right. The third contains too many unknowns to be of use as evidence one way or the other, though what little it does tell us or seem to imply is certainly susceptible of various expla-nations that accord with the fourth evangelist's claim.

In addition to the foregoing, Smallwood suggests that there are two other pieces of evidence that the Sanhedrin had power to carry out executions, namely John 19.6, "Pilate's own proposal that the Jews should try and sentence Christ themselves," and John 8.3–7, the story of the woman taken in adultery, "whom Christ, no breaker of Roman law, invited the Jews to put to death."[22] With all respect to a fine historian, these suggestions both involve an evident misunderstanding of the text.

In its context, as commentators have consistently pointed out, John 19.6 is a *taunt* that at once fixes responsibility for Jesus' death with his accusers and forces them to confess the humiliating fact that *imperium* lies not with them but with Rome.[23] The best analogy to 19.6 is therefore Pilate's question to the high priests later in the same dialogue: "Shall I crucify your king?" (19.15b)— likewise certainly not implying any real recognition of royal authority in Jesus but rather intended to force from them, as it does, the humiliating concession "We have no king but Caesar" (19.15c). In any case, the notion implied by Smallwood's view of 19.6 that the Sanhedrin did not know its own rights is at least as absurd as would be the notion that Pilate did not know them.

By contrast, the story of the woman taken in adultery (not a part of John, as most translations now indicate) does not even mention the Sanhedrin. It is entirely possible that it intends to describe a situation in which a group of Pharisees and the mob, fired with Phinehas-like zeal for the law (Num. 25.6–18; 1 Macc. 2.26) were about to stone the woman without any due process at all, and certainly without regard to Roman law.[24] (One might, perhaps, compare the actions of those who murder doctors and nurses who perform abortions, in zeal, as they see it, for "God's law" and in manifest defiance of U.S. law.) Jesus' words at 8.7 are in their context clearly ironic, intended to *prevent* the woman's death, not encourage it—as the event shows. To take them, therefore, as evidence of Jesus' or the fourth evangelist's view of Roman law in Judea under the prefects is totally to misunderstand them.

In other words, there really is not the slightest reason to suppose that, in the case of the Sanhedrin, Rome had yielded what A. N. Sherwin-White describes as "the most jealously guarded of all the attributes of government."[25]

5

Jesus' Followers and the Roman Empire

Paul

Jesus said that God's sovereignty would be manifested "with power" in the lifetime of some who knew him. "And he said to them [the disciples], 'Truly, I say to you, there are some standing here who will not taste death before they see that the kingdom of God has come with power'" (Mark 9.1). According to his followers, what happened was Jesus' own vindication and exaltation, their experience of the Holy Spirit, the proclamation of the Word going forth from Zion, and the incorporation of gentiles into the people of God. No doubt that left much to anticipate. It was, as Paul put it (and, later, Polycarp), a "down payment" (*arrabōn*) (2 Cor. 1.22, 5.5; compare Eph. 1.14, Pol. *Phil.* 8.1). "The sufferings of this present time" were not ended (Rom. 8.18). Equally clearly, it provided enough sense of Israel renewed and restored to vindicate Jesus as, among other things, a true prophet and to convince his followers that in his ministry and the events that followed from it, God's sovereignty had indeed been manifested in a new and decisive way. Jesus had accomplished his "exodus" (NRSV "departure") in Jerusalem (Luke 9.31).[1] But still, as Paul put it, the final and full day of that manifestation was only "near" (Rom. 13.11; compare Rom. 8.19–25). In that sense, then, even for Jesus' followers, the exile continued. And Rome still ruled over them, as over everyone else. What, then, was their attitude toward that rule?

Let us begin with Paul.

The Letter to the Romans

Paul wrote the longest and, many would argue, the greatest of his letters to believers who lived in Rome: in other words, to those who, however humble their lot may have seemed in terms of their own society, from his viewpoint were a part of the metropolitan center of the world. Perhaps the way he begins his address reflects not only (as he makes explicit) his awareness that he is speaking to a church he has not founded but also, implicitly, that other awareness—that those to whom he speaks live at the empire's heart; he has, he says, often intended to visit the believers at Rome, "in order that I may reap some harvest among you as I have among the rest of the Gentiles" (Rom. 1.8–13).

Be that as it may, discussions of the specifics of Paul's attitude to Roman *imperium* usually begin by looking at Romans 13.1–7, and this is appropriate, provided we are careful to understand that passage within its wider context, for it is only one part of one section of Paul's closing exhortation.[2] That exhortation began at 12.1 with the words "I beseech you *therefore*, brothers and sisters, by the mercies of God"—in other words, that exhortation is itself based on all that Paul has said in the first eleven chapters of Romans about "my gospel" (2.16), which is above all the story of God's justice and mercy toward all. On that basis, and no other, Paul now goes on to speak of the justice and mercy that must "therefore" characterize both the believers' relationships with one another within the fellowship of Christ (12.3–12.13) and their relationships with those who are outside that fellowship (12.14–13.7).

Paul begins consideration of this latter group with what might seem to be the extreme case of those "outside": "Bless those who persecute [you]—bless, and do not curse them!" (12.14). Perhaps he begins there because that is where he began himself. But he moves on, urging among his hearers a concern for "what is noble in the sight of all," encouraging them, so far as possible, to live "peaceably with all, never avenging yourselves, beloved, but leave it to the wrath of God, for it is written, 'Vengeance is mine, I will repay,' says the Lord" (12.16b–19). Far from pursuing vendetta, " 'if your enemy is hungry, feed him; if he is thirsty, give him drink; for by so doing you will heap burning coals upon his head.' Do not be overcome by the evil, but overcome the evil with the good" (12.20–21).

It is in this context, as a part of his discussion of the graceful attitude that should characterize the believers' relationships with the world at large, that Paul then moves to the question of believers' relationships with what we would call "the state." "Let every person be subject to the governing authorities" (13.1a).[3] It is at once obvious that, in common with the broad consensus of biblical thinking that we have examined (and, as it happens, in concert with pagan thinking, too), Paul regards such institutions as related to divine authority: "for there is no authority except from God," and therefore "the authorities" with which the faithful in Rome must deal—that is, the Roman emperor and his servants and officials—"have been instituted by God" (13.1b).[4] Paul's view of Roman rule therefore points in two directions, just as the biblical and prophetic tradition has always done. On the one hand, it accepts and holds as legitimate Roman authority; on the other, it leaves Roman authority in principle open to prophetic challenge wherever and whenever it has claimed too much for itself or betrayed the purposes for which it was instituted. Paul never writes save on the basis of theological conviction, and such convictions as these are the driving force behind what he writes here.

Still, it is the case that at the time when Paul was writing, the new emperor, Nero, was regarded with high hopes. That, no doubt, made it easier for Paul to continue as he did:

> Therefore whoever resists authority resists what God has appointed,
> and those who resist will incur judgment. For rulers are not a terror
> to good conduct, but to bad. Do you [singular] wish to have no fear
> of the authority? Then do what is good, and you [singular] will re-
> ceive its approval; for it is God's minister [*diakonos*] for your [singu-
> lar] good. But if you [singular] do what is wrong, you should be
> afraid, for the authority does not bear the sword in vain! It is the
> minister [*diakonos*] of God to execute wrath on the wrongdoer.
> (13.2–4)

As John N. Collins has shown in the course of an extensive survey of the entire literature,[5] the basic sense of the noun *diakonos* and its cognates is not to do with "waiting at table" (though that claim is still sometimes heard) but to do with "going between," as a representative, agent, or attendant. Hence, when, at 13.4, Paul speaks of the Roman civil administration as God's *diakonos*, his words carry an assertion that, although pagan, the office involves a sacred appointment, since the administrator (like Cyrus—whether he knows it or not) is "God's minister" toward believers "for good"—which includes the execution of "wrath" against wrongdoers, for which reason they "bear the sword." Various commentators have connected "bear the sword" with the Roman *ius gladii*. In Paul's day, however, *ius gladii* referred only to the right of provincial governors to condemn to death a Roman citizen serving in the armed forces under their command,[6] and so, as an allusion, it was hardly likely to be relevant to those whom Paul addressed. His words are probably better understood as a loose reference to the general life-and-death power of the Roman *imperium*. In other words, given that human administrations are commissioned by God for the sake of those administered, "therefore one must be subject, not only in consideration of God's wrath, but also for the sake of conscience" (13.5).

At the risk of being tedious, let me again point out that such an attitude toward civil authority must also serve to make that authority entirely limited and *relative*. If it is instituted by God, and serves as a "minister" (*diakonos*) of God, then it is subject to God and may not claim for itself the honor that is God's alone. Hence, Paul's advocacy of submission "for the sake of conscience" cannot (or, at least, should not) be understood as implying blind submission to *any* rule, however tyrannous or unjust.

So much may be said broadly about the implications of Romans 13.1–7. There may have been two other, more specific issues in Paul's mind.

First, Jeremiah instructed the exiles to "seek the good" of the pagan city wherein they found themselves. Paul's exhortation to "do what is good" (*to agathon poiein*) so as to receive "praise" (*epainon*) from the civil authority (13.3) appears to be a restatement of the same principle in terms of euergetism. As Bruce Winter has pointed out, the phrase "to do good" (*to agathon poiein*) appears linked to public benefaction and service in a number of inscriptions: thus, for example, the people of Athens are found praising a certain Menelaus, "because he is a good man and does whatever good he can [*kai poiei hoti dunatai agathon*] for the people of Athens . . . it is resolved that Menelaus be considered a benefactor" (*SIG* 174).[7] Paul's expressions would then most naturally have been heard by his audience—and intended by him—as a reference to their duties as citizens to act, according to their means, not merely in accordance with the laws but also as *patrons* and *benefactors* to the community at large, actively seeking "the welfare of the city" (Jer. 29.7)—whereby they would gain "honor" not simply for themselves but for the church and for the gospel. In this connection, the use of the second-person singular ("Would you [singular] have no fear of the authorities?") may be particularly significant, making clear that this injunction is addressed to individuals, rather than to the church as a whole: for it would be evident that only persons of considerable means could undertake the kind of benefactions that would expect, and receive, public praise.

Second, according to Tacitus, there were at this period growing complaints in society at large about taxation—so much so that, in 58, Nero responded by proposing to abolish all indirect taxation (*Annals* 13.50–51). Was Paul anxious lest believers, living, as they knew themselves to be, in the new age, have strong feelings about this—and be tempted to resist payment? Did he fear that they might bring themselves into dispute with the authorities over an issue that did not have any direct bearing on their witness to the gospel? If so, his next words were appropriate to such concerns: "for the same reason you also pay taxes, for the authorities are God's public servants [*leitougoi*],[8] busy with this very thing" (Rom. 13.6). Paul is exactly at one with the rabbis—"the law of the emperor is the Law"—though his precise choice of expression, indeed, leads one to wonder whether he had not in mind specifically Jesus' response to the question about the payment of *tributum capitis*. "Pay [*apodote*][9] to all what is due to them, taxes to whom taxes are due, revenue to whom revenue is due" (13. 7). Such subjection to the "authorities" is not, moreover, merely a matter of the proper settlement in cash or goods; it is also a matter of "respect" and "honor." As believers are concerned with the proper honor of God and of those within the believing community, so they are concerned with the honor of those beyond it, paying "respect to whom respect" is due and "honor to whom honor" (13.7b)—for all, potentially, are members of God's people.

Having encouraged the believers at Rome to proper behavior toward those inside and those outside the church, Paul plays on the notion of what is "due" (*opheilas*) to bring him full circle back to the point from which he began. It is all—even paying the proper taxes, and certainly the giving of proper honor—a part of love:

> Owe [*opheilete*] no one anything, save to love one another; for who-
> ever loves the other has fulfilled the Law. For "Thou shalt not com-
> mit adultery, Thou shalt not kill, Thou shalt not steal, Thou shalt
> not covet," and whatever other commandment there is, is summed
> up in this one word, "Thou shalt love thy neighbor as thyself" [cit-
> ing LXX Leviticus 19.18]. Love does not work evil against the neigh-
> bor. Therefore love is the fulfillment of the Law. (13.8–10)

In the passage from Leviticus that Paul cites, it is evident that the "neighbor" in question is a fellow member of God's people (LXX Leviticus 19.18), and that is no small thing. In Paul's context, however, it is naturally extended to any human contact—since all, potentially, are members of God's people.

Finally, we should note—indeed, Paul insists on drawing our attention to it—the *context* in which the Romans are to live in this way: it is the context of God's saving act in Christ, "knowing the time, that it is high time for you to awake out of sleep. For salvation is nearer to us now than when we first be-lieved" (13.11). The laws of the Empire are to be obeyed and Christians are to seek to be good citizens, *not* because life never changes and God's kingdom is only a dream but precisely *because* the new age is already beginning. Already believers are like those who stretch and blink and prepare to begin a new day:

"the night is far gone, the day is at hand" (13.12). Still they are exiles, but they know that the end of their exile is near. Their gracious behavior to those around them, including the pagan empire, will reflect this consciousness.

> Let us therefore cast off the works of darkness and put on us the armor of light; let us conduct ourselves becomingly [euschēmonōs— that is, with grace and dignity], as in the day, not in reveling and drunkenness, not in debauchery and licentiousness, not in quarrelling and jealousy, but put on the Lord Jesus Christ, and make no provision for the flesh, to gratify its desires. (Rom. 13.12b–14)

The Rhetoric of Paul's Gospel

There is a distinct language of Pauline proclamation—I mean Paul's talk of "good news" (euaggelion), of Jesus who is "lord" (kurios) and "son of God" (huios thou) and who gives gifts of "salvation" (sōtēria), "justice" (dikaiosunē), and "peace" (eirēnē). All this, as biblical critics have long pointed out, resonates with biblical tradition and, more precisely, with the language and imagery of the Septuagint. It would also have resonated with the rhetoric of imperial Rome. Augustus, too, was declared "son of god" (by virtue of his kinship to the deified Julius Caesar). He too was spoken of as one who brought "salvation," "justice," and "peace" to the world—rhetoric that was understandable enough, in view of the dreadful civil wars that had followed the assassination of Julius Caesar in BC 29 and continued to tear the empire apart until Augustus assumed control and put an end to them. As the corporation of Greek citizens of Asia expressed it, in reply to a letter from the proconsul proposing that they honor the emperor's birthday, Caesar

> has realized the hopes of our ancestors . . . not only has he surpassed earlier benefactors of humanity, but he leaves no hope to those of the future that they might surpass him. The god's [birthday] was for the world the beginning of the good news [euaggelion] that he brought.[10]

Other elements in Pauline rhetoric about the gospel seem not to be biblical (Septuagintal) at all and would have resonated only with those who were familiar with the imperial rhetoric. An example of this is the thought of Jesus' final parousia (his "coming" or "visitation" to his people) (1 Cor. 15:23; 1 Thess. 2.19, 3:13). There is no parallel to this kind of language in the Septuagint, but we do find such language in the Hellenistic rhetoric of divine manifestation, or that surrounding the formal visit of a sovereign—rhetoric that was certainly adopted and used by Rome. Thus, an inscription from Tegea is dated in "the sixty-ninth year of the first *parousia* of the god Hadrian in Greece."[11] Critics have, again, long been aware of these parallels. In a discussion published in 1911, commenting on the words of the Greek citizens of Asia cited earlier, Jean Rouffiac pointed out that "this text would not have needed much adjustment for a Christian fifty years later to have been able to apply it to Christ. . . . The idea that a 'good news' began for the world with the birth of Augustus is one of the most remarkable points of contact between our inscription and the NT, because no word received the imprint of Christianity more profoundly than the word *evangel*."[12]

So much, then, is reasonably clear. But what is its significance? According to Horsley and a number of other scholars, "by applying this key imperial language to Jesus, Paul was making him into the alternative or real emperor of the world, the head of an anti-imperial international alternative society."[13] But was Paul doing that? Here, once again, we are on much slippier ground. The key phrase is "anti-imperial." The view put forward is that to have *made use* of the imperial rhetoric was therefore to be *in confrontation* with it. But was it?

Let us consider a rather striking example of Paul's use of imperial rhetoric—arguably, the most striking in all his letters. It occurs in the Letter to the Philippians, a letter evidently written when Paul was in a Roman prison—in other words, at a time when he, if any one, might have had good reason to feel jaundiced about Roman rule (1.12–26).[14] (Precisely where and when this particular imprisonment was taking place and whether it was before or after he wrote the Letter to the Romans are much more difficult questions to answer, but they need not affect our argument here.) At Philippians 3.20–4.1, we have then, from Paul the Roman prisoner, a particularly striking image of Christ as Savior.

> But our citizenship [*politeuma*][15] is in heaven, and it is from there
> that we are expecting a Savior [*sōter*],[16] the Lord Jesus Christ. He will
> transform the body of our humiliation that it may be conformed to
> the body of his glory, by the power that also enables him to make all
> things subject to himself. Therefore, my brothers and sisters, whom
> I love and long for, my joy and crown, stand firm in the Lord in this
> way, my beloved.

The origin of this image is clear. It is springs from the notion of Roman citizenship (*politeuma*) under an emperor who comes from Rome as "savior" (*sōter*) to assist and fortify a Roman community—perhaps a Roman army or a

Roman colony—that is in difficulty. Thus, the emperor Claudius "came to the assistance" of the legions under Aulus Plautius that were experiencing "difficulties" during the British campaign of 43 AD (Dio Cassius 60.22; *ILS* 216).[17] This is an image that would have been especially well understood at Philippi, which was itself a Roman colony with *ius Italica*. It was settled, at least in some measure, by Roman veterans[18] and intended, no doubt, to be a beacon of Roman order and justice to the society around it, just as Christians were supposed to shine like "lights in the world" to those around them (Phil. 2.15). Some members of the church would themselves have been Roman citizens,[19] and for all of them, citizens or not, citizenship would have been an issue that was, in Peter Oakes's words, "never irrelevant" with regard to their position in society.[20] Paul's point is, then, clear. As Christians, the Philippians have "citizenship" under a much greater "savior" than Augustus or his successors. Such a "savior" will be able to sustain and vindicate his followers at Philippi, not merely in the face of Rome's enemies, but in the face even of sin and death.

Where, then, does Paul direct the Philippians' thoughts in the light of this image? Does he say that they are to deny or resist the claims of the lesser "savior"? Does he say that if they are members of the church they cannot be members of the Roman state? Those are exactly the things that he does *not* say. On the contrary, he at once directs their attention to their *own* life together and to specific details of that life: "I exhort Euodia and I exhort Syntache"— the double "exhort" showing how important this is for Paul—"*to agree with one another in the Lord*" (4:2).[21] Paul's concern, in other words, is *for the Philippian church*, and his argument is an example of that good old rabbinic favorite, *qal va-chomer* ("light and heavy"): "if this . . . then by how much more that . . . !" If the Philippians know what might be due from them and to them merely as citizens of Rome, *then by how much more* they should know what is due from them and to them as citizens of a realm whose emperor is lord of lords and king of kings! What, then, of the apostle's attitude to the Roman *imperium*? So far from implying confrontation with Rome, the fact that, like the centurion in the gospels,[22] he points to behavior owed in a Roman context as a model for behavior owed "in Christ" appears to imply the complete opposite.

Hence, despite my admiration for Oakes's careful assembly of evidence showing the connection between Philippians 3.20–1 and Roman imperial rhetoric,[23] in this respect I must differ from his conclusion. According to Oakes, Philippians 3.20–21 means that "the Philippian Christians belong to another state. Not only that, but this is the *only* state to which they belong: ἡμῶν . . . τὸ πολίτευμα . . . (verse 20)" (my italics).[24] If Oakes is saying what I think he is saying—that the Philippian Christians, including those who possessed citizenship, were no longer to think of themselves as in any sense subject to Rome *because they were now Christians*—then I must reply that one might as logically argue that because Christians are members of "the household of God," they cannot belong to any ordinary human household, or because a Christian is a "child" of God, a Christian cannot be the child of any ordinary earthly parent. Such assertions would manifestly be nonsense and involve a simple failure to appreciate the nature of metaphor. Christians are not *literally* citizens of heaven (which is not *literally* a state or a realm), any more than they are *literally* children of God (who is not *literally* a parent) or the church is *literally* a household. But just as "member of a household" expresses something of what we believe to be our relationship to God and God's people in terms of shared belonging and loyalties, and "child" does so in terms of love and dependence, so "citizenship" does in terms of required action and allegiance. Therefore, we use such language to express our faith and our hopes.[25] This is what Paul is doing at Philippians 3.20–21, and to treat his expressions there as if he were talking literally about citizenship is to make a serious—and possibly rather dangerous—mistake.

Another passage in Philippians that, in the view of some scholars, involves a parody of imperial rhetoric is the famous "Philippians hymn":

> Let the same mind be in you that was in Christ Jesus,
> who, though he was in the form of God,
> did not regard equality with God as something to be exploited,
> but emptied himself, taking the form of a slave,
> being born in human likeness.
> And being found in human form,
> he humbled himself and became obedient to the point of death,
> even death on a cross.
> Therefore God also highly exalted [*hyperupsōsen*] him
> and gave him the name that is above every name,
> so that at the name of Jesus every knee should bend [*pan gonu
> kampsē[i]*],
> in heaven and on earth and under the earth,
> and every tongue should confess [*pasa glōssa exomologēsetai*] that
> Jesus Christ is Lord,
> to the glory of God the Father.
> (Phil. 2.5–11)

Peter Oakes has, again, assembled an impressive list of parallels between the sequence of events associated with ascension to the imperial throne and the sequence of events in the hymn's description of Christ's exaltation.[26] His conclusion is, "Jesus receives the Name that is above every name. All knees bow to him. Every tongue acknowledges him as Lord. A Graeco-Roman hearer would probably hear this as a comparison with the Emperor."[27]

There are, however, some problems with this identification, more so than with Philippians 3.20–21. The most obvious is that, as Richard Bauckham has recently reminded us, at virtually every point a case can also be made for seeing Philippians 2.5–11 as a Christian interpretation of Isaiah 45 and 52.13–53.12.[28] Thus, the important phrases *pan gonu kampsē[i]* and *pasa glōssa exomologēsetai* do not occur in any example of imperial rhetoric known to us but are manifestly references to LXX Isaiah 45.23. (Oakes is therefore correct in noting that "Paul has not chosen them because they coincide with material about the Emperor.")[29] The key word *huperupsoō* also does not occur any known example of imperial rhetoric. Indeed, it does not occur in *any* extant Greek literature, except here in Philippians and at LXX Ps. 96.9,[30] where it is used to describe God, who alone is "highly exalted": the same theme that dominates Isaiah 45— and, indeed, the Philippians hymn, since for a Jew such as Paul there is certainly only one "name that is above every name." (The cognate verb *hupsoō* is used, however, to describe the deutero-Isaianic Servant at LXX Isaiah 52.13.) Even the "therefore" (*dio kai*) of Philippians 2.9, of which Oakes makes much as parallel to the Senate's granting Caesar his authority "for a reason,"[31] also has a perfectly good parallel in the "therefore" (*dia touto*) of LXX Isaiah 53.12, whereby the Servant is lifted up because he has been humiliated for the sake of others.[32]

In addition to the *identification* of Jesus with the Deutero-Isaianic servant implied by the foregoing, many critics have seen in Philippians 2.5–11 an implicit *contrast* with Adam.[33] There is certainly no reason why both sets of allusions should not be allowed, although, in view of the striking linguistic parallels with Isaiah, the Adam allusion must surely have been experienced as the more indirect and marginal of the two.[34] Still, if Paul had taught the Philippians about Adam in anything like the way in which he seems to meditate on the Adam story in Romans and 1 Corinthians (Rom. 1.18–23, 5.12–21; 1 Cor. 15.20–22),[35] the implied counterpoint between

> Adam, who chose to be as God,
> And arrogantly disobeyed,
> Therefore God has utterly humbled him
> *and*
> Christ, who was in the form of God but did not exploit Godhead,
> And humbly obeyed,
> Therefore God has highly exalted him

could have been expected to work well, both as literary form and as a challenging and deeply biblical theological insight.

Still, none of this gives us any reason to deny that there are also parallels between the exaltation of Christ as described in the Philippians hymn and the narrative sequence of imperial propaganda, as Oakes has pointed out. It is therefore possible that, as well as noticing the identification of Christ with the Isaianic servant of the Lord and the contrast between Christ and Adam, the Philippians would have seen these imperial parallels, too, and been expected to see them. The Adam image and the emperor image are not, after all, entirely unrelated. There is, N. T. Wright suggests, a sense in which the Adam image itself could be applied to an arrogant Caesar—or, indeed, to an Alexander or to any other arrogant emperor. "Jesus succeeded where Adam failed; he completed the task assigned to Israel; and he is the reality of which Caesar is the parody."[36]

All this, then, we may grant. What then? For our present purpose, the important question that remains is not "To whom *could* these expressions be applied?" but "Of whom or what did Paul *want* to the Philippians to think when he used them?" In other words, what was the actual purpose of this imagery—the Servant, Adam, imperial, whatever? What did Paul actually want the Philippians to do? And here we are fortunate, since Paul answers those questions for us. He has just exhorted his hearers to

> be of the same mind, having the same love, being in full accord and of one mind. Do nothing from selfish ambition or conceit, but in humility regard others as better than yourselves. Let each of you look not to your own interests, but to the interests of others. (Phil. 2.2–4)

Then he introduces the "hymn" with words that the NRSV translates as "Have this mind among you which is also in Christ Jesus" (Phil. 2.5). The expression is not without its difficulties,[37] but in its context the overall thrust is surely clear: *the Philippians were not to be thinking of someone else's arrogant claims to greatness, not even Adam's or Caesar's, but of Christ's humility, and how they might strive to identify with it.* While I am not quite so suspicious of the notion of Christ as *exemplum* here as are some[38] (does not Paul cite Christ as *exemplum* at Romans 15.1–7?), still, Cousar probably has the balance about right: "The story of Christ in Philippians 2:6–11 is a concrete description of the Lord in whom the Philippians believe. But in its context (1:27–2:18) appropriate analogies are drawn from it that are applicable to their situation. Christ's actions become the warrant as well as the paradigm for the actions Paul urges on his readers."[39] So Paul at once proceeds to exhort the Philippians to "work out [their] own salvation." And what does that mean in practical terms? "Do everything without quarrels and arguments!" (2.14). The Philippians hymn is, then, a plank in Paul's exhortation to the Philippians—and perhaps to the two leaders Euodia and Syntache in particular[40]—to stand firm and, above all, to stand united, which is in its turn an element playing its part in Paul's overall rhetorical purpose, to offer "consolation" (paramuthia) to the believers at Philippi.[41]

Another passage in Philippians that has been regarded as anti-imperial is Philippians 3.18–19.

> For many live as enemies of the cross of Christ; I have often told you of them, and now I tell you even with tears. Their end is destruction; their god is the belly; and their glory is in their shame; their minds are set on earthly things.

Richard J. Cassidy, in the course of two studies that present a series of theses regarding Jesus' response to Roman rule and the subsequent unfolding of various disciples' responses to it,[42] claims that Philippians presents a "trenchant and sustained" criticism of the Roman ethos, and that 3.18–19 is part of it.[43] The question of the identity of those of whom Paul speaks with such fierce polemic in chapter 3 is indeed complex,[44] and I do not propose to attempt a solution to it here. Given the language Paul uses, however, Cassidy's particular proposal appears intrinsically unlikely. The polemic at 3.18–19 is typically the language of Jewish religious polemic, a rhetoric of blame applied to those whom the speaker considers to be apostate. So we find it used by Philo, and by the authors of 3 Maccabees and of the Testaments of the Twelve Patriarchs (Philo, On the Virtues, 182; 3 Macc.7.11; Testament of Moses 7.4) as well, of course, as by Paul himself at Romans 16.18.[45] It would, then, be very surprising indeed if Paul had here applied that kind of language to pagans, whatever he thought of them. Cassidy suggests that Paul would have disapproved of Nero's propensity for "murder and licentiousness," as well his obsession with his own titles and honors.[46] No doubt, Paul did disapprove of these things (as, incidentally, did a good many who were neither Jews nor Christians). That, surely, does not need to be debated. It does not follow, however, that that was what he was talking about at Philippians 3.18–19. There, I suspect, he had in mind the same "opponents" of whom he had already spoken in 3.1b to 4a, that is, those who "mutilate the flesh." As for them, whatever may have been the precise nature of their views—and as I have said, the question is complex and cannot be solved here—still, what Paul objected to about them clearly had something to do with Judaism.[47] They are therefore exactly the types of person whom we should expect to be targets for this kind of rhetoric.

There is an earlier passage in Philippians where Paul refers to "opponents."

> Only, live your life in a manner worthy of the gospel of Christ, so
> that, whether I come and see you or am absent and hear about you,
> I will know that you are standing firm in one spirit, striving side by
> side with one mind for the faith of the gospel, and are in no way
> intimidated by your opponents. For them this is evidence of their
> destruction, but of your salvation. And this is God's doing. For he
> has graciously granted you the privilege not only of believing in
> Christ, but of suffering for him as well—since you are having the
> same struggle that you saw I had and now hear that I still have.
> (Phil. 1.27–30)

It is the opinion of a good many scholars that here, too, Paul was referring to those to whom he would refer again in chapter 3—to those who "mutilate the flesh"—and that is certainly a possibility.[48] At this point, however, it seems to me more likely that Paul was indeed speaking of some kind of trouble with local civic authorities. It is perfectly possible that, as Morna D. Hooker and Charles B. Cousar have both suggested, something was happening after the nature of the problems described in Acts 16: local "businessmen" objecting to and harassing the Christian movement because it seemed likely to undermine their financial interests.[49] Hebrews speaks to its addressees of the "plundering of possessions" (10.34) even though in their struggle against sin they had "not yet resisted to the point of shedding [their] blood" (12.4). In Oakes's view, "since Paul mentions no deaths or other very dramatic forms of suffering at Philippi, we can safely assume that the suffering is of an unspectacular kind. Such suffering is likely to have had a strong economic component."[50] That, needless to say, would not have made that suffering any less significant or serious for those undergoing it. It does mean, however, that there is not the slightest reason to connect it to an alleged Christian resistance to Roman *imperium*, or anything of that kind.

Am I then saying that there was no connection at all between imperial ideologies and such local harassment as we are envisaging? Of course I am not! There is always a connection between elements in the dominant ideologies of a society and local behaviors, however sporadic and apparently unconnected, just as there is a connection between the political, social, and economic disadvantaging of black Americans that has marked so much of U.S. history, and certain elements in the U.S. Constitution and the nation's self-perception that go back to the founding fathers themselves.[51] I *am* saying, however, that there is no evidence that Paul—or the Philippian Christians—objected to the institution of the Roman state in and of itself or desired to replace it by some other human political institution. Again, Martin Luther King provides a useful analogy. While King's words and deeds demonstrate at every turn his protest against the disadvantages suffered by his people under American institutions, *at no point* do they reflect a rejection of those institutions—in marked contrast, it may be noted, to other African-American leaders such as Malcolm X. On the contrary, King *appealed* to those institutions, simply demanding that "the American dream" be available to his people as it is to white Americans.[52]

The Problem of Religious Language

One final caution must be offered in the present connection. I began this part of my discussion by noting that much of the vocabulary of imperial rhetoric also resonated with the language of the Septuagint. I conclude by again recalling that point and by further noting that, to a considerable extent, the translators of the Septuagint were themselves using the language that they found to hand, which is to say the religious language of Hellenism. Not only Jews and Christians but also pagans spoke of the divine, of salvation, of sons of God. The various forms of imperial cult,[53] and the Hellenistic monarchy cults that were their forerunners, also made use of that religious vocabulary. As is evident, I think that Paul did at times deliberately make use of a rhetoric that he derived from the rhetoric of the Roman Empire. But, to be sure of that claim in any particular case (as I think we can be reasonably sure in the case of Philippians 3.19–4.1), we have to *earn* it. The mere fact of a linguistic parallel does not allow us to *assume* it. In this area, as in others, we should beware of what Samuel Sandmel wittily characterized as "parallelomania."[54] Those before Paul who translated the Jewish scriptures into Greek, those who associated Hellenistic kings and Roman emperors with divinity, and Paul himself all had at least one thing in common. They all had to use *some* vocabulary and concepts to speak of the things that they held sacred, and if they were to communicate at all, they all had to draw on more or less the same vocabulary and concepts as everyone else. Hence, there were bound to be parallels between them. That is a part of the nature of discourse. We should be very careful indeed about what conclusions, if any, we draw from it.

Thus, as we have already observed, Romans spoke of living emperors as "son of god," "lord," and "savior." Paul and other Christians did the same for Jesus. Does it follow, as Crossan and Reed claim, that for Christians "to proclaim Jesus as Son of God was deliberately denying Caesar his highest title, and that to announce Jesus as Lord and Savior was calculated treason"?[55] No, it does not. Certainly Christians were using some of the same words about Jesus as pagans used about Caesar, but they were hardly using them in the same context, or meaning anything like the same thing by them. The Romans, on the one hand, had called Octavius Caesar "divi filius" (son of a god) because he was heir to the deified Julius—a position that bestowed on him immense prestige in the Greco-Roman world.[56] Paul, on the other hand, called Jesus "son of God" because he believed him to have been "sent" in the fullness of time by the one God of Israel and declared "son of God in power" by God's own Spirit "through resurrection from the dead" (Gal. 4.4, Rom. 1.4). Paul claimed, moreover, that Jesus' followers were *also* "sons" of God, by virtue of their union with Jesus through baptism (Rom. 8.15–16; Gal. 3.26-28, 4.6–7). Two more different scenarios could hardly be imagined. Why then did Paul choose to speak of Jesus as "son of God" at all? Surely the reason is not hard to find. *Paul was a Jew.* Articulations of the divine sonship of God's people (Exod. 4.22, Deut. 14.1, Isa. 1.2, Jer. 3.22, Hos. 1.10, 11.1, Wisd. of Sol. 12.21, 16.10, 26; 18.4, 13, *Ps. Sol.* 18.4, Isa. 1.2, 64.7), the divine sonship of the just (Wisd. of Sol. 2.18, 5.5; Sir. 4.10; *Pss. Sol.* 13.9, 18.4), and the divine sonship of the Lord's anointed (2 Sam. 7.4, Ps. 2.7, 89.26–27, 4Q174 [4QFlorilegium], 4Q246) were deeply rooted in Israel's tradition.[57] Some of them long predated any Caesar. No doubt Paul was aware of claims made for Caesar, and no doubt, as a Jew, he believed that pagans spoke in ignorance and folly (Romans 1.22-23!). But to suggest therefore that when he spoke of Jesus as "the son of God, who loved me and gave himself for me" (Gal. 2.20), or when he told the Galatians that "God has sent the Spirit of his Son into our hearts, crying 'Abba! Father!'" (Gal. 4.6)—to suggest that at such moments as these Paul was concerned with denying something to Caesar is surely a spectacular example of placing the cart before the horse. Yes, Paul was in some senses a Greek. Yes, he was, like all who lived in his world, affected by Rome. Perhaps, as some insist (not I), he was anti-Roman. But above all Paul was a *Jew*, who believed that he had found the Messiah; and it is to his likely understanding of the promises of God that we must first look to explain anything that he says about the Messiah.[58] Doubtless we will continue to debate whether or not Paul was interested in challenging Roman rule. There can be no debate at all about his interest in the fulfillment of God's promise Israel.

My concern in this section has been to talk about Paul's attitude to Rome, not Rome's attitude to Paul or his fellow Christians. Still, for what it is worth, perhaps even here I should point out that it is in any case extremely unlikely that imperial authorities *would* have regarded talk of Jesus as "savior," "lord," or "son of God" as in itself "treason," or "denying Caesar." Such a view of emperor worship treats it, I suspect, far too much as if it were a phenomenon like Christianity. Greco-Roman religion (from which emperor worship should not be separated[59]) did not, essentially, involve a body of doctrine and belief as does Christianity, but was rather a practice of honoring the gods. It flourished in a world in which, as Paul noted, there were "many gods and many lords" (1 Cor. 8.5). Why then (from the Roman point of view) should not Jesus be one of them? According to Tertullian, Tiberius had no problem with that—and even if Tertullian's story of Tiberius proposing Jesus' deification to the Roman senate is not true,[60] the point remains, for Tertullian certainly had some understanding of how Romans thought (Tertullian, *Apology* 5.2). The fact is, even at the height of the persecutions, Rome's problem with Christianity appears generally to have had nothing to do with what Christians believed or claimed about Jesus and everything to do with Christians' refusal to honor the Roman gods. But of that, I plan to say more at a later point in this book.[61]

Conclusions

Paul proclaimed a Messiah crucified, "a stumbling block to Jews and foolishness to Gentiles, but to those who are the called, both Jews and Greeks, Christ the power of God and the wisdom of God" (1 Cor. 1.23–24). And, of course, that proclamation, like Jesus' proclamation of the kingdom, made relative all earthly rule, Caesar's or anyone else's. That surely went without saying. "Then comes the end, when Christ hands over the kingdom to his God and Father, when he has destroyed every sovereignty and every authority and power" (1 Cor. 15:24). But that also remained precisely the point. These proclamations were the end of *all* earthly rule—*every* sovereignty and authority and power. Paul's proclamation is therefore "political," in the same way in which, as we have repeatedly seen, the entire biblical tradition is "political," which is to say it asserts that there is One who is above all earthly powers, even within their own spheres, and who will hold them accountable. To that One every knee will bow, and that, as Oakes points out, "presumably, includes the Emperor's own knee."[62] So the proclamation of Christ's universal authority has "social and political consequences."[63] It is a challenge to rulers to understand the basis of their authority and a call to them to seek God's justice for those whom they rule. It is a reminder to them that they stand on notice.

But that in itself need not mean the *rejection* of those rulers, any more than Martin Luther King's challenge to the government of the United States to give to his people the rights that it had hitherto denied them constituted a rejection of the government of the United States. So Paul's proclamation is *not* "political" insofar as "politics" is understood as having to do with replacing or reorganizing specific structures, refusing to consider oneself subject to the authority of a specific state or sovereign, "regime change," and the like. Specifically, the idea that Paul was interested in seeing an end to Roman rule in the sense in which, say, Judas the Galilean was interested in that agenda is without any basis whatever. Romans 13.1–7 is the only passage we have that *certainly* expresses a Pauline view of the Roman state, and it is, as we have seen, broadly favorable to it.

6

Jesus' Followers and the Roman Empire

Luke-Acts, 1 Peter, and Revelation

Luke-Acts and the Roman Empire

What was Luke's[1] attitude to the empire? New Testament scholarship is as divided over this as over any question before it. By way of beginning my own discussion, therefore, I would note four opinions of the matter—four apparently very different opinions—all of which have been seriously canvassed in recent decades. These are (1) that Luke has no particular concern about the empire at all, since his chief concern is to show that God has acted in Jesus Christ, that God has thereby been faithful to the promises made to Israel, and that the church was and is therefore the true heir to those promises; (2) that Luke is concerned to prepare his hearers for the suffering that may come to them, either from the empire or elsewhere, as a result of their Christian profession; (3) that Luke is concerned to present an apologia for the empire to the church; and (4) that Luke is concerned to present an apologia for the church to the empire.

None of these positions appears to me to be without merit, or without some support in Luke's text. Yet each, if presented in a (so to speak) "pure" form, is in danger of omitting or ignoring other elements that are also present. Thus, I am sure that Jacob Jervell and Luke Timothy Johnson are right to stress that Luke's fundamental concern is theological. I am less comfortable, however, with their virtually omitting consideration of other issues, as if theological concern must necessarily exclude all lesser matters.[2] C. K. Barrett, who also sees Luke's chief purpose as theological ("Christian faith is the truth, the truth of God: magna est, et praevalebit"), is right to be more nuanced in his discussion.[3] Again, I think that Richard Cassidy is right to stress Luke's determination to prepare those whom he addresses for the suffering that may come to them at the hands of imperial officials and others.[4] But still, as Steve Walton and Gregory E. Sterling suggest, he should perhaps take more account of those occasions when Luke has quite positive things to say about Roman officials and their actions.[5] I intend to say more of these "positive things" at a later point in this chapter. For the present, suffice it to note that they do indeed stand as evidence for the case presented by Paul C. Walawsky and Robert M. Maddox: that Luke would not have wanted his Christian hearers to regard the Roman Empire as their enemy.[6] But again, taken in the context of Luke-Acts as a whole, they are hardly evidence that pro-Roman apologetic was Luke's main purpose: if it were, why would he have introduced into his narrative negative elements about Roman officials, such as Pilate's brutality in the matter of the Galilean pilgrims or the greed and superficiality of Felix? Nevertheless, the "positive things" that are said about Rome also lead me to think that Luke would have been happy to persuade respectable Romans of the middle or upper rank that there was nothing subversive about Christianity, if only so that such considerations need not be a barrier to their conversion or to their continuing loyalty to their new faith.[7] Again, however, this element—as proponents generally concede—hardly allows us to suppose that Luke intended his work as a whole to be in any formal sense an apologia or legal defense to be presented to Roman officials. As regards that suggestion, C. K. Barrett's tart observation, "no Roman court could be expected to wade through so much Jewish religious nonsense in order to find half a dozen fragments of legally significant material," remains unanswerable.[8] The form of pro-church "apologetic" that we do find in Luke-Acts is rather, as Philip F. Esler has pointed out (distinguishing his view from the normal "apologetic" position), a matter of "legitimation": a social process necessary for those who become members of a new order, and who need to have that order explained and justified to them, especially if they have ties and commitments that are important to them and that still bind them to the old order.[9] Insofar, then, as Luke-Acts is addressed to Romans, it is addressed to Romans who are already members of the church or at least thinking seriously of becoming such.[10]

Given this complexity, what then should we say of Luke's attitude to the Roman Empire?

In the sixth month the angel Gabriel was sent by God to town in Galilee called Nazareth to a virgin engaged to a man whose name

was Joseph, of the house of David. The virgin's name was Mary.
(Luke 1.11-13a)

The first thing, as Barrett, Johnson, and Jervell have said, is that Rome and its concerns are not, for Luke, the center of his narrative, or even necessary to it. Like the other three evangelists, Luke wishes to tell a story that is essentially about God and God's action. In particular, he wishes to tell the story to which Mary bears prophetic witness in the Magnificat (Luke 1.46-55): how God "has looked with favor on the lowliness of his servant" and how, from the beginning until this day,

> his mercy is for those who fear him,
> in every generation.
> He has shown strength with his arm;
> he has scattered those who were arrogant in the thoughts of their
>   hearts . . .
> He has helped Israel his servant,
> remembering his mercy,
> according to his promise to our fathers,
> to Abraham and to his descendants for ever. (Luke 1.48, 50–55)

Needless to say, this continued outpouring of God's mercy upon Israel and the world has meant the overthrowing of much that is great by human standards and the reversal of much that the world (including Israel) has usually taken for granted:

> He has cast down mighty ones [dunastas] from their thrones
> and lifted up the lowly;
> he has filled hungry people with good things,
> and sent the rich away empty handed. (Luke 1.52–53)

And now in Jesus this long history has reached a climax and fulfillment, pointed to by the prophetic witness of Simeon:

> For my eyes have seen your salvation,
> which you have prepared before the face of all peoples:
> a light for revelation to the nations,
> and the glory of your people Israel. (Luke 2.30–32)

All these, then, are "the events that have been fulfilled among us," about which Luke wishes his audience to know "the truth" (asphaleia) (Luke 1.4); and in that purpose he evidently has much in common with the other three evangelists. That granted, it should be noted, nonetheless, that Luke's insistence that his faith involved the fulfillment of God's promises to Israel—in other words, that it was a continuation of the ancient faith—although a claim important to Christian witness for many reasons, would not have been unimportant even in Roman eyes. It is clear that the Romans valued antiquity, and it was because of Judaism's antiquity, if for no other reason, that some Romans were prepared to tolerate it (Tacitus, *Histories* 5.4–5; Origen, *Against Celsus* 5.25).[11]

Yet there is more to be said. The fact is, one might read for some time in Matthew, Mark, and John without even realizing that there *was* such a thing as the Roman Empire. Not so with Luke, for whom its presence is felt and named early in the story, even before the child Jesus is born.

> In those days a decree went out from Emperor Augustus that all the empire [*pasan tēn oikoumenēn*[12]] should be registered. This was the first registration and was taken while Quirinius was governor of Syria. All went to their own towns to be registered. Joseph also went from the town of Nazareth in Galilee to Judea, to the city of David called Bethlehem, because he was descended from the house and family of David. He went to be registered with Mary, to whom he was engaged and who was expecting a child. (Luke 2.1–5)

There are obvious problems with this passage, not least that Publius Sulpicius Quirinius does not appear to have been governor of Syria prior to his appointment in AD 6, when he was indeed sent to Judea as Augustus' *legatus* to conduct the census to which Judas the Galilean objected. But whatever the solution to these problems—and I agree with Luke Timothy Johnson that "to obsess over Luke's chronological accuracy" is "to miss the point"[13]—one thing is perfectly clear: Luke here shows Mary and Joseph loyally obeying Caesar Augustus' decree, and in so doing, *identifying* themselves with the Roman Empire. We should not ignore the implications, both theological (Numbers 1.26!) and political, of a census. Horsley is quite right to connect it with the Roman requirement (normal in antiquity) that subject peoples pay tribute to their conquerors.[14] Nevertheless, those other commentators are not wrong who point out that in Luke's view, here at least are faithful Jews who find no difficulty in giving to Caesar what is Caesar's while at the same time giving to God what is God's.[15] It remains to be seen whether or not Caesar is to be numbered among those "mighty ones" whom God has in the past (and therefore presumably can and will again in the future) "cast down" from their thrones. If the biblical and prophetic witness is to be taken as seriously as Luke seems to take it, that will depend in part on Caesar's behavior. But whatever may be the end of *that* particular story, Mary appears to see no contradiction between God's power over such "mighty ones" and her own obedience to Caesar's decree. Nor is it incorrect to note that in this case (far from being in opposition to obedience to God), it is obedience to Caesar that actually brings Mary to Bethlehem, the city of David wherein the Messiah ought to be born.[16] By showing how Caesar's decrees serve to fulfill God's purposes even without Caesar's knowing it, Luke does, indeed, also *relativize* Caesar's power in comparison with God's power. In the same way, later in the birth narrative, by showing Jesus as the "lord" (*kurios*) who alone brings true "peace" (*eirēnē*) to the world, Luke relativizes the merely political peace that Caesar brought (Luke 2.11, 14).[17] But to relativize is not necessarily to deny. It is merely to place in proper perspective—the very perspective to which Mary has already drawn our attention by her prophetic witness to the God who "has scattered the arrogant" and who, as a part of that process, "has cast down mighty ones from their thrones."

So, then, to the main gospel story, the story of Jesus. Luke's Jesus is not a rebel seeking to replace one *polis* with another, nor is he a Gandhi, counseling nonviolent noncooperation with imperial authorities.[18] On the contrary, when confronted with a Jew who collects taxes for the Romans, Jesus rejoices in the man's almsgiving and his acts of penitence for extortion, but notably does *not* tell him to stop working for the empire (Luke 19.1–10). In response to a question about paying tax to Rome, Jesus declares, just as he does in Matthew and Mark, that Caesar must be given back what is owed to him, just as God must be given what God is owed (Luke 20.25).[19] When interrogated by Pilate Jesus is, to be sure, neither obsequious nor deferential, but he does not refuse to answer Pilate's question (Luke 23.3–4), and—again notably—he challenges neither the imperial representative's right to ask him the question nor his right to sit in judgment upon him (a marked contrast to Gandhi!). All this is not to say that Luke does not see resistance—and even perhaps violent resistance—as an option for Jesus. Luke's description of the second temptation (4.6–7) and his description of Jesus' arrest (22.50–51) seem to show Jesus twice faced with just such a possibility, and refusing it.

In connection with all this we may usefully consider the programmatic prophecy of the jubilee "year of the Lord's favor" that Luke tells us was quoted by Jesus in the synagogue at Nazareth at the beginning of his ministry.

> "The Spirit of the Lord is upon me, because he has anointed me to bring good news to the poor. He has sent me to proclaim release to the captives and recovery of sight to the blind, to let the oppressed go free, to proclaim the year of the Lord's favor." (Luke 4.18–19, citing Isaiah 61.1–2)

Here, truly, is a revolutionary program! And that prophecy, Jesus goes on to say, is *already* being fulfilled (4.21). So what is the prophecy about? Evidently, it does not refer to the replacement of Roman *imperium*. Or, if it does, then Luke has Jesus talking nonsense, since the *imperium* is still in place. But that is not to say that it refers to something merely "spiritual" or "inward." Jesus is speaking, as the original prophet was surely speaking, of the people whom he was addressing. This the townspeople in the synagogue evidently understand very well, for they respond gracefully to Jesus' message. But then they realize that the reordering he describes will by its nature allow a place in God's compassion for those whom they have hitherto despised—the gentiles—and that will involve for them a change of social and political attitudes that they are not prepared to contemplate. At that point they seek to kill Jesus (Luke 4.22–29). When, much nearer to the end of Luke's story, Paul will present virtually the same call to his people—"Then [the Lord] said to me, 'Go, for I will send you far away to the Gentiles' "—the result will be the same (Acts 22.21). This, then, is evidently a key issue for Luke, and it not an exhortation to enmity toward Rome—or, indeed, toward anyone.

But the account of Jesus' preaching in the synagogue at Nazareth contains a further element. Any among Luke's hearers who knew the story of Naaman to which Jesus referred, or was interested enough to inquire (and there is no reason to suppose there would not have been such), would know that it was the story of a pagan soldier serving a pagan government, who in the process of his service was from time to time obliged to be present at pagan worship. And they would know that when he confessed his faith in the God of Israel, but pleaded the pressure on him to be present with his master at ceremonies of pagan worship, he was told, "Go in peace" (2 Kings 5.17–19). What better news, or what better precedent, could have been offered for the comfort of a converted soldier like Cornelius, or a converted civil servant such as Sergius Paulus, both of whom, virtually as a part of their work, would from time to time need to be present at pagan imperial ceremonies?[20]

A later scene in the gospel offers a striking critique of all human claims to and abuse of power, a critique that amplifies and develops the implications of Mary's prophetic word in the Magnificat:

A dispute also arose among [the disciples] as to which one of them was to be regarded as the greatest. But [Jesus] said to them, "The kings of the Gentiles lord it over them; and those in authority over them are called benefactors. But not so with you; rather the greatest among you must become like the youngest, and the leader like one who serves. For who is greater, the one who is at the table or the one who serves? Is it not the one at the table? But I am among you as one who serves. (Luke 22.24–27)

Again there is, of course, nothing specifically anti-*Roman* about that critique. Rather, it criticizes the general understanding of power in the Greco-Roman world. In its context, insofar as it is specific at all, it is aimed at the life of Jesus' followers—that is, at the church. Subsequently, in his picture in Acts of the community of believers with "all things in common" (Acts 4.32–37) (in some ways, the ideal Hellenistic society of friends) Luke describes for us just such a community as would follow from taking seriously the implications of Luke 1.52–53 and 22.24–27. Because that community is the work of God in Christ through the gift of the Spirit, to deceive or cheat it is a terrible thing. That is why the story of Annas and Sapphira is so harsh, so contrary to what seems to us the general spirit of Luke (Acts 5.1–11). What Annas and Sapphira do is terrible, because it involves direct defiance of God's grace. In Luke's view, nothing that comes from *outside* the church can really damage the church. But the church *can* be damaged from within, when it fails to listen to the call of God's grace. Needless to say, the very existence in the world of such a group as Luke describes would (and sometimes actually does) constitute a challenge to and critique of all other exercises and structures of power (including naturally therefore the Roman) just as Nathan constituted such a challenge and critique for David. But that does not mean that its purpose is to overthrow or replace such structures, any more than Nathan's was. Its purpose is to be faithful to the best of its ability, and by that faithfulness it inevitably challenges all who are in power to perform the work for which God gives them power.

For Luke, the Roman Empire in itself is not an obstacle to the spreading of the Good News. In his account of Jesus' trial, Luke more than any other of the evangelists appears to be saying that Jesus' unjust condemnation comes about not because Pilate is Roman, but because of Pilate's *failure* to uphold Roman order (Luke 23.3–16). It is much the same with Felix in Acts. When the orator Tertullus offers his address to Felix (Acts 24.2–4), we hear, and are no doubt intended to hear, irony in the offering of such flattery to the venial and self-serving Roman governor. Luke's irony, we may note, also provides us with a fine example of the "public transcript of power," skillfully manipulated by those who are subject to it, while being, no doubt, entirely different from their "hidden transcript."[21] But here again, as with Pilate, Luke makes clear that the problem with Felix is *not* the Roman imperial system, but his own weakness—in this case, his personal greed (Acts 24.26); and even Felix gives Paul a measure of liberty and allows his friends to visit him (Acts 24.23).

These negative examples are, moreover, balanced throughout Luke-Acts—and I would incline to say, rather more than balanced—by a whole chain of other Roman establishment figures who generally appear in a good light, and who (most importantly for Luke's purposes) are in some measure supportive of God's people. Thus, while the episode of the centurion's servant occurs in both Matthew and Luke, it is Luke who emphasizes the centurion's *goodness*: "he loves our nation and has built us a synagogue" (Luke 7.1–10; compare— and contrast—Matt. 8.5–13). Similarly Luke 23:47 accentuates Mark's centurion at the cross. Luke's centurion actually "glorified God," saying, "Surely this was a just man" (Luke 23.47; compare—and again contrast—Mark 15.39). Luke alone includes in his narrative a third centurion—Cornelius, of the *cohors Italica*. He is the gentile whose prayers are heard by God, and he and his household are blessed in the gentile Pentecost (Acts 10.1–48). (In general connection with Roman soldiers, it is perhaps not irrelevant to note further that Luke *omits* a section in Mark that describes Jesus being mocked by Roman soldiers [Mark 15.16–20], but adds a section of his own that describes Jesus receiving such treatment at the hands of Herod and his, presumably, Jewish soldiers [Luke 23.6-12].[22]) Other Roman establishment figures who appear in Luke's narrative in a favorable light are Sergius Paulus, governor of Cyprus, who "believed," being "astonished at the teaching about the Lord" (13.4–12); Gallio, proconsul of Achaia, who refuses to hear the accusations against Paul (18.12–17);[23] Julius, a centurion of the *cohors Augusta*, who protects Paul (27.1–44); and Publius, the "leading man of the island"[24] of Malta, who shows kindness to Paul and his companions after their shipwreck (28.1–10).

Insofar as Acts has a "hero," it is, in the second half at least, obviously Paul. Richard Cassidy quite correctly points out that there is nothing in Luke's portrait to suggest that Paul was anti-Roman or deliberately disrupted Roman order, even though "in the situations that Luke describes Paul is *de facto* a disturber of the Roman order."[25] And that, evidently, is a concern for Luke, for throughout this part of his narrative he goes out of his way to claim that it is those (whether Jews or gentiles) who *oppose* Paul who disturb Roman order, *not* Paul himself (Acts 13.50, 14.4–5, 19.23–41, 21.27–31, 22.22–23).

Cassidy also observes that in Acts, from Paul's arrest onward, he appears most of the time to be in chains, and suggests that Luke's Paul is only a "reluctant" Roman citizen.[26] With regard to the former, evidently, being in chains was an extremely unpleasant and shameful circumstance, and Luke makes no attempt to hide it (e.g. Acts 26.29). On the other hand, Luke also makes perfectly clear that were it *not* for Paul's Roman custody, he would be not in chains, but dead (Acts 22.22). Moreover, as Robert O'Toole has pointed out, the last section of Acts (26.30–31) does not mention chains or speak of imprisonment, and ends with the word "unhindered," which seems to speak rather hopefully of Christianity's place in the Roman world.[27]

With regard to Paul's citizenship, while I am not sure that I can go so far in the opposite direction from Cassidy as does Esler, who speaks of Luke's "apparent delight" in playing "the trump card" of Paul's Roman citizenship,[28] and while I grant that Paul is nowhere seen boasting of his Roman citizenship, in the way that he proudly declares his identity as a Pharisee and as a servant of Christ, still, I am also bound to note that Paul appeals to his Roman citizenship when it suits him (Acts 16.37–39, 22.28, 25.11–12) and that his response to the tribune, "But I was born a citizen" (Acts 22.28), certainly does not appear to reflect any reluctance about the matter.[29] Moreover, as O'Toole says, "Paul's citizenship is a dominant factor in the final chapters of Acts. It explains Lysias' considerate treatment of him, the journey to Caesarea and Felix, the appeal before Festus and the voyage to Rome. . . . For Luke, Paul's citizenship is a significant part of his theme of Christians fitting well into the Roman world."[30] This appears to me to be undeniable. To put it another way, one effect of the story of Paul's citizenship is further "legitimation." Here we are shown the great apostle of Christ actually *claiming* to be a citizen, and being protected by the empire (Acts 22.23–29, 24.12–35). Such persons as Cornelius and Sergius Paulus could hardly be furnished with clearer evidence that as Christians they do not need to reject the empire and can even, on occasion, claim to be part of it and look to it for protection from God's enemies.

Is it then the case that Paul in Acts is shown as slavishly obedient to Rome, so that whatever Rome does must be right? Is it the case that the Roman Empire is seen simply as "a benign and enabling context for the rise of a supposedly innocuous new religious movement that became Christianity"?[31] By no means! The Paul of Acts is in this respect completely consistent with the biblical tradition (which includes, as we have seen, the Paul of Romans 13). The governing authorities have a job to do, and *Luke's Paul expects them to do it*. Therefore when Paul is wrongly arrested and beaten in Philippi, he is not content to be shipped out of town quietly (*lathra*), as the authorities would like. On the contrary, he demands—and receives—a public apology (Acts 16:35–40).[32] To put it another way, when he and his fellow missionaries, and therefore the gospel that they represent, have been put to shame publicly (*dēmosia*) by being stripped, beaten, and imprisoned, he insists on an equally public restoration of honor: "Let them come and take us out themselves" (16.37).[33] When Paul is standing before Caesar's tribunal, under the laws of Rome, he expects Caesar's tribunal to do its work; when Caesar's servant on that tribunal suggests a way whereby he might avoid that work, *Paul appeals to Caesar*—which is to say, Paul does not hesitate to put even the Emperor himself on the spot (Acts 25:8–12). So later, after Paul has made his defense before King Agrippa and Queen Bernice,

Then the king got up, and with him the governor and Bernice and
those who had been seated with them; and as they were leaving,
they said to one another, "This man is doing nothing to deserve
death or imprisonment." Agrippa said to Festus, "This man could
have been set free if he had not appealed to Caesar." (Acts 26.31–32)

Perhaps so! But that, apparently, is not good enough for the Paul of Acts, who
will insist on putting his question. Will the Emperor fulfill the purpose for
which God has given him power (Isa. 44:28), or not?

In connection with Acts, Horsley asks a question: "Why were Roman officials regularly arresting Paul and other apostles and keeping them in jail, on
the grounds that 'they are acting contrary to the decrees of the emperor, saying
that there is another king named Jesus?' (Acts 17:7)."[34] Why indeed? The question cannot meaningfully be answered, for it involves at least two false assumptions. First, it assumes "regular" arrests of Paul and the other apostles
by the Romans—in fact, throughout the whole of Acts, Paul is arrested *once*
by the Roman authorities, following a semi-riot, and is released the following
day (16:16–24, 35–40); he is *once* taken into protective custody by the Romans,
without which it seems likely he would have been lynched (21:27–40).[35] Second,
the quotation from Acts that is offered as Roman "grounds" for arresting the
apostles is actually presented by Acts as a summary of *Jewish* charges, which
the "Roman officials," for their part, pretty well ignore (17:8–9). The last part
of Acts (24–28) shows Paul being repeatedly examined by Roman tribunals
and repeatedly acquitted, so that the climax, with Paul teaching in Rome "without hindrance," is not unexpected (Acts 28.31). If therefore we propose to draw
upon Acts in this discussion, the question that ought to be asked is, "Why does
Luke show Roman officials repeatedly releasing or acquitting Paul and the
other apostles (Acts 17:8–9, 18.12–17, 24:1–28:31 passim, cf. 19:31), despite
charges by the hierarchy in Jerusalem that 'they are acting contrary to the
decrees of the emperor, saying that there is another king named Jesus?' (Acts
17:7)?"[36] That is the *real* question. In answering it, broadly speaking, I agree
with John Dominic Crossan and Jonathan L. Reed: Luke wants to suggest that
hostility to the Christians invariably arises from one of two causes, "pagan
greed" or "Jewish jealousy," and *not* from imperial suspicion or disapproval.[37]
As Esler says, "The general impression communicated by this politically sensitive material is that Jesus and his followers did not contravene Roman law
and were therefore not a threat to the empire, even though Jewish authorities
repeatedly initiated proceedings designed to prove the opposite and occasionally enjoyed some measure of success before Roman officials whose weakness
or self-seeking prevented the judicial system they administered from operating

effectively."[38] How much that was merely the way in which Luke chose to interpret the story, and how much it represented historical reality, is no doubt matter for discussion. My own suspicion is that, for the period about which he was writing—that is, prior to Nero's change of policy (Suetonius, *Nero* 16.2)—as far as relates to Rome's attitude to Christianity, Luke probably got it about right. That is to say, while I do not doubt there was during this period a measure of harassment of the new minority by both pagans and Jews, I suspect that imperial officials were, on the whole, inclined to be protective of a Jewish sect that appeared to them to be eliminating from Jewish messianic tradition precisely those politically violent, anti-Roman elements that Rome feared. (Of course, throughout most of this period, those same officials could have had no idea that this sect would eventually make far more converts outside of Judea than it ever made within.) But whether I am right or wrong about all that, it appears to me that there really is not much room for argument about what Luke is *claiming*. "I have," says Paul, "committed no crime either against the Jewish law or against the temple *or against Caesar*" (Acts 25.8). Exactly! Christianity is not, says Luke, and has no intention of being, the enemy of Rome; and there is not the slightest reason for Rome to be the enemy of the church. What is more, sensible Roman administrators are perfectly well aware of that, and so are sensible Christians.

1 Peter

Here we have the work of someone very much in the Pauline tradition, sharply conscious of the "already" and the "not yet" of Christianity. Those in Asia to whom Peter[39] writes, perhaps from Rome, perhaps at some time in the 90s of the first Christian century, have already received from God "a new birth into a living hope through the resurrection of Jesus Christ from the dead, and into an inheritance that is imperishable, undefiled, and unfading." Nevertheless, that inheritance is not yet in their hands. It is, for the present, "kept in heaven for you, who are being protected by the power of God through faith for a salvation ready to be revealed in the last time" (1 Peter 1.3–5). Therefore, they are still "exiles of the dispersion," even though they have been "chosen and destined by God the Father and sanctified by the Spirit to be obedient to Jesus Christ and to be sprinkled with his blood" (1.1–2). That situation of exile can and does at times involve suffering and even, from time to time, "fiery ordeal" (4.12), referring, in the view of most recent commentators (I think correctly), not to persecution by the state but rather to the more intermittent local harassment that could arise simply from local communities that resented those whose customs and lifestyle were different from their own;[40]as the writer says, "They are surprised that you no longer join them in the same excesses of dissipation, and so they malign you" (4.4). In that situation, the duty of the baptized is still clear. The author has already stated it:

> Beloved, I urge you as aliens and exiles to abstain from the desires of the flesh that wage war against the soul. Conduct yourselves honorably among the Gentiles, so that, though they malign you as evildoers, they may see your honorable deeds and glorify God when he comes to judge. For the Lord's sake accept the authority of every human institution, whether of the emperor as supreme, or of governors, as sent by him to punish those who do wrong and to praise those who do right [agathopoiōn]. For it is God's will that by doing right [agathopoiountas] you should silence the ignorance of the foolish. As servants of God, live as free people, yet do not use your freedom as a pretext for evil. Honor everyone. Love the family of believers. Fear God. Honor the emperor. (1 Peter 2.11–17)

While Peter does not tell his hearers to pray for the pagan city in which they find themselves, the conducting of oneself "honorably" among pagans is partly owed to continuing hope that pagans, too, when confronted with the judgment of the living God, will be able to "glorify" God as is fitting. On the other hand, it is noticeable that, while conduct among pagans involves honor, and believers must "honor" the emperor, still they are to "fear" no one but God. "The concluding verse of this section thus establishes a hierarchy of values and allegiances: all people, including the emperor, are to be shown due honor and respect; fellow Christians are to be regarded as members of one's own family and shown appropriate love; God alone is to be shown reverence" (Paul Achtemeier).[41] If you know the right thing to fear, you have no need to fear anything else.

As we have already noticed in our examination of Romans 13, the phrase "to do good" (to agathon poiein) appears linked to public benefaction and service in a number of inscriptions.[42] Thus, it is possible that in 1 Peter, too, Christian obligation to public service was a part of the issue in the exhortation to "do good." As in Romans, we should understand the commitment first in the light of Jeremiah's injunctions to the exiles to "seek the welfare of the city where I have sent you into exile" (Jer. 29.7) and second in connection with dominical injunctions, such as that in Matthew to "let your light so shine before others that they may see your noble works [kala erga], and give glory to your father in heaven" (Matt. 5.16).[43] We should note, moreover, that it is precisely in view of their future hope that Peter (like Paul) exhorts believers to perform what even those who traduce them will have to recognize as "noble works." Thus, he keeps eschatological and social concerns bound inseparably together. It is not in spite of the fact that they are already citizens of a greater kingdom that is coming but precisely because of it that they are to be, as far as in them lies, good citizens and respectful subjects of Rome.

The Revelation to John

The seer of Revelation, who wrote from Patmos to the churches of Asia at a time perhaps not very distant from that of I Peter, is surely the one obvious and explicit enemy of Rome in the New Testament. Nonetheless, I wrote in my *Preface to Romans* that, "for all the well-nigh unbridgeable difference of *attitude* and *emotion* between Paul and the Apocalypse, it does not seem to me that there is here an essential *theological* difference."[44] I believe that I was right. Revelation, in being an exception to the rest of the New Testament in its attitude to Rome, is also (in the proper sense of the proverb) an exception that proves (tests, puts to proof) the rule.

The important thing here is to perceive correctly the object of John's attack. This means that we must examine it using the correct lens: the correct lens will enable us to see it more clearly, whereas the wrong lens will obscure it. In this particular case, the postcolonial lens is not helpful, for the chief object of John's attack is not, as it happens, the notion of empire. On the contrary, like the prophetic tradition in general, and like Jesus, John is entirely capable of using "empire" as a positive image of God's own rule, and does (22.24–26). The object of John's attack is not even the *Roman* Empire, in and of itself. The object of John's attack is the *worship* of emperor and empire. Above all, John is concerned with *idolatry*. Certainly (and in good Jewish fashion) he believes that idolatry leads to injustice, exploitation, and abuse, and that these things will be punished. But the root of them all is idolatry. This, of course, is exactly Paul's view. To put it another way—and though I am generally wary of "what-would-have happened-if" statements, I will venture this one—if Paul had perceived Roman imperial rhetoric as John perceived it, he would have judged it as John did. He was every bit as clear as John that it is sin—indeed, it is the archetypal sin—to worship and serve the creature rather than the creator (Rom. I.25). The proper role of humanity in relation to the creation not to worship it but "to till it and keep it" (Gen. 2.15).[45]

Precisely what led John the seer to this particular view of Rome is a matter of deep disagreement in current scholarship. In the opinion of Adela Yarbro Collins, social pressure (*not* state coercion[46]) to join in some form of emperor worship was only one among several traumatic experiences that Christians in Asia Minor were undergoing with respect to Roman rule. Other pressures on the Christian community were the destruction of the temple and of Jerusalem, the deaths of many Christians at Rome under Nero in the mid-sixties, the martyrdom of Antipas (Rev. 2.13), and John's own exile to Patmos—none of which, in themselves, were more than examples of "the usual sporadic repression suffered by Christians in the first two centuries."[47] Elizabeth Schüssler Fiorenza sees more or less the same scenario as Collins but paints it in much bleaker colors. In her view, Christian refusal to participate in emperor worship in Asia Minor merely made an already bad situation worse. Most of those who lived in the province were already "staggering under the colonial injustices of oppressive taxation often combined with ruinous interest rates." They were fearful of "Roman repression of disturbances, paranoid prohibition of private associations, and suspicious surveillance by neighbors and informants," and they were suffering from "colonial abuses of power, exploitation, slavery, and famine."[48]

Leonard L. Thompson, by contrast, sees "little evidence" for any of this. "The writer of the Book of Revelation may urge his readers to see conflicts in their urban setting and to think of Roman society as 'the enemy,' but those conflicts do not reside in Asian social structures. The urban setting in which Christians worshipped and lived was stable and beneficial to all who participated in its social and economic institutions."[49] Imperial government was, in Thomson's view, generally popular among the lower classes, who were sometimes protected by its representatives from the depredations of the wealthy; and it was valued by the wealthy because it offered avenues to prestige. Therefore the problems reflected in Revelation arose not so much from any actual evils in society as from John's perception of them. John wished to provoke his hearers so as to alienate them from the society around them. "In comparison to the public knowledge embodied in the empire, John reveals a deviant knowledge, that is, one that deviates from public knowledge taken for granted in everyday Roman life."[50] Similarly Robert M. Royalty sees scant evidence of "oppression by the Roman authorities"[51] and reads Revelation not as "the description of a struggle between Christians and Romans" but rather as "between Christians. The key issue in this struggle is who should have authority within the Christian communities—John and his prophets, or other teachers, and officials."[52]

For my present purpose, it is not necessary to adopt one or other of these widely divergent views of the situation addressed by John. What is important is, rather, the one point upon which all are agreed, namely, *the significance for John of his perception*. Paul, as we have observed, counseled respect for the state perceived as God's agent and so stood in line with the prophets. The Apocalypse, particularly in chapters 13 to 19, opposes the state *perceived as claiming for itself divine honors* and so also stands in line with the prophets. Regardless of the accuracy or inaccuracy of John's perceptions, it remains that his chief concern is with the empire perceived as claiming divinity. As Richard Bauckham says, "From John's prophetic standpoint Rome's evil lay primarily in absolutizing her own power and prosperity. . . . The special contribution of Christian martyrdom is that it makes the issue clear. Those who bear witness to the one true God, the only true absolute, to whom all political power is subject, expose Rome's idolatrous self-deification for what it is."[53] Exactly so. Nor, for John the seer to have had such a standpoint, are we required to posit a great increase in imperial cultic activity at the time of his writing, or (if Irenaeus was right about the date of Revelation [*Adv. Haer.* 5.30.3; cited Eusebius, *HE* 3.18][54]) any particular outbreak of persecution under Domitian, or any special claims to divinity by him.[55] We may even suppose that there was general content with the social and political situation, not only on the part of the elite but also on the part of the general populace and even of most Christians, since that, as it happens, is precisely what John himself seems to claim: "In amazement the whole earth followed the beast. They worshiped the dragon, for he had given his authority to the beast, and they worshiped the beast, saying, 'Who is like the beast, and who can fight against it?'" (Rev. 13.3b–4). In speaking therefore of the seer's concerns about the "divinity" of emperor and empire, we are simply speaking of *his* particular view of the situation, no more than that, but also no less. So Revelation 13.1–18 may quite well be seen, and perhaps should be seen, as a *minority* discourse. It challenged the majority view by portraying the powers-that-be in dramatically unflattering terms: terms that were no doubt quite different from those in which they were normally portrayed, or in which they sought to portray themselves.

As to Revelation's view of the end of those who are outside God's people: here, too, opinions differ. Robert M. Royalty sees Revelation as having no vision of redemption for those whom it sees as oppressors, only judgment for them—a "judgment with no justice, crisis without catharsis."[56] Wilfred Harrington, by contrast, sees Revelation as asserting only that there is "no negative eschaton," and that for anyone who, "faced with evil, can choose to embrace evil" there can be no future "because evil has no future. Good has an eternal future."[57] But here, too, for our present purposes we do not need to make a decision. It is sufficient to notice that, while John does not tell his exiles to pray for the good of their city or to "do good" in it—and to that extent he does stand aside from the prophetic and Pauline tradition—still he does not counsel them to attack the pagan empire, or even to reject its authority, save in the matter of worship. He counsels no violence. He tells them simply "do not fear" and "be faithful until death" (2.10; see also 2.25, 3.5, 3.11). Those "under the altar" who have already died for the faith are told only "to rest a little longer, until the number would be complete both of their fellow servants and of their brothers and sisters, who were soon to be killed as they themselves had been killed" (6.9, 11). It is God, not the people of God, who through Christ will bring about the fall of "Babylon the Great" (18.2; see 18–19). It is God who through Christ will finally "repay according to everyone's work" (22.12). Here, too, the seer of Revelation is at one with Paul, who tells the Romans that, "the God of peace will shortly crush Satan under your feet" (Rom. 16.20a). But it is not believers who are to do the crushing. God will do it.[58] Therefore "war broke out in heaven; Michael and his angels fought against the dragon. The dragon and his angels fought back, but they were defeated, and there was no longer any place for them in heaven" (Rev. 12.7–8).

But what of those who do not persist in rebellion? Here is matter for poetry—for images of holy city, bride and groom (Rev. 21.9–12). And among those images, it is striking that, despite his anger with Rome and its claims, one image that John brings to rebirth is that of empire: "The nations will walk by its light, and the kings of the earth will bring their glory into it. Its gates will never be shut by day—and there will be no night there. People will bring into it the glory and the honor of the nations" (Rev. 21.24–26). This empire will be what all earthly empires—David's or Solomon's, Cyrus' or Caesar's—have at their best merely dreamed of being. It will be that, because it will know its Lord. "I saw no temple in the city, for its temple is the Lord God the Almighty and the Lamb. And the city has no need of sun or moon to shine on it, for the glory of God is its light, and its lamp is the Lamb" (Rev. 21.22–23).[59]

Conclusions

Here then are three more witnesses to early Christian attitudes toward the Roman *imperium*. If the usual scholarly dating of these writers—which I have followed in each case—is even approximately correct, then all wrote between the death of Nero and the death of Domitian. As regards Rome's treatment of Christianity, much of that period seems to have been marked in general by peace for the church. Indeed, if those who dispute the extent, and even the reality, of Domitian's alleged persecutions are correct, then perhaps all of it was.[60] What attitudes, then, do our three writers take? All fall within the general biblical understanding of pagan empire: that is to say, all see it as within and dependent upon God's will. That tradition, as we have observed, sees empire as having the potential either to be supportive of God's people or else to be self-absolutizing and therefore the enemy of God's people. Here our witnesses differ. Luke and 1 Peter still seem to see the possibility of Rome being placed in the former category. One can easily enough imagine them agreeing with the author of the Pastorals, who (perhaps writing at about the same time[61]) asks that prayers be offered for the Emperor and all in authority, "in order that we may lead a quiet and tranquil life in all devotion and dignity" (1 Tim. 2.2). The seer of Revelation, by contrast, has no doubt that Rome is the enemy of God's people, and therefore he rebukes any church that actually does seem to be leading "a quiet and tranquil life" under the imperial regime (Rev. 3.1–2, 14–19). It is not so much that he speaks of actual persecution—though he is sure that for the faithful persecution will come—as that he sees in Rome a seductive temptress (the imagery is his[62]), and he fears that his people will succumb to her wiles before God has exposed her for what she is.

None of our three writers, however—not even the author of Revelation—counsels resistance to the empire. Even John is clear that if Rome serves Satan, it is God, not Christians, who will overthrow Satan and Rome alike.

7

Empires Ancient and Modern

Richard Horsley uses as an epigraph to the Introduction to his book *Jesus and Empire* a quotation from Edward W. Said's seminal postcolonial study, *Culture and Imperialism*: "Texts are tied to circumstances and to politics large and small, and these require attention and criticism. . . . We cannot deal with the literature of the peripheries without also attending to the literature of the metropolitan centers."[1] Horsley sees a connection between the insights of postcolonialism and the examination of Roman *imperium* that is to follow—a connection, indeed, to which he had already drawn attention in his earlier study, *Jesus and the Spiral of Violence*.[2]

In my introduction to the present discussion, I suggested, however, that there are questions that must be asked about this connection. One such question has already been asked, at least implicitly, in connection with Scott's identification of hidden and public agendas and its applicability to the ancient situation. As we noted, the problem with that application is that we cannot do the kind of research among first-century Galilean peasants that Scott was able to do among his Malaysian villagers. In other words, we are bound to ask how far techniques that were developed for social analysis, as frameworks for collecting and reflecting upon data, may properly be used in historical research, where inevitably they function not really as analytic tools but rather (and perhaps primarily) as means of *reconstruction* through which we try to make good the enormous holes in what we actually know. Evidently, they can be so used only with care, and with limited results. But there is a further question. How far can techniques of analysis that were developed in connection with the post-Enlightenment colonial—to be precise, *post*colonial—experience of cultures formerly subject to nineteenth- and twentieth-century Western domination be applied *at all* to the ancient, largely Mediterranean world of the Roman Empire?

To this latter question we must now turn. Let me say at once that I do not doubt that there *are* parallels between ancient and modern experiences of imperial power. As is evident, I have at more than one point in this book drawn upon postcolonial studies where they appeared to me to help our examination of the ancient situation, either by way of illustration or clarification. Nevertheless, I have tried to proceed with caution, for as well as parallels, there are also profound differences between the two situations. I do not mean merely technical differences, such as the speed of modern communication, the efficiency of modern methods of warfare, and—perhaps above all—the effects of global capitalism, although they are obviously important. Horsley draws our attention to the significance of the last of these in particular, noting that whereas Roman dominance was based on politics and military power, modern Western dominance is based largely on economics—that is, the "needs" of global capital. And while it is true that Rome, like all other ancient polities, exploited its subjects in order to provide wealth and resources for itself, still "the proportion of the world's goods consumed by ancient Rome never even approached the 75% of the world's resources currently being consumed by Americans."[3] All this may be granted. Nevertheless, in speaking of profound differences between Roman *imperium* and post-Enlightenment *imperium*, I have in mind other differences than these.

Assumptions of the Rulers and the Ruled

However much the Romans may have been hated by those whom they conquered, and however much the Romans may have despised those they conquered, the two groups clearly had in common a range of shared assumptions and understanding that is virtually incomprehensible to most people in the twenty-first century West—shared assumptions and understanding about matters such as honor and shame, patronage, patriarchy, solidarity and kinship, sacrifice, the significance of purity, and the intimate relationship between religion and society. Such shared assumptions and understanding are something that Western, post-Enlightenment oppressors of the "third world" generally do *not* have in common with their "subjects" at all.[4] Moreover, the Romans themselves, who clearly were not *always* hated and clearly did not *always* despise their subjects, were not a monolith. The experience of empire itself clearly "prompted new ways of defining what was 'Roman,' new ways of thinking about what was to count as 'Roman' and what was not."[5] Talk of "the Romans," like talk of "the Jews," can easily become talk about nothing so much as our own construct. Thus, it is not hard to find examples of the Romans stereotyping Greeks as untrustworthy, immoral, and (as we would say) generally "lightweight"—*"natio comoeda est"* (it's a nation of playactors), according to Juvenal (*Satires* 3.100). Such an outlook is reflected and, indeed, appealed to by Josephus in his defense of the antiquity and *gravitas* of his own people (*War* 1.13–16; *Ant.* 1.121, 20.262–63; *Life* 40).[6] Nevertheless, many Romans were far from regarding the Greeks and their civilization as peripheral to them, in the way that British, French, and American imperialisms in the nineteenth and twentieth centuries would later regard—or rather disregard—the "native" cultures of the Native Americans, or of Africa, Australia, or Central and South America.[7] Many Romans—including some among the intellectual elite of Rome—were drawn to and even overawed by Greek intellectual and artistic achievement and consciously made it the basis of their own artistic and intellectual world. So, alongside Juvenal, we should set Pliny the Younger, writing to his friend Maximus, who has been appointed to govern Achaia: "Just think of it! You have been sent to the province of Achaia, to the true and genuine Greece, where civilization and literature, and agriculture too, are believed to have originated. . . . Bear in mind that this is the land that provided us with justice and gave us laws" (*Letters* 8.24.2, 4).[8]

This difference in shared assumptions between ourselves and the ancients—Jew, Christian, and pagan, Roman and non-Roman—is nowhere more clearly illustrated than in the strife that arose in the course of time between Christianity and the Roman Empire. We, naturally, tend to think of such strife in terms of our own "imperial" concerns with what we perceive as "security threats"—terrorists, suicide bombers, and the like. But, as we noted earlier, even the seer of Revelation, the most obviously anti-Roman of all the writers in the New Testament, never urges believers to take matters into their own hands or indulge in any acts of violence.[9] And through all the three centuries of conflict between Rome and Christianity—a conflict, to be sure, that only occasionally reached a high level of intensity—there is scarcely any evidence at all (indeed, there is a great deal to the contrary) that Jesus or his followers regarded themselves or were regarded as security threats to the empire in the sense in which we think of security threats—or, indeed, in the sense in which the Romans themselves obviously and correctly regarded those whom Josephus calls *lēstai* as security threats. Christians, by contrast, protested that they *prayed* for the emperor (1 *Clement* 60.4–61.3; Tertullian, *Apology*, 30.1.4–5, 32.1, 33.1[10];

Martyrdom of Appollonius 4; *Acts of St. Cyprian* 1 Eusebius, *Ecclesiastical History* 7.11.8) and were taught to render honor to him and to those in authority under him (*Martyrdom of Polycarp* 9.2). There were, it is true, varieties of Christians, and there are exceptions to this picture. The Montanists at the time of Marcus Aurelius did indeed urge hostility toward the empire: at which point we have Celsus' comparing (c. 177) Jesus to a *lēstarchos* ("rebel leader") (Origen, *Against Celsus*, 2.12, also 8.14). But it is notable that it is at precisely this period that we also find other Christians—such as Apollinaris of Hierapolis, Melito of Sardis, and Athenagoras of Athens—producing "apologies" to explain the Christian position—and they all affirm their loyalty to the emperor and the empire.[11] Origen argues against Celsus that the Christians by their prayers "fight on behalf of the emperor" (*Against Celsus* 8.73), and even Tatian, bitterly hostile as he is toward Greco-Roman culture, nonetheless insists that he pays his taxes and gives due honor to the emperor (*Oration against the Greeks* 4).[12]

Why, then, was Rome hostile to Christianity? Various factors may be pointed to in a situation whose origins are unclear and that in any case evolved. One factor would have been (as Luke says and Paul may reflect) local economic interests that were threatened by the activities of the new minority group (Acts 19; Philippians 1.27–30[13]). Another would have involved personal animosities that could conveniently be worked out against those who were members of a little understood minority: such, it seems, was the curious tangle of marital jealousies and intrigue described by Justin Martyr in his *Second Apology* (2).[14] Another would have involved misunderstandings and distortions of Christian faith and practice, such as the suggestion that Christians practised cannibalism and incest at their assemblies (Athenagoras, *Embassy*, 3.1, 31–33; Eusebius, *Hist. eccl.*, 5.1.14, 26, 52; 9.5.2; compare Pliny, *Letters*, 10.96.2,7).[15] The sheer persistence of Christians in their beliefs would have been seen by many Romans as *contumacia* (arrogance, meaning, in this context, wilful refusal to obey a judicial order), naturally meriting chastisement by the magistrate's *coercitio* (power to administer summary punishment) (Pliny, *Letters*, 10.96.3).[16] At a later stage, the sheer size of the growing Christian community would have been a factor.[17]

All these elements would, then, have played a part. Yet all fade into relative insignificance when weighed against the single consistent charge that the Roman Empire regularly brought against the Church. What the Romans charged the Christians with was *superstitio* (irregular and/or improper relationship to the gods) (Tacitus, *Annals*, 15.44.5; Suetonius, *Nero*, 16.2; Pliny, *Letters*, 10.96.8); surprising though it may be to us, accustomed as we are to our (imagined) separation of religion from politics,[18] they meant it.[19] The Romans—or, at least, a sufficient number of them—did not think that the strength and security of Rome depended finally upon the wisdom of her leaders or the effectiveness of "the Roman fighting-man." Traditional Romans believed that *pax Romana* finally depended upon *pax deorum*. Rome's part in that was *religio*, and *religio* meant showing *pietas*, the respect and honor for the gods that was their due as Rome's benefactors. That is why Virgil's Aeneas is the ideal Roman hero: he is not marked by *mētis* ("wiliness" or "stratagem") as is the Greek hero Odysseus, but he *is* pious, *pius Aeneas*, as Virgil repeatedly calls him: which is to say, he honors the gods. Christians, however, on their own admission, did not honor the gods.[20] They were guilty of *impietas*. Therefore, and in that sense, they were a security threat. In saying that, were the Romans merely putting on an act? We have not the slightest grounds for such a claim. As Robert L. Wilken has pointed out,

> the Roman belief in divine Providence, in the necessity of religious observance for the well-being of society, and in the efficacy of traditional rites and practices, was no less sincere than the beliefs of the Christians. As a Roman proconsul put it at the trial of a Christian in North Africa, "If you make fun of things we hold sacred I will not allow you to speak." How presumptuous, thought the Romans, that the Christians considered themselves alone religious. As a Roman official aptly remarked at the trial of the Scillitan martyrs, "We too are a religious people." We must take these claims seriously. As tempting as it may be to those who have been nurtured on the personal religion of our culture, Roman religion cannot be reduced, as Augustine attempted, to politics or statecraft.[21]

That recognition does not mean, however, that we should jump to an equal and opposite error, that of supposing that Roman religion involved a body of beliefs and theology—perhaps even sacred texts—analogous to, even if different from, those of Christianity or Judaism. That is quite to misunderstand the matter. In Christianity, rituals without faith are nothing. Roman religion was in this respect precisely opposite. The ritual was what mattered, rather than any doctrinal or theological rationale. There was no such thing as "Roman imperial theology."[22] Indeed, there was in a general sense no such thing as "Roman theology" at all. That is not to say that individual Romans would not have thought from time to time about the relationship of the divine to the human, or about what it meant for the Emperor to become a god; no doubt they did, and works such as Cicero's *On the Nature of the Gods* represent such thoughts. But there is little or no indication that such texts, or such thinking, had more than a marginal influence on the actual *practice* of Roman religion.[23] In Roman religion there were rites, and the rites constituted the reality. So it was that even at the height of Roman persecution of Christianity, the Romans consistently displayed almost no interest at all in what Christians *believed*. They displayed considerable interest, however, in what Christians *did*, or rather refused to do, in the matter of showing respect to the Roman gods. As Ittai Gradel says,

> what Roman governors trying Christian defendants demanded of them was not any specific belief, cosmology, reasoning, or philosophy, but simply an action: sacrifice. . . . Sacrifice . . . did not need to be pinned onto a dogmatic or philosophical system to be defended. With impressive tradition behind it, it had always, or so it must have seemed, been the natural way to honour the vastly superior powers of the gods: sacrifice was the core element in divine worship.[24]

Anyone who doubts all this has only to read through a collection of accounts of the deaths of early Christian martyrs, such as those in Herbert Musurillo's *Acts of the Christian Martyrs*.[25] These records, in many ways so deeply moving, are from this point of view almost monotonous. The Christians talk about their faith, and the imperial officials talk about sacrifice. Whatever else was here (and there was much else) there was certainly a complete nonmeeting of minds.

So, for pious Romans, Christians who refused to sacrifice were evidently *atheoi*—atheists. And atheists were a security threat.

While it would be an exaggeration to describe Roman persecution of Christians as merely a result of Roman anxieties about the state of the empire, it is surely no coincidence that after generations of relative peace for the church, major persecutions started under Decius, Valerian, and Diocletian, at precisely those periods when various serious difficulties—political, military, and economic—threatened the empire. That those difficulties had arisen because the empire was allowing people—that is, Christians—to dishonor the gods was a conclusion only too easy to draw.[26] Eventually, Christians succeeded in putting their own stamp upon the words *religio* and *superstitio* and persuaded Rome's emperors that Christianity was *religio* and faith in the gods *superstitio*. Let two facts stand to remind us, however, that from the viewpoint of those who lived in those times, such a conclusion can have seemed by no means either inevitable or obvious. One fact is Julian, a man clearly possessed of education, intelligence, and piety. He turned *from* Christianity *to* paganism and afterward became emperor (361–363).[27] Christians called him "the Apostate," but from his own viewpoint he was apostate only in the sense that Paul was apostate from Judaism, which is to say he followed where it seemed to him that divine calling and his own religious experience led him. It is simply not enough to claim of the gods of Greece and Rome that "their hold on the intelligentsia, even on the priests themselves, was waning. They could no longer satisfy."[28] The fact is, pagan religion *could* satisfy some; it remained a force that could at any time challenge Christianity. The other fact is that when Rome fell to Alaric the Visigoth in 410, decades after Constantine had given peace to the church, Augustine *still* had to struggle in his *City of God* to persuade his contemporaries that the disaster had not come about because Rome had forsaken its gods. The ancient faiths of Rome did not die easily and were ever ready to rise again.

The Brutality of the Ancient World

We certainly need not dispute that the Roman Empire as an institution was often violent, brutal, and exploitative. That it was notably *more* violent, brutal, or exploitative than other polities of its time (including the Jewish, in those periods when Jews had some freedom to run their own affairs) would, however, be hard to demonstrate. When "Pompey and the other Roman warlords conquered various Middle Eastern peoples,"[29] they did not, in general—certainly not in Israel—replace a benevolent and kindly state with something else. Israel in the century before the coming of Pompey had been the scene of vicious internecine Jewish conflict among those who stood for differing political and religious loyalties. The Hasmonean king Alexander Jannaeus (107–76 BC) crucified hundreds, including many Pharisees (Josephus, *War*, 1.97; *Antiquities*, 13.380). Alexander Jannaeus' sons Hyrcanus II and Aristobulus II then fought against each other, ripping the country to shreds. Nor was that all. Economic exploitation bearing heavily on the poorest members of the community had been a characteristic of society in the Middle East (certainly including Israel) for centuries before Pompey arrived.[30] The entire phenomenon of Hasmonean expansionism that had taken place in the century preceding Pompey's arrival was, in Schwartz's view, in many respects simply "a small scale version of Roman imperialism."[31] The Romans (at worst) merely replaced one self-seeking form of economic exploitation with another. At no time may we forget what Horsley speaks of as "the extreme gulf that existed between rulers and ruled in the ancient world, which gulf has recently been more clearly discerned by classical historians."[32]

We do not, moreover, have to be an Achilles Tatius to see that the Roman Empire did have its positive elements. I am aware that at present it is academically unfashionable, at least among New Testament scholars, to dwell on those elements. Thus, Cassidy gives a lengthy description of the evils and violence of imperial rule and the riches it brought to Rome,[33] followed by a mere paragraph outlining the "tangible benefits" that it brought to the subjugated territories—such as harbors, water supplies, road systems, and public baths—of which he has nothing to say save that their provision was "scarcely a decisive consideration" for "those who ruled the empire."[34] Warren Carter has almost twenty pages on the evils of the Roman imperial system,[35] qualified by *one sentence* conceding Rome's "vested interest in limiting the amount of plunder"![36]

I confess that when I read this kind of thing I am reminded of that marvelously funny "What have the Romans ever done for us?" scene in *Life of Brian*.[37] More seriously, I am left wondering just how we could *know* that such things as harbors and road systems were "scarcely a decisive consideration" for those who ran the empire? I suspect that some Roman administrators—including even some emperors, such as Vespasian, Trajan, Hadrian, and Marcus Aurelius—cared very much about the roads and the aqueducts that they built, just as some British administrators and engineers in nineteenth-century India and Africa cared very much about the roads and railways and bridges that *they* built. As Edward Said points out:

> In the expansion of the great Western Empires, profit and hope of further profit were obviously tremendously important. . . . But there is more than that to imperialism and colonialism. There was a commitment to them over and above profit, a commitment in constant circulation and recirculation, which, on the one hand, allowed decent men and women to accept the notion that distant territories and their native peoples *should* be subjugated, and, on the other, replenished metropolitan energies so that these decent people could think of the *imperium* as a protracted, almost physical obligation to rule subordinate, inferior, or less advanced peoples. We must not forget that there was very little domestic resistance to these empires, although they were very frequently established and maintained under adverse and even disadvantageous conditions.[38]

If this was sometimes true (and it was) of nineteenth- and twentieth-century imperialisms, we have absolutely no reason to suppose that it was never true of Roman imperialism twenty centuries earlier. Hence, while it is correct to note the extent to which Cicero, in appealing to Roman expansionism, stressed the material advantages it would bring to Rome, we are quite wrong—indeed, we ignore something fundamental about the way in which Cicero structured his appeal or his hearers would have understood it—to ignore the extent to which Cicero also appealed to the Romans' sense of *honor*, of what was their *duty* (*On the Manilian Law* 9–16).[39] So Virgil, in the famous passage that I quoted at the beginning of this book:

> Hae tibi erunt artes: pacisque imponere morem
> Parcere subiectis et debellare superbos.
> [Be these your arts, to crown peace with justice,
> to spare the vanquished and crush the proud.]
> (Virgil, *Aeneid*, 6.852–53)

And so Pliny the Younger in a letter to his friend Maximus, in which he sets out his vision of the responsibilities of imperial rule over other nations:

> Revere the gods their founders, and the names of those gods. Honor their ancient glory and their very age, which in a person is worthy of veneration, in cities is sacred. Honor their antiquity, their heroic deeds, and the legends of their past. Do not take away from anyone dignity, liberty, or even pride. Bear in mind that this is the land that provided us with justice and gave us laws, not after conquering us, but because we sought them; that it is Athens to which you go, and Sparta that you rule. To rob them of the name and shadow of freedom, which is all that now remains to them, is cruel, uncivilized, and barbarous. . . . Recall what each city once was, but not so as to look down on it for being so no longer. Do not allow yourself to be hard or domineering. Have no fear that you will be despised for this. Are any who bear the insignia of *imperium* despised, unless their own meanness and ignominy show that they first despise themselves? It is a wretched thing if authority makes trial of its power by insults to others, a wretched thing if respect is won by terror! Love is far more effective than fear in obtaining what you wish. Fear disappears when you depart. Love endures, and whereas fear turns into hatred, love turns into genuine regard. Again, and again— yes, I have to repeat this—you must remember the title of your office and understand what it means: you must remember what it is, and how great a thing it is, to establish order in the constitution of free cities. For what is more important for a city than ordered rule, and what more precious than liberty? (Pliny, *Letters* 8.24.3–7)[40]

Virgil's and Pliny's vision of empire cannot be ours, for it is based upon assumptions about the right (and even the duty) of one nation to govern another that we no longer share; but to suggest therefore that it was a vision devoid of honor, idealism, or a sense of duty would manifestly be false, as would be the suggestion that no Roman took it seriously or attempted to live by it. One Roman who did take it seriously was, undoubtedly, Pliny himself.[41] Another was probably P. Petronius, legate of Syria under Augustus. He gets good press from both Josephus (*War* 2.184–87, 192–203; *Antiquities* 18.261–309) and Philo (*Laws* 188, 198–348) for the part he played in Gaius' attack on the Temple (neither Philo nor Josephus being, as we have noted, reluctant to criticize Roman governors when it suited them). In Smallwood's view, "Petronius comes out of the story with great credit both for the tact with which he handled the Jews and for his courage in risking disgrace and the ruin of his career in order to safeguard the Jewish religion and maintain the peace of the East."[42] Of Petronius, and of his predecessor Vitellius, she suggests that "if the province of Judea had been under the direct rule of men of their caliber, its history during the first century AD might well have been very different."[43] Indeed it might.

Finally, perhaps we should concede that decent roads and harbors, a water supply, and (above all) a measure of peace and security are things more easily despised by North American and Western European academics who (despite September 11, 2001) still have the luxury of taking them largely for granted, than by those in other parts of the world who do not. Peace and stability are blessings as precious for the poor and vulnerable as for the rich, or more so, for the poor cannot escape in times of strife, whereas the rich sometimes can. Roman peace certainly came at a price, yet it is evident that many within the empire's borders thought the bargain worth it. At a distance of twenty centuries we do well to be cautious about dismissing all who made such choices simply as charlatans, profiteers, or victims.

To put it another way, perhaps we need to beware of a colonizing attitude of our own—a colonizing attitude *to the past*.[44] Are we *really* interested in Jesus or Josephus, the Romans or the Jews, for their own sake? Are we actually trying to listen to their experiences, their aspirations, and their questions, in all their complexity, *as they understood them,* so as to see what implications they might have for us—possibly implications that we did not expect? Or are we approaching them with *our* agendas, *our* concerns, seeking to use them for *our* purposes, defining them in *our* terms, fitting their perceptions of their situations to *our* perceptions of *our* situations, and so, in effect, colonizing them, looking to them only for the loot that we may bring back from them to our own (intellectual) "metropolitan center"? Of course, it is not possible for us to answer such questions about our own work. No doubt we are all guilty of some degree of self-interest. "Objectivity" is a myth. But still we must do our best to hold each other, and ourselves, accountable. If the disciplines of historical criticism have taught us anything, it is surely that we must be cautious in assuming that the concerns, categories, and values of the ancients were the same as ours. That is *not* to say that they have nothing to say to us. Quite the contrary! But we ignore at our peril the extent to which their expectations and understanding of the world were different from ours, and the grounds therefore on which they described their situations, and their intentions and hopes in doing so, were also different.

8

Unscientific Postscript

On the Significance (or Otherwise) of Structures

I have, I believe, demonstrated the conclusion that I promised. I have shown that the biblical tradition is in general concerned neither with the forms nor with the origins of human power structures. It is not even concerned whether those in positions of power are formally members of God's people. ("It is," as Archbishop William Temple said, "a mistake to suppose that God is only, or even chiefly, concerned with religion.")[1] The biblical tradition *is* concerned, however, with the purposes for which power structures are ordained, and it is concerned that those in positions of power should fulfill those purposes. Thus, the biblical tradition subverts human order not by attempting to dismantle it or replace it with other structures but by consistently confronting its representatives with the truth about its origin and its purpose. Its origin is that God wills it, and its purpose is to serve God's glory by promoting God's peace and God's justice for all. Powers and superpowers are allowed to exist, and may even be approved, but they are always on notice. Biblical tradition is therefore utterly opposed to the absolutizing of governmental authority (Dan. 3:4–6!) or to the exercise of that authority without concern for those who are subject. Insofar as the representatives of any human order—in the world or in the church—take these things seriously, they may do quite well. Insofar as they do not, they do ill, and God will shorten their days. Florence Morgan

Gillman cites a story of Bishop Hugh Latimer preaching in Westminster Abbey before King Henry VIII:

> In the pulpit, Latimer soliloquised, "Latimer! Latimer! Latimer! Be careful what you say. The king of England is here!" Then he went on, "Latimer! Latimer! Latimer! Be careful what you say. The King of Kings is here."[2]

Exactly.

There is not a shred of evidence that Jesus stood aside from this tradition, or that his followers did. Which is to say, Jesus made no common cause with those whose primary agenda (for whatever motive) was to exchange one structure—imperial Roman rule—for another—Jewish home rule. Neither did his followers. The traditions of the words and works of both in general do, however, indicate a concern that those who have power understand it as God's gift to them, given for the sake of God's people and the world. If such an attitude is regarded as political and revolutionary (and perhaps it should be), then Jesus and his followers were political and revolutionary. Their traditions do not, however, indicate the slightest interest in the forms or structures of temporal power, the choice of one system of government over another, or questions as to whether those who rule are believers or pagans. This attitude is consistently maintained on every occasion where they are seen dealing with those who have temporal authority. So, for the most part, it was to remain throughout the whole period of imperial Rome's war with the church. That war was about religion, about the proper honor due to God and/or the gods. The Catholic Church never claimed to be Rome's enemy in the sense that it was attempting to overthrow or change the structures of the Roman state. There were never any freedom fighters for Jesus.

The currently fashionable desire to make Jesus into such a freedom fighter (even if nonviolent), such a zealot for structure, is merely the latest in the long chain of human attempts to recreate Jesus in our own image. We ourselves are deeply preoccupied, perhaps even obsessed, by structure, and so we would like to think that Jesus was similarly preoccupied. In the West—and particularly in the Anglo-Saxon West—we seem at present to be especially obsessed with the structure that we call "democracy." Let me make myself clear. I do believe that structures are important, and that some structures can work better than others for the well-being of those involved in them. I also believe that there is a good deal to be said for democracy. I am even inclined to give some credence to Michael Doyle's claim that the rise of liberal democracies throughout the world can lead to increasing peace and stability, because liberal democracies will not fight each other.[3] All that granted, it is still nonsense—nonsense as idle and idolatrous as anything the Romans ever said of their Caesars as "lords" and "saviors"—to claim that the mere form of democracy can of itself bring God's peace or justice to the world or deliver humankind from its extraordinary capacity for evil. (By no means irrelevant here is the simple consideration that in the sphere of political structure, as in others, mere form may in fact be divorced from reality.[4]) Jesus and the prophetic tradition, however, show no interest in structures, democratic or any other. They are only interested in *how* power is exercised, and *to what end.*

There is, however, an equal and opposite error to which we can tend—and this error is the particular temptation of those who have become suspicious of our preoccupation with power and our concern with structure. In most matters, of course, we are indeed powerless and had better not forget it. From potentate to peasant, we cannot by worrying add a cubit to our height (Matt. 6.27) or avoid the certainty of death. Yet, in some matters, from time to time, we are given power, as Adam was given power (and therefore also responsibility) to "till and to keep" the garden. The error is to suppose that on such occasions we may *abandon* that power. We may not abandon it. "The powers that be are ordained by God" (Rom. 13.1) is an assertion that does not cut only one way. Power, like any gift from God, is a sacred trust, and when those who have received it abandon their responsibility, the result is chaos. The church has, at its best, realized this, and to dismiss such awareness of responsibility as "neo-Constantinian" or as "owing more to pagan philosophy than the church" simply will not do.[5] Nathan's challenge to David—"You are the man!"—implicitly *demands* responsibility in the exercise of power, as do the words of the Johannine Christ to Pilate: "You would have no power over me unless it had been given you from above" (2 Sam. 12.7; John 19.11). Matthew's picture of Pilate washing his hands is—and is meant to be—contemptible (Matt. 27.24). The governor is no more "innocent" of Jesus' blood after that act than he was before. One cannot by the renunciation of power become "innocent" of something that one had the power to prevent. The parables of the talents and the pounds, in their own way, make the same point. Not to use one's gifts and powers, to act as if one did not have them or was not responsible for them, is merely to "bury" them, and that is to incur God's wrath (Matt. 25.14–30; Luke 19.12–27).

Anyone who does not understand this could do worse than to meditate for a while on Shakespeare's *King Lear*, for Shakespeare evidently understood these issues very well. Lear's tragedy—and the concomitant disaster for virtually everyone around him—springs from one initial wrong action: his renunciation of the power to which he has been anointed. The king says, "'Tis our fast intent / To shake all cares and business from our age, / Conferring them on younger strengths, while we / Unburthened crawl towards death" (1.1.40–43).

But that, in the view of Shakespeare and his contemporaries, who in this respect are thoroughly biblical, is something that he, as king, has absolutely no right to do.[6] If you are Caesar, you must not claim to be God, but you may no more step aside from being Caesar than a mother may abandon her children or a captain the ship. Of course, it is true that talk of "responsibility" can be used as a cloak for evil motives—what talk cannot be so used, including the talk of prayer and piety? It is, nevertheless, an utter mistake to dismiss the notion of "responsibility" in relation to power—or, rather, to deceive ourselves into imagining that we can dismiss it. Insofar as we have power (and we have), then we are responsible for its exercise, whether we like it or not, just as Pilate, and the man with one talent, and Lear were all responsible, whether they liked it or not.

Exodus and Exile: The Problem of Violence

Closely associated with the foregoing is a theological question, or, more precisely, a question of theological models. A striking feature of the Bible is that it offers two models for the life of the people of God, and they stand in evident tension with one another. One is the life of those who are in exile; the other is the life of those who are part of an exodus community. It is the case that the people of God as exiles are virtually by definition *powerless*. It is equally the case that the exodus is a sign pointing to renewed *power* among God's people. Do we, can we, or should we choose one of these models over against the other? The answer is plainly no. Christians are neither required nor permitted to make such a choice.[7] For Christians are precisely those who live in an "already" that is also a "not yet." *Already* we have been redeemed: we are an exodus and resurrection people. But we also continue to live in hope of a consummation that is *not yet*: we are still exiles. In the midst of that tension, in the very uncomfortable place where those two images meet, is where we are called to take our stand politically and socially, as well as spiritually, for our theology does not allow us to cordon off these areas from one another. For Christians to attempt to live *either* as if we were not exiles *or* as if our exodus had not happened in that Christ has been raised from the dead is for us to attempt to live a lie.

In a post–September 11 Western world, one must note that part of the tension of which I speak pertains to the issue of violence. We are, or ought to be, appalled by violence. All violence is an assault upon God's creation. Yet the Exodus story is in many respects a violent image, giving rise to the possibility that on occasion, in a world that is "in Adam," God's will can be fulfilled only through violence. Rabbinic tradition shows itself well aware of the awful danger and the terrible ambiguity involved in this aspect of the Exodus. The practice of spilling drops of wine at Pesach when the plagues are enumerated reminds Israel that its rejoicing, even over its deliverance from Egypt, must be limited by its awareness of the griefs that fell upon its enemies, so rendering its joy incomplete.[8] In the same way, on the last six days of Pesach, only half-Hallel is recited, in accordance with the tradition that, when the Egyptians were drowning in the Red Sea, "The ministering angels wanted to chant their hymns, but the Holy One, blessed be He, said, 'The work of my hands is being drowned in the sea, and shall you chant hymns?'" (b. Megillah 10b).[9]

Christian tradition, from Augustine onward, continues to wrestle with the problem of the justifiable use of force. It should. There are, indeed, ways of avoiding the problem that in the short run may seem easier to live with. The church may cease to wrestle, simply blessing the guns and the bombs and rendering all to Caesar. That is a particular temptation for "respectable" churches, churches that are in some sense or other "by law established." Or the church may dismiss all such wrestling as "neo-Constantinian" and refuse to participate at all, leaving the guns and the bombs, again, to Caesar. That is a particular temptation for nonconformity and dissent. Neither will do— though the latter perhaps has some theological justification in that it challenges the former to be honest. In the long run, however, so long as we are given a measure of power (and we are), we shall be forced to ask how, when, and (on any given occasion) whether we are supposed to use it. No doubt even the best decision we can make must, like the Exodus itself, be grievous and sinful, especially when it involves the deaths of those who are also the work of God's hands. War, as William J. Danaher says, "is always a cause for lamentation, and even when a particular war is justified, our consciences are never clear but at best comforted."[10]

Construal of Power

God faces the powers that be in the present age with the questions with which God has always faced such powers: "Do you acknowledge that I am the One who has given you this power? Do you use it only for your own aggrandizement, or do you use it to bring justice to God's people and the world?" It is a major part of the church's task to be one instrument whereby the powers that be are repeatedly faced with such questions. Some years ago, during the time of apartheid in South Africa, I remember watching on the BBC News an encounter between Archbishop Desmond Tutu (just released, as I recall, from South African police custody) and a television journalist. The journalist asked, "How long do you intend to go on defying the South African government?" With a gentle smile, the Archbishop replied, "But we are not defying anyone. We are simply trying to obey God!" Those were the words of a prophet in the biblical tradition. He by no means denied or defied the South African government; yet such a church as he led, by the mere fact of its being and its constant witness, constituted a challenge to that government to do its job and in the end was instrumental in bringing about one of the most remarkable (largely nonviolent) revolutions of the modern era.[11] Such witness is not, of course, only a task for Archbishops! Anna Elisabeth Rosmus, a laywoman, has tirelessly demanded honesty from her fellow citizens about Germany's history during the Nazi era, beginning with her own city. Though she has often met with hostility and resistance, I do not doubt that she has in the long run contributed much to the spiritual and moral health of twenty-first-century Germany and hence to the spiritual and moral health of Europe. In 1986, Rosmus, then aged twenty-six, wrote,

> I so much would like to live among a people [Volk] that does not fear or suppress the truth, a nation that admits to its past mistakes. I would so much like to live in a nation where somebody who thinks "against the stream" can be an adversary but not necessarily the enemy. I would like to live among people who can take criticism, among people who will try to right their wrongs instead of trying to hide them. I would like to live in a country whose official representatives help to expose dangers and fight against them instead of pretending they don't exist. In my view the sovereignty of a nation reveals itself in precisely these attributes, and not in the question of where a territorial authority recognizes its limits. I would like to live among a people who see each person as an individual, and I would like to see each human being be allowed to be just that, a human being. Why are terms such as "nation," "religion," "heritage," and "prosperity" so significant? I would like it if people could simply be here for each other. It doesn't really matter what we might call such a nation, so long as that nation measures the value of its citizens according to those standards. That is the country I would like to live in.[12]

My friend and colleague William J. Danaher, having read that passage aloud in Rosmus's presence, added, "I, too, would like to live in a country like that." So would I. My point, however, is this: Such witness—modest and self-deprecating, no doubt (for we ourselves are never free from the evils that we presume to challenge) but nonetheless insistent—is always the task of those who claim to be heirs of the prophetic tradition, and especially the task of those who claim to follow Jesus of Nazareth.

For the kingdom of God is at hand.

And God is not mocked.

Notes

PROLOGUE

1. Theodor Mommsen, *The History of Rome*, William Purdie Jackson, trans. (altered) (New York: Charles Scribner's Sons, 1900), 5.3–4.

2. Edward Said, *Culture and Imperialism* (New York: Knopf, 1993), 9–10.

3. Walter Carruthers Sellar and Robert Julian Yeatman, *1066 and All That: A Memorable History of England, Comprising All the Parts You Can Remember Including One Hundred and Three Good Things, Five Bad Things and Two Genuine Dates* (London: Methuen, 1931).

4. M. A. C. Warren, *Caesar the Beloved Enemy: Three Studies in the Relation of Church and State* (London: SCM Press/Chicago: Alec R. Allenson, 1955), 27.

5. Warren, *Caesar the Beloved Enemy*, 28. To do Warren justice, I should make clear that he was by no means merely starry-eyed about imperialism. On the contrary, he pointed out that there is also "a 'demonology' of imperialism [that] has to be taken seriously, as seriously indeed as the doctrine of original sin to which in fact it is closely related." He claimed, nonetheless, that God remains "the Lord of history" and that "history has much to say about imperialism, not all of it bad" (10).

6. Richard A. Horsley, *Jesus and Empire: The Kingdom of God and the New World Disorder* (Minneapolis: Fortress Press, 2003).

7. Ibid., 6; see also 154, n. 7.

8. Ibid., 7.

9. Ibid., 10.

10. Ibid., 35; see the whole section, 35–54. See also Richard A. Horsley, *Jesus and the Spiral of Violence: Popular Jewish Resistance in Roman Palestine* (Minneapolis: Fortress Press, 1993).

11. Horsley, *Jesus and Empire*, 13.

12. Ibid., 104.

13. "Postcolonial studies emerged as a way of engaging with the textual, histori-cal, and cultural articulations of societies disturbed and transformed by the historical reality of colonial presence. In this respect, in its earlier incarnation, postcolonialism was never conceived as a grand theory, but as creative literature and as a resistance discourse in the former colonies of the Western empires. Postcolonialism as a meth-odological category and as a critical practice followed later. There were two aspects: first, to analyze the diverse strategies by which the colonizers constructed images of the colonized; and second, to study how the colonized themselves made use of and went beyond many of those strategies in order to articulate their identity, self-worth, and empowerment. Postcolonialism has been taking a long historical look at both old and new forms of domination. Its insight lies in understanding how the past informs the present" (R. S. Sugirtharajah, *Postcolonial Criticism and Biblical Studies* [Oxford: Oxford University Press, 2002], 11).

14. John P. Meier, *A Marginal Jew: Rethinking the Historical Jesus*, vol. 1, *The Roots of the Problem and the Person* (New York: Doubleday, 1991), 21–40.

15. For a brief presentation of my view of Scripture as revelation, as inspired, and as authoritative, and the implications of that for our understanding and study of it, see my *And God Spoke: The Authority of the Bible for the Church Today* (Cambridge, Mass.: Cowley, 2002).

16. Cited by Alois Grillmeier, *The Divine Inspiration and the Interpretation of Sa-cred Scripture*, in *Commentary on the Documents of Vatican II*, Herbert Vorgrimler, ed. (New York: Herder and Herder, 1969), vol. 3, 205.

17. George Kennedy, "Classical and Christian Source Criticism," in *The Relation-ships among the Gospels: An Interdisciplinary Dialogue*, William O. Walker, Jr., ed. Trin-ity University Monograph Series in Religion 5 (San Antonio, Texas: Trinity University Press, 1978), 126.

18. Morton Smith, "Palestinian Judaism in the First Century," in *Israel: Its Role in Civilization*, Moshe Davis, ed. (New York: Jewish Theological Seminary, 1956), 67–81, esp. 75–77.

19. Steve Mason, *Flavius Josephus on the Pharisees: A Composition Critical Study* (Leiden: E. J. Brill, 1991), 308.

20. Louis H. Feldman, *Studies in Hellenistic Judaism* (Leiden: E. J. Brill, 1996), 4.

21. See David Aune, *The New Testament in Its Literary Environment* (Philadelphia: Westminster Press, 1987), 88; also 107–9. Cicero claimed, "historia . . . opus unum oratorium maxime" (history is one task that is above all for orators) (*De legibus* 1.5; see also *De oratore* esp. 2.53–54 and 62).

22. See, for example, Feldman, *Studies in Hellenistic Judaism*, 1–33; Per Bilde, *Flavius Josephus between Jerusalem and Rome: His Life, His Works, and Their Impor-tance*, JSPSS, 2 (Sheffield: JSOT/Sheffield Academic, 1988), 191–200; Tessa Rajak, *Jo-sephus* (London: Duckworth, 1983), 229; Steve Mason, *Josephus and the New Testament*, 2nd ed. (Peabody, Mass.: Hendrickson, 2003), 37–41, 45–46, 81–99; *Flavius Josephus: Life of Josephus* (Boston, Mass., and Leiden: Brill, 2003), xxxvi–xli. Relevant here, and

in my view complementary, is Gregory E. Sterling's categorization of Josephus' *Antiquities* as "apologetic historiography." Written by priestly members (such as the Babylonian Berossus, the Eyptian Manetho, and Josephus himself) of ethnic subgroups in the Hellenistic world, apologetic historiography represented a native oriental response to Greek ethnography. The author of such a work "follows the group's own traditions but Hellenizes them in an effort to establish the identity of the group within the setting of the larger world" (Sterling, *Historiography and Self-Definition: Josephos, Luke-Acts, and Apologetic Historiography* [Leiden: Brill, 1992], 17). Hence Josephus in the *Antiquities* is concerned above all to present to the outside world a positive view of Israel's history and culture: "I believe that in my writing of the *Antiquitates* . . . I have made perfectly clear to any who read it that the Jewish race is most ancient, is originally of pure stock, and how it settled the land which we now possess" (Josephus, *Contra Apion* 1.1; cited Sterling, *Apologetic Historiography*, 297; see 297–308).

23. See *Jesus and Empire*, 6–9, 147–49; also K. C. Hanson and Douglas E. Oakman, *Palestine in the Time of Jesus: Social Structures and Social Conflicts* (Minneapolis: Fortress Press, 1998), 125.

CHAPTER I

1. Said, *Imperialism and Culture*, 83–97.

2. Ibid., 96. There is, I think, little reason to doubt that Jane Austen herself was opposed to the slave trade. Jane Fairfax, a young woman of whose principles and opinions Austen obviously intends us to think highly, at one point refers to the trade, speaking (in an aside, admittedly, but nonetheless unequivocally) of the "guilt of those who carry it on" and the "misery of the victims" (Jane Austen, *Emma* [London: John Murray, 1816], in *The Oxford Illustrated Jane Austen*, R. W. Chapman, ed., 5 vols. [Oxford: Oxford University Press, 1923], 300–301). As regards the issue of race, it is also interesting to note that Austen appears to contemplate with complete equanimity a match between Sir Edward Denham, an English baronet, and Miss Lambe, "half Mulatto, chilly and tender," from the West Indies (*Sanditon*, in *The Oxford Illustrated Jane Austen*, 6.421). To be sure (and as Austen makes clear with her usual irony), the considerations involved for those who seek this match are scarcely noble—indeed, they are entirely pecuniary! But, still, it is striking that it does not seem to occur to Austen or to those whom she describes that *race* might be a consideration, one way or the other (idem. 6.421–22). That fact alone places Austen generations, indeed centuries, ahead of many who had vastly the advantage of her in their opportunities to learn about the world and humanity.

3. Ibid.

4. James C. Scott, *Domination and the Arts of Resistance* (New Haven: Yale University Press, 1990), xii.

5. Ibid., xi.

6. Ibid., 15; also James C. Scott, *Weapons of the Weak: Everyday Forms of Peasant Resistance* (New Haven and London: Yale University Press, 1985), xv–xvi.

7. Scott, *Weapons of the Weak*, xv. For a fictional construction of the attitudes involved here, see the Botswana stories of Alexander McCall Smith, for example, *The No. 1 Ladies Detective Agency* (London: Polygon, 1998), 18.

8. Walter Brueggemann, *Theology of the Old Testament: Testimony, Dispute, Advocacy* (Minneapolis: Fortress Press, 1997), 504; the entire section 492–527 is relevant to the issues raised in this chapter, as also is Oliver O'Donovan, *The Desire of the Nations* (Cambridge: Cambridge Unversity Press, 1996), esp. 68–73.

9. Daniel L. Smith, *The Religion of the Landless: The Social Context of the Babylonian Exile* (Bloomington, Ind.: Meyer-Stone, 1989), 136.

10. Walter Eichrodt, *Theology of the Old Testament*, vol. 3, John Baker, trans. (London: SCM/Philadelphia: Westminster, 1967), 248.

11. Said, *Imperialism and Culture*, xxi; as it happens, Warren had made the same point in *Caesar the Beloved Enemy*, 27; see also Daniel Smith-Christopher, "Prayers and Dreams: Power and Diaspora Identities in the Social Setting of the Daniel Tales," in *The Book of Daniel: Composition and Reception*, John J. Collins and Peter W. Flint, eds., 2 vols. (Leiden: Brill, 2001), 266–67 and n. 1.

12. O'Donovan, *Desire of the Nations*, 87.

13. Since I am attempting to describe the perceptions of those who wrote our texts and the theological conclusions to which they came on the basis of those perceptions, I believe that I do not need to decide between widely differing views as to what was *actually* going on during, say, the Babylonian exile. Thus, H. Barstadt emphasizes the continuity of Jewish cultural life at this period and (incidentally) sees Babylon's right to rule in almost Mommsen-esque terms (see *The Myth of the Empty Land* [Symbolae Osloenses Fasc. 28 (Oslo: Scandinavian University Press, 1996)], 63–46). Smith-Christopher, by contrast, while granting the continuing vitality of Jewish religious practice, believes nonetheless that one cannot "radically dismiss all the biblical and archaeological evidence that we have with regard to the enormity of the disaster, [and] the depth of the spiritual and social crises that resulted" ("Prayers and Dreams," 273, n. 23). Similarly with the Greek period, Antiochus IV presents a puzzle. Even 1 and 2 Maccabees themselves differ considerably as to the motivation and nature of Antiochus' persecution, which in many ways was uncharacteristic of Greek imperial practice (see, for example, Robert Doran, "The First Book of Maccabees," *NIB*, vol. 4 [Nashville: Abingdon, 1996], 8–12).

14. In fact, one does not have to read even the books of Maccabees very carefully to see that, militarily, the Hasmonean rebellion was by no means an unmixed success: see, for example, Seth Schwartz, *Imperialism and Jewish Society, 200 B.C.E. to 640 C.E.* (Princeton and Oxford: Princeton University Press, 2001), 32–33.

15. Smith-Christopher, "Prayers and Dreams," 289.

16. That there are significant connections and parallels (as well, of course, as significant differences) between the court narratives of Joseph and Daniel is a matter of general scholarly consensus: see Louis F. Hartmann, C.SS.R. and Alexander A. di Lella, O.F.M., *The Book of Daniel* (Garden City, N.Y.: Doubleday, 1978), 56, 145, 171, 190; John E. Goldingay, *Daniel* WBC 30 (Dallas, Texas: Word, 1989), 7, 37, 41–43; John J. Collins and Adela Yarbro Collins, *Daniel*. Hermeneia. (Minneapolis: Fortress

Press, 1993), 39–40; Daniel Smith-Christopher, "The Book of Daniel," *NIB*, vol. 7 (Nashville: Abingdon, 1996), 21.

17. Schwartz, *Imperialism and Jewish Society*, 20–22; Jon L. Berquist, *Judaism in Persia's Shadow* (Minneapolis: Fortress Press, 1995), v, 51, 81, and passim; Smith, *Religion of the Landless*, 17–47; Martin Noth, *The History of Israel*, Stanley Godman, trans. (London: Adam and Charles Black, 1958), 301–15.

18. I speak, as usual, of what appears to be the dominant strain at this point in the tradition, represented in Haggai, Zechariah, Ezekiel, and the Chronicler: here, too, however, there were clearly other voices: see, for example, Paul D. Hanson, *The Dawn of Apocalyptic: The Historical and Sociological Roots of Jewish Apocalyptic Eschatology* (Philadelphia: Fortress Press, 1979), 226–79, and (for a somewhat different approach) Smith, *Religion of the Landless*, 179–97.

19. O'Donovan, *Desire of the Nations*, 85.

20. Ibid., 72; contrast Warren, *Caesar the Beloved Enemy*, 10.

21. O'Donovan, *Desire of the Nations* 35.

22. Martin Hengel, *Judaism and Hellenism: Studies in Their Encounter in Palestine during the Early Hellenistic Period*, John Bowden, trans. (London: SCM, 1974 [19732]), 1.29.

23. See R. J. H. Shutt, *Letter of Aristeas*, in *The Old Testament Pseudepigrapha*, vol.2, James H. Charlesworth, ed. (New York: Doubleday, 1985), 8–9; Emil Schürer, *The History of the Jewish People in the Age of Jesus*, revised by Geza Vermes, Fergus Millar, and Martin Goodman, 3 vols. (Edinburgh: T. & T. Clark, 1973–87), vol. 3, pt. 1, 677–85, esp. 679–84.

24. Paul D. Hanson, *The Diversity of Scripture* (Philadelphia: Fortress Press, 1982), 26. Thus, Norman K. Gottwald argues that the pressure toward monarchy came originally from the wealthy, who sought a strong, centralized form of government that would give legitimacy to and protection for their economic and political advantages (see Gottwald, "The Participation of Free Agrarians in the Introduction of Monarchy to Ancient Israel: An Application of H. A. Landsberger's Framework for the Analysis of Peasant Movements," *Semeia* 37 [1986]: 77–106). If Gottwald were right, then the institution of Israelite kingship would be an early example of a familiar political maneuver—an external threat being used as an expedient for bringing about internal change for political advantage; the origins of Israelite kingship would also, of course, be an example of Gottwald's wider thesis, that what "proved to be distinctive of ancient Israel was not its politics but rather its literature and religion" (*The Politics of Ancient Israel* [Louisville, Ken.: Westminster John Knox, 2001], 247). But the reality may be more complicated than Gottwald assumes. The Philistines were, after all, a real threat, not imaginary. As Hanson says, "staring into the jaws of the Philistine war machine," Israel faced something that simply could not be defeated by "Hebrew militia under the charismatic šôpet." So the Israelites "felt the force of world politics driving them away from the constant application of egalitarian ideals derived from their experience of deliverance, and casting them into the ambiguities of civil maturity." "Thus the Bible, in preserving this diversity, is more complex and, I think, more profound than uncritical liberationists who speak only of revolution and forget the

concomitant human need for security, nurture, order and form" (Hanson, *Diversity of Scripture*, 24–25).

25. O'Donovan, *Desire of the Nations*, 35–41.

26. See Brueggemann, *Theology of the Old Testament*, 519–20.

27. Ibid., 518.

28. See Christopher R. Seitz, "Isaiah 40–66," *NIB* vol. 6 (Nashville: Abingdon, 2001), 393–95.

29. Klaus Baltzer, *Deutero-Isaiah: A Commentary on Isaiah 40–55*. Hermeneia (Minneapolis: Fortress Press, 2001), 224–25.

30. Seitz, "Isaiah 40–66," 394.

CHAPTER 2

1. Philo's *Embassy* is essentially a plea to the Emperor Claudius, composed early in his reign, asking him to follow not the policies of Gaius as regards the Jews but those of Augustus and Tiberius. Philo consistently asserts that the Jews desire to be peaceful and loyal members of the Empire, asking no more than that their hallowed ancestral laws be respected (so, for example, *Embassy* 160, 230–32, 236; also *In Flaccum* 48). For discussion see E. R. Goodenough, *The Politics of Philo Judaeus* (Hildesheim: Georg Olms, 1967), 19–20; J. P. Lémenon, *Pilate et le gouvernement de la Judée: textes et monuments*, Études bibliques (Paris: Gabalda, 1981), 207–8; D. R. Schwarz, "Josephus and Philo on Pontius Pilate," *Jerusalem Cathedra* 3 (1983): 32.

2. See, for example, Horsley, *Jesus and Empire*, 10–11.

3. Samuel Sandmel, *Judaism and Christian Beginnings* (New York: Oxford University Press, 1978), 15.

4. Schwartz, *Imperialism and Jewish Society*, 49–74. "In fact, all surviving Jewish literature shares a basic set of concerns, which separates it sharply from other corpora of ancient literature and marks its participation in a common, if only loosely centralized, ideological system" (12). "In trying to make sense of the many specific differences between these texts, we should not forget their commonalities" (ibid.).

5. Meier, *Marginal Jew*, 3.617; N. T. Wright, *Christian Origins and the Question of God*, vol. 1, *The New Testament and the People of God*, corrected edition (London: SPCK/ Philadelphia: Fortress Press, 1993), 215-23, 403-9. I do not here concern myself with the vexed problem of the origins of this narrative, especially its eschatological elements, or its relationship to the covenantal nomism implied by the complex of God, Torah, and Temple. Definitive solutions to these problems may be forever beyond scholarly grasp; in any case, what matters for my purposes is simply that, "by the first century, if not earlier, the myth was a more or less fully naturalized part of the ideology of Judaism" (Schwartz, *Imperialism and Jewish Society*, 81; see further 74–87).

6. On the "kingdom of God" in the first-century Palestinian synagogue, see Bruce Chilton, *The Glory of Israel* (Sheffield: JSOT, 1983); also N. T. Wright, *Christian Origins and the Question of God*, vol. 2, *Jesus and the Victory of God* (London: SPCK/ Minneapolis: Fortress Press, 1996), 202–9; Meier, *Marginal Jew*, 2.241–70.

7. N. T. Wright, *Christian Origins and the Question of God*, vol. 2, *The Resurrection of the Son of God* (London: SPCK/Minneapolis: Fortress Press, 2003), 85–206.

8. A classic example of this is Luke's account of Peter's speech on the day of Pentecost, where the apostle is shown using all the apocalyptic and earth-shattering imagery that one could imagine to speak of events—the resurrection of the Christ and the gift and call of God to and through the Church—that have manifestly taken place *within the ordinary course of history*, since obviously the Romans are still running Palestine, and the world in general is carrying on business as usual (Acts 2.14–36); on the whole subject, see further N. T. Wright, *New Testament and the People of God*, 145–338, esp. 280–338; Wright, *Victory of God*, 202–209; also (and in some respects seminally) G. B. Caird, *The Language and Imagery of the Bible* (London: Duckworth, 1980), 243–71.

9. Horsley, *Jesus and Empire*, 81. Part of the problem here has been, and continues to be, the confused and confusing way in which we regularly use the words "literal" and "metaphorical" ("When she discovered what I had done, the air *literally* turned blue!"). A dose of useful and highly entertaining common sense is available, again, in Caird, *Language and Imagery of the Bible*, 131–97.

10. See further Wright, *Victory of God*, 152–55; Raymond Brown, *The Death of the Messiah: From Gesthemane to the Grave*, 2 vols. (New York: Doubleday, 1993), 1.684–86; E. P. Sanders, *Jesus and Judaism* (Philadelphia: Fortress Press, 1985), 271; Richard A. Horsley, " 'Like One of the Prophets of Old': Two Types of Popular Prophets at the Time of Jesus," *CBQ* 47 (1985): 435–63; Hanson and Oakman, *Palestine in the Time of Jesus*, 85–86.

11. Brown, *Death of the Messiah* 1.677–79; Lémonon, *Pilate et le gouvernement de la Judée*, 21–22.

12. The discovery, in 1961, of an inscription in which Pilate refers to himself as "prefect of Judea" appears to confirm this as a title for the governors of Judea at this period, contra Tacitus, *Annals* 15.44. See, for example, Brown, *Death of the Messiah*, 1.336–37; E. Mary Smallwood, *The Jews under Roman Rule: From Pompey to Diocletian* (Leiden: Brill, 1976), 145; Louisa Prandi, "Una nuova ipotesi sull'iscrizione di Ponzio Pilato," *Civiltà classica e cristiana* 2 (1981): 26.

13. See Smallwood. *Jews under Roman Rule*, 147–48. This, however, is a surmise. We do not know the exact date when the practice began, and it might have been under Herod the Great.

14. See Schürer, *Jewish People in the Age of Jesus Christ*, revised Vermes et al., 1.343; Smallwood, *Jews under Roman Rule*, 184; Hanson and Oakman, *Palestine in the Time of Jesus*, 82–85. For a thoughtful reconstruction of the problems that faced Augustus Caesar as he made these arrangements, see Peter Richardson, *Herod: King of the Jews and Friend of the Romans* (Columbia: University of South Carolina Press, 1996), 20–32.

15. Some authorities link these passages to Agrippa II, his son, but probably they refer to Agrippa I: see Schürer, *Jewish People in the Age of Christ*, revised Vermes et al., 1.446–47.

16. Seán Freyne, "Bandits in Galilee: A Contribution to the Study of Social Con-

ditions in First-Century Palestine," in *The Social World of Formative Christianity and Judaism*, Jacob Neusner et al., eds. (Philadelphia: Fortress Press, 1982), 50–68; also Horsley, *Jesus and the Spiral of Violence*, 20–146; Brown, *Death of the Messiah*, 1.680–93.

17. Horsley, *Jesus and Empire*, 35.

18. Ibid., 41–42.

19. Freyne, "Bandits in Galilee," 58. The archetypal social bandit is the Robin Hood of legend, fighting a powerful ruling elite that has robbed him of his land and stealing from that elite in order to give to the poor. On the phenomenon of social banditry from the view point of social science, see the convenient summary in Hanson and Oakman, *Palestine in the Time of Jesus*, 86–89, noting only that the short section wherein they suggest that Jesus, though not a social bandit, is nonetheless to be "linked" to "the issue of social banditry" (88) is vague and unconvincing, citing texts that appear to have little relationship to the issue.

20. Horsley, *Jesus and Empire*, 53.

21. Ibid., 54.

22. "Difficile est dictu, quirites, quanto in odio simus apud exteras nationes propter eorum quos ad eas per hos annos cum imperio misimus, libidines et iniurias" (Cicero, *On the Manilian Law*, 65).

23. A. E. Harvey, *Jesus and the Constraints of History* (Philadelphia: Westminster, 1982), 85; Brown, *Death of the Messiah*, 1.677–79.

24. Freyne, "Bandits in Galilee," 54. Meier's view of the situation under Herod Antipas not very different from Freyne's: "To be sure we moderns, accustomed to democracy, due process, and standards of social justice would have found Antipas' rule intolerable. But there is no hard proof that Antipas' rule was any more politically unjust, socially exploitative, or economically burdensome than most other regimes in the ancient Near East before or after him. The ancient Near East was always a very rough neighborhood. That Antipas was the second-longest reigning Herodian monarch in ancient history and that his reign came to an abrupt end not because of internal rebellion but because of his ill-advised request to the Emperor Caligula to make him a king witnesses to the relatively stable and peaceful nature of his reign. To state that this peace and stability were the result of an iron fist, as the death of the Baptist shows, and not of concern for human rights and democracy, is simply to state the obvious: Antipas ruled in the ancient Near East, where stability and peace were achieved in only one way" (*A Marginal Jew*, 3.619).

25. H. St. J. Thackeray for Josephus, *Life* 28, and passim uses "brigands"; Steve Mason, *Josephus: Life* 21 and passim uses "bandits."

26. BDAG λῃστής, 1 and 2.

27. Martin Hengel, *The Zealots: Investigations into the Jewish Freedom Movement in the Period from Herod I until 70 A.D.*, David Smith, trans. (Edinburgh: T. & T. Clark, 1989 [1976²], 45; see 41–46.

28. Horsley, *Jesus and the Spiral of Violence* 37; see 37–39. On social banditry, see n. 19.

29. Freyne, "Bandits in Galilee," 50–65.

30. Schwartz, *Imperialism and Jewish Society*, 89.

31. Brent D. Shaw, "Bandits in the Roman Empire," *Past and Present* 105 (1984), 3–52; cited in Mason, *Josephus: Life* 32. Mason's own note on "bandit" and its cognates is excellent (31–32).

32. Shaye J. D. Cohen, *From the Maccabees to the Mishnah* (Philadelphia: Westminster, 1987), 32; for the rabbinic material to which Cohen refers, see Jacob Neusner, *Development of a Legend* (Leiden: Brill, 1970). Not without humor, Cohen goes on to note, "The rabbi neglected to inform the Roman that the next verse of the prophecy begins with the messianic prediction 'There shall come forth a shoot from the stump of Jesse.' Had Vespasian known the Bible of the Jews he might not have received the rabbi so kindly."

33. Jacob Neusner, *From Politics to Piety: The Emergence of Pharisaic Judaism*, 2nd ed. (New York: KTAV, 1979), 137.

34. Horsley, *Jesus and Empire*, 137–49. In a similar vein, though somewhat more obliquely, John Dominic Crossan and Jonathan Reed hint at parallels between the "new world order" alleged by some American politicians following the collapse of the Soviet bloc and Roman claims for the order that had been brought by the Caesars: see *In Search of Paul: How Jesus's Apostle Opposed Rome's Empire with God's Kingdom* (New York: HarperSanFrancisco, 2004), 11–12.

35. He makes the same point elsewhere: "How can we possibly know what motivated peasants or other common people, when they left no literature or other records of their thoughts and motives?" (*Jesus and the Spiral of Violence*, 129).

36. See page 12; Horsley draws attention to Scott's work: see *Jesus and Empire*, 53–54, 160, n. 25, 26.

37. Scott, *Weapons of the Weak*, xvii and passim.

38. Gisgala (Heb. גוש חלב) means "fat soil," and Gischala was famous for the high quality of its oil (Josephus, *Life*, 13.74–75; *War* 2.591–92; *b. Men.* 85b).

39. Scott, *Weapons of the Weak*, xvi.

40. Ibid., xv.

41. Ibid., xv. He is citing Eric Hobsbawm, "Peasants and Politics," *Journal of Peasant Studies* 1.1 (1973): 3–22. His following paragraph, though not strictly relevant to my discussion, is also, I believe, worth bearing in mind: "for all their importance when they do occur, peasant rebellions—let alone revolutions—are few and far between. Most such rebellions are crushed unceremoniously. When, more rarely, they do succeed, it is a melancholy fact that the consequences are seldom what the peasantry had in mind. Whatever else revolutions may achieve—and I have no desire to gainsay those achievements—they also typically bring into being a vaster and more dominant state apparatus that is capable of battening itself on its peasant subjects even more effectively than its predecessors" (*Weapons of the Weak*, xv–xvi).

42. Perhaps including, according to his lights, Herod the Great himself: see Richardson, *Herod*, 264–73.

43. See pages 41–42.

44. Mason, *Josephus and the New Testament*, 85.

45. See Schwartz, *Imperialism and Jewish Society*, 103–28.

46. Erwin R. Goodenough, *Jewish Symbols in the Greco-Roman Period*, 13 vols. (Princeton: Princeton University Press, 1953–68); but note significant caveats by Louis

H. Feldman, *Studies in Hellenistic Judaism,* 30–31 and (implicitly) 577–602. Even if Goodenough was right about the limits of rabbinic influence, it does not follow that he was right in the alternative picture of Jewish life that he drew on his own account— a life marked by mysticism and Platonism and classically represented by Philo of Alexandria. That picture depended on Goodenough's own interpretation of the art that he examined. Though he asserted that it should be interpreted without reference to literary commentary, there is perhaps some justice in Jacob Neusner's complaint that what he actually did was interpret it in the light of one particular body of texts, namely the writings of Philo of Alexandria and other Greek-speaking Jews, while leaving out of account *all* Jewish texts in Aramaic and Hebrew. See Neusner, *Method and Meaning in Ancient Judaism,* 3rd ser. (Chico, Calif.: Scholars Press, 1981), 143–51.

47. Neusner, *From Politics to Piety,* 97–98.

48. For the Bar Kokbha war, our sources of information are much less detailed than is Josephus on the war of 66–74, and the causes that led to it remain obscure to us. Three different sources—Dio Cassius, the author of *Historia Augusta,* and the Babylonian Talmud—suggest that it was sparked by aggressive Roman action against the Jewish religion (Dio Cassius, 66.12–15; *Historia Augusta: Life of Hadrian,* 14.2; *b. Megillah* 9b). Hence, rabbinic tradition sees in Hadrian another Antiochus Epiphanes: a gentile king trying to destroy Judaism. The sources differ, however, as to what the Roman action was, and no doubt there were also internal factors. One was economic: the earlier defeat had led to Roman confiscation of much Jewish land and hence the creation of a landless peasantry that provided Bar Kokhba with a good deal of his support. A second was religious: Bar Kokhba was perceived by Aqiba (generally recognized as the greatest rabbi of his day) as God's anointed, who would fulfill God's purposes by destroying the Romans and rebuilding the Temple. In this, no doubt, the memory of the Maccabees and the memory of Jeremiah's prophecy (Jer. 29:10) both played their part: it was about seventy years since the destruction of the Temple. See, for example, Schürer, *Jewish People in the Age of Jesus Christ,* revised Vermes et al., 1.534–45; Yigael Yadin, *Bar-Kokhba: The Rediscovery of the Legendary Hero of the Second Jewish Revolt against Rome* (New York: Random House, 1971), 18–27

49. Neusner, *From Politics to Piety* 133–34.

CHAPTER 3

1. See BDAG, τέκτων; Meier, *Marginal Jew,* 1.280–81. Celsus derided Christianity for having a working man as its founder: see Origen, *Against Celsus* 6.34, 36. (Origen's response, alas, is as replete with Hellenistic snobbery as is Celsus' attack.) Whether therefore Jesus is appropriately called a "peasant" depends on what one means by "peasant": see the discussion in Meier, *Marginal Jew,* 1.287–280 (although Meier himself seems to have become less patient with the word by 3.620!) and the note in Hanson and Oakman, *Palestine in the Time of Jesus,* 201. My own feeling is that both popular and academic uses of the word "peasant" are in general so confused and confusing that, in connection with Jesus, the word is best avoided, unless it is precisely defined for a specific purpose.

2. Hanson and Oakman, *Palestine in the Time of Jesus*, 19–60.

3. See Meier, *Marginal Jew*, 1.281–85, 3.620. Considering the origin of some of Jesus's disciples, it is worth noting that *fishermen* were a prime target of tax collection. This in itself is an indication that fishermen were perceived as not without means: there is no point in taxing people who have nothing to tax. That does not, of course, mean that the system of tax collection was not exploitative or that it was not designed for the benefit of the *really* wealthy and powerful: like most taxation in the ancient world, it was clearly both. See further K. C. Hanson, "The Galilean Fishing Economy and the Jesus Tradition," *Biblical Theology Bulletin: A Journal of Bible and Theology* 27.3 (1997): 99–111.

4. It is a striking and rather serious omission that Hanson and Oakman in their study of social structures and conflicts in Jesus' Palestine do not once refer to Luke 8.1–3, even in their section "Politics and Patronage" (63–97).

5. For this view see, broadly, Martin Hengel, *The Charismatic Leader and His Followers*, James C. G. Greig, trans. (Edinburgh: T. & T. Clark, 1981[1968]), esp. 38–83; Harvey, *Jesus and the Constraints of History*, 57–65, 131–34; E. P. Sanders, *Jesus and Judaism* (Philadelphia: Fortress Press, 1985), 237–41; N. T. Wright, *Christian Origins and the Question of God*, vol. 2, *Jesus and the Victory of God* (London: SPCK; Minneapolis: Fortress Press, 1996), 147–243; Meier, *A Marginal Jew*, 2.1044–45.

6. John the Baptist was (presumably) celibate, as (presumably) were the ascetics of Qumran (1 QS1.6) and (presumably) Bannus, claimed by Josephus as his teacher (*Life* 11), but in no case, as my qualifications indicate, is the evidence absolutely clear. On Matthew 19.12, see further W. D. Davies and Dale C. Allison, *A Critical and Exegetical Commentary on the Gospel according to Saint Matthew*, 3 vols. (Edinburgh: T. & T. Clark, 1988–97), 3.24–26.

7. Meier, *A Marginal Jew*, 3.622; see further 3.73–80.

8. In thus interpreting the so-called cleansing of the Temple, I am in broad general agreement with Bond (see Helen K. Bond, *Caiaphas: Friend of Rome and Judge of Jesus* [Louisville, Ken./London: Westminster John Knox, 2004], 64–67), N. T. Wright (see *Victory of God*, 413–28), E. P. Sanders (see *Jesus and Judaism*, 61–76), and John Dominic Crossan (see *The Historical Jesus: The Life of a Mediterranean Jewish Peasant* [New York: HarperSanFrancisco, 1991], 357–58). As to the *motives* for this destruction—prelude to restoration (Sanders), reaction to the nonegalitarian and oppressive system (Crossan), or prophetic symbol of its imminent destruction (Wright, Bond)—there is no such agreement. Wright's discussion is, in my opinion, the most helpful.

9. I am aware that in this sentence I have cut a *very* long story *extremely* short! For the understanding of Jesus' teaching about the kingdom of God implicit here (including the vexed problems of "realized" and "futurist" eschatologies and their variants) see Meier, *A Marginal Jew*, 2.289–454; Wright, *Jesus and the Victory of God*, 443–474; and, seminally, G. B. Caird, *The Language and Imagery of the Bible* (London: Duckworth, 1980), 243–71.

10. For a useful discussion of Caiaphas' probable attitude, see Helen K. Bond, *Caiaphas: Friend of Rome and Judge of Jesus?* (Louisville, Ken./London: Westminster John Knox, 2004), 51–55.

11. John Howard Yoder, *The Politics of Jesus: Behold the Man! Our Victorious Lamb*, 2nd ed. (Grand Rapids, Mich.: Eerdmans; Carlisle: Paternoster, 1994), 43; see the entire section, 21–59.

12. But as regards Jesus and violence, see Appendix A, "Jesus, Violence, and Nonviolence."

13. R. S. Sugirtharajah, *Postcolonial Criticism and Biblical Interpretation* (Oxford: Oxford University Press, 2002), 88.

14. See Smallwood, *Jews under Roman Rule*, 150–53.

15. BDAG, ἀρχιτελώνης.

16. Smallwood, *Jews under Roman Rule*, 152. Levi, in Capernaum (Mark 2.13–17//), by contrast, would have been working directly for Herod Antipas, who collected his own taxes, and then paid tribute to Rome.

17. Sugirtharajah, *Postcolonial Criticism*, 90.

18. Horsley, *Jesus and Empire*, 98–99; for more or less the same argument see S. G. F. Brandon, *Jesus and the Zealots* (Manchester: Manchester University Press, 1967), 345–46.

19. Horsley, *Jesus and the Spiral of Violence*, 311. Even N. T. Wright, though his discussion is more nuanced than Horsley's, still appears to assume that "liason with Rome" and "heavily compromised" (in terms of commitment to Israel's God) have to go together for all who consider themselves loyal Israelites, and that "the two Judases, Maccabean and Galilean[,]" would have provided for such persons the *only* "echo chamber in which questions of kingdom and freedom such as this brief exchange must be heard" (*Jesus and the Victory of God*, 502). As we have seen, the entire biblical tradition, from Joseph onward, provides evidence that that was not necessarily the case. Why should they not have heard such questions in the "echo chamber" offered by stories such as those of Joseph, Nehemiah, and Daniel? Philo certainly thought of himself as a faithful Jew, and yet he was prepared to speak of Augustus as one "whose every virtue outshone human nature . . . almost the whole human race would have been destroyed in internecine conflicts and disappeared completely, had it not been for one man, one princeps, Augustus, who deserves the title 'Averter of Evil' . . . 'wonderful benefactor'" (*Embassy* 143–48).

20. See page 36. This, perhaps, is a suitable place to mention David J. A. Clines's suggestion—the opposite of Horsley's—that "paying tax is not forbidden" because "the law (and the scribal tradition, as far as I know) have nothing to say about Caesar, or about paying taxes to foreign rulers" ("Ethics as Deconstruction and, the Ethics of Deconstruction," in *The Bible in Ethics*, John W. Rogerson, Margaret Davies, and M. Daniel Caroll R, eds., JSOTSS 207 [Sheffield: Sheffield University, 1995], 90–91 and footnote 30). Suffice it to say that in this matter, evidently, there is a great deal that Clines does not "know"!

21. The word "Herodians" (Ἡρῳδιανοί) is not without its difficulties. Nonetheless, the most sensible conclusion as regards its meaning is that it refers to "household servants or slaves of Herod, his officials or courtiers (high officials sometimes being ex-slaves), and more generally all the supporters of Herod's regime, whether or not they belonged to an organized group or party" (Meier, *Marginal Jew*, 3.561; see the entire section 560–65).

22. See pages 27–28. I am aware how surprising is the combination of Pharisees and Herodians (see Meier, *Marginal Jew*, 3.562–65). Still, politics do sometimes produce unlikely bedfellows, and we must in any case, at least as a first step, do our best to interpret the text that Mark has given us. Francis J. Moloney, S.D.B., suggests, not unreasonably, that the "hypocrisy" discerned by Jesus lies in the fact of these two "incompatible parties" coming together to ask him "a question that divided them" (*The Gospel of Mark: A Commentary* [Peabody, Mass.: Hendrickson], 236.

23. O'Donovan, *Desire of the Nations*, 92.

24. Ibid., 93.

25. Horsley, *Jesus and Empire* 12.

26. Ben Witherington III argues for much the same kind of conclusion as O'Donovan: Jesus' words are ironic and mean, in effect, "O.K. Give Caesar back these worthless pieces of metal he claims, but know that we are to render to God all things since God alone is divine and to God belong all things" (*The Gospel of Mark: A Socio-Rhetorical Commentary* [Grand Rapids, Mich./Cambridge: Eerdmans, 2001], 326). The emphasis here—on true ownership, rather than on transience—is slightly different from that of O'Donovan's proposal, but the problem with it is virtually the same: the claims of religion are treated as essentially separate from those of the social and political order. How very convenient for Caesar! But if all things (including, of course, Caesar's coinage) truly belong to God, then it really *does* matter, to God and to us, what we do with them *now*. The Pharisees' and Herodians' question remains a real one, and how people answered it was important. Judas the Galilean saw that, and so did Jesus, however different (as I believe) their answers may have been.

27. See Witherington, *Mark*, 324; C. E. B. Cranfield, *The Gospel according to Saint Mark* (Cambridge: Cambridge University Press, 1959), 371; Vincent Taylor, *The Gospel according to Saint Mark* (London: Macmillan, 1957), 479.

28. BDAG δίδωμι 1; see the entire article.

29. BDAG ἔξεστιν; Witherington, *Mark*, 324.

30. BDAG εἰκών, esp. 1, 2.

31. While Hanson and Oakman are no doubt correct in saying that "most peasants would be unfamiliar with the coin" (*Palestine in the Time of Jesus*, 124), their suggestion that this is "a point at issue" here (ibid.) is evidently mistaken. Both the rhetoric and the dynamic of the passage not only allow but demand that all involved know precisely what a denarius is like. Jesus is setting a trap for his opponents. Its brilliance depends on the fact that at each stage he leaves them no alternative but to walk further into it, and he and they know it.

32. Tiberius' denarius has on its obverse a bust of the Emperor and on its reverse a representation of his mother, Livia. On the obverse, the inscription reads, TI[BERIUS] CAESAR DIVI AUG[USTI] F[ILIUS] AUGUSTUS (Tiberius Caesar, Son of the Divine Augustus, Augustus); on the reverse it reads, PONTIFEX MAXIMUS.

33. BDAG ἀποδίδωμι, especially 2 and 3; see John R. Donahue, S.J. and Daniel J. Harrington, S.J., *The Gospel of Mark*, SP 2 (Collegeville, Minn.: Liturgical Press, 2002), 345; Morna Hooker, *The Gospel according to St. Mark* (London: A. & C. Black, 1991), 281; Cranfield, *Mark*, 372; Taylor, *Mark*, 479. Hence Paul's expression at Romans 13.7, "ἀπόδοτε πᾶσιν τὰς ὀφειλάς" (pay to all what is due them) is precise. In-

deed, I am inclined to suspect that the entire passage, Romans 13.1–8, represents Paul's reflections on the "word of the Lord" that is preserved for us at Mark 12.17 //. If it is, then Paul clearly understood that "word" in the sense in which I have interpreted it above. On Romans 13.1–8, see further below, pages 80–81. In Greek, of course, just as in English, the notion of "payback" could be used in a negative, retributional sense—though it appears that when such a negative sense was intended, it was expressed more commonly by the cognate ἀνταποδίδωμι than by ἀποδίδωμι (compare BDAG ἀνταποδίδωμι 2). In any case, in Greek as in English, the negative sense when there is one is always perfectly clear from the context (e.g. LXX Deut. 32.35; Ps. 136.8; 1 Macc. 2.68; Rev. 18.6): and that, of course, is precisely what is *not* the case at Mark 12.17. If it were clear, we would have no problem. (It is, incidentally, because the KJV translators—as so often, subtler than their successors—preserved the distinction between δίδωμι and ἀποδίδωμι, that I have used their version in the title and epigraph to this book, rather than that of the NRSV.)

34. So Horsley, *Jesus and Empire*, 99.

35. Hooker, *Mark*, 281.

36. *Pace* Ched Myers, it is both wrong and misleading to say that "no Jew could have allowed for a valid *analogy* between the debt Israel owed to Yahweh and any other human claim" (*Binding the Strong Man: A Political Reading of Mark's Story of Jesus* [Mayknoll, N.Y.: Orbis, 1990], 312). On the contrary, the entire rabbinic system of teaching about God's sovereignty by parable *depended* on the validity of such analogy, as is made clear by the formulae commonly associated with that teaching: namely, the introductory formula, "to what shall we compare it" (?מָשָׁל לְמָה הַדָּבָר דּוֹמֶה) or simply "it is like" (מָשָׁל לְ); and the concluding formula of application (נִמְשַׁל), introduced by "likewise, similarly" (כָּךְ). See further Arland J. Hultgren, *The Parables of Jesus: A Commentary* (Grand Rapids, Mich./Cambridge: Eerdmans, 2000), 5–14. Indeed, without analogy it is impossible to say anything about God at all. Of course, as any competent rabbi or theologian knows, no analogy or group of analogies can be completely *adequate* to the sovereignty of God, but that is another matter. See further Robert W. Jenson, *Systematic Theology* (Oxford: Oxford University Press, 1999), 2.36–38, 161–62.

37. So, again correctly, Morna Hooker: Jesus' opponents "have as usual concentrated on a minor question—the payment of taxes—and so ignored the fundamental question, which was whether or not they were paying to God what they owed to him" (*Mark* 281).

38. See page 12.

39. E.g. Richard J. Cassidy, *Christians and Roman Rule in the New Testament: New Perspectives* (New York: Crossroad, 2001), 27; see also Cassidy, *Jesus, Politics, and Society* (Maryknoll: Orbis, 1978), 61.

40. "The characteristics of the later jurisdiction *extra ordinem* are three in number. First, there is the free formulation of charges and penalties. . . . The second is the insistence on a proper formal act of accusation by the interested party. Third, the cases are heard by the holder of *imperium* in person on his tribunal, and assisted by his advisory cabinet or *consilium* of friends and officials . . . [T]here is insistence upon independent prosecution by third parties. The system is not inquisitorial. There must be a prosecutor. This comes out well in the affair of the Christians. Trajan insists in

his well-known reply to Pliny that all charges must be properly made by the usual process of *delatio* ("conquirendi non sunt, si deferantur et arguantur puniendi sunt" (they are not be sought out; if they are accused and convicted, they ought to be punished) Pliny, *Letters* 10.97.1). The business had indeed begun in this very manner, when the Christians were haled before Pliny by independent accusers ("ad me tamquam Christiani deferebantur" [they were accused before me as Christians] 96.2)" (A. N. Sherwin-White, *Roman Society and Roman Law in the New Testament* [Oxford: Oxford University Press, 1963], 17, 18; the entire section, 12–23, is relevant). So much for Roman practice; as it happens, the same basic pattern—plaintiff, defendant, and adjudicating judge (or judges)—appears in what appear to be reflections of purely Jewish practice from antiquity, e.g. 2 Samuel 12.1–11 (where, of course, the irony is that the king thinks he is the adjudicating judge and then discovers that he is also the defendant), 1 Kings 3.16–28, Daniel 13.1–63 (Susanna and the Elders), Sirach 35.10–18, and Luke 18.2–8.

41. Horsley, *Jesus and Empire*, 13.

42. Ibid., 107.

43. Horsley's cites the Qumran War Scroll as a parallel (*Jesus and Empire*, 101; compare 84–85), and certainly the scroll presents a vivid and unambiguous picture of Rome (the "Kittim") under the sway of Darkness until the time of God's visitation, "at which time the community itself would join the forces of Light in successful battle against the 'Kittim' . . . and the forces of darkness" (84). The gospels, however, while they are certainly clear that in Jesus' work the forces of darkness are being overcome (Mark 3.20–30), conspicuously do *not* identify those forces with any *particular* political structure. That is one obvious difference between the gospels and the Qumran War Scroll. That others made such an identification I do not question. It does not follow, however, that Jesus made it.

44. Horsley, *Jesus and Empire*, 108.

45. See Hooker, *Mark*, 143; Taylor, *Mark*, 281; Cranfield, *Saint Mark*, 178; note, however, cautions offered by Donahue and Harrington, *Mark*, 166.

46. Sugirtharajah, *Postcolonial Criticism*, 93.

47. See Smallwood, *Jews under Roman Rule*, 146–47 on Roman recruitment in Judea.

48. Sugirtharajah, *Postcolonial Criticism*, 94.

49. Horsley, *Jesus and Empire*, 108.

50. Ibid., 109.

51. Sugirtharajah's summary, so far as it goes, is correct: "Jesus' response to an oppressive structure had more to do with personalizing the issue and appealing directly to individuals to act fairly than with calling for a radical overhaul of the system. Jesus challenged the system by appealing to the moral conviction of individuals, and raising their consciousness" (*Postcolonial Criticism*, 90).

52. *Pace* Sugirtharajah, 90, "fox" in both Greek and rabbinical literature implies "crafty," "sly," and "deceitful" (for example, Plutarch, *Solon* 95e [3.2]; Epictetus 1.3.7; *b. Ber.* 61b): see BDAG ἀλώπηξ 2. So, correctly, Florence Mark Gillman, *Herodias: At Home in That Fox's Den* (Collegeville, Minn.: Liturgical Press, 2003), xiii–xiv.

53. See page 41, and n. 8.

54. See Edward W. Said, *Out of Place: A Memoir* (New York: Alfred A. Knopf, 1999), esp. 44–45, 80–106.

55. Said, *Culture and Imperialism*, xxii.

56. Ibid., xxvi.

57. Ibid., 96. Such generosity of spirit is, incidentally, exactly what leads to such a film as the wonderfully postcolonial *Bend It Like Beckham* (Gurinda Chadha, dir. Twentieth Century Fox, 2002), which, while it does not seek to hide anyone's pain— British and Indian, English and Irish, Hindu and Muslim, Caucasian and African, straight and gay, parents and adolescents, elder siblings who manage (more or less) to do what their parents want and younger siblings who keep getting it wrong, protectors of tradition and dreamers of new dreams—yet somehow manages to be generous to all.

58. Meier, *Marginal Jew*, 3.646.

APPENDIX TO CHAPTER 3

1. Horsely, *Jesus and the Spiral of Violence*, 263; see further 261–64 and the entire section 59–145.

2. Ibid., 104.

3. Ibid., 45–47.

4. Ulrich Luz, *Matthew 1–7*, Wilhelm C. Linss, trans. (Minneapolis: Fortress Press, 1989 [1985]), 330; also, with varying emphases, Hengel, *The Zealots*, 181, n. 180; Hans Dieter Betz, *The Sermon on the Mount* (Minneapolis: Fortress Press, 1995), 309; Davies and Allison, *Saint Matthew*, 1.542–43; Wright, *Jesus and the Victory of God*, 290; also Yoder, *Politics of Jesus*, 202, n. 14. Daniel Harrington, S.J., notes, however, that the issue as to "whether it [Matt. 5.39] can be transposed to the social or political realms is a matter of ongoing debate" (*The Gospel of Matthew*, SP1 [Collegeville, Minn.: Liturgical Press, 1991], 88).

5. Michael Battle, *Reconciliation: The Ubunto Theology of Desmond Tutu* (Cleveland, Ohio: Pilgrim Press, 1997), 144.

6. Desmond Tutu, "Spirituality: Christian and African," in *Resistance and Hope: South African Essays in Honour of Beyers Naudé*, Charles Villa–Vicencio and John de Gruchy, eds. (Cape Town: David Philips, 1985), 163.

7. S. G. F. Brandon, *Jesus and the Zealots* (Manchester: Manchester University, 1947).

8. For various responses, see, however, the symposium edited by Ernst Bammel and C. F. D. Moule, *Jesus and the Politics of His Day* (Cambridge: Cambridge University Press, 1984).

CHAPTER 4

1. Horsley, *Jesus and Empire*, 131–32.

2. That Jesus prophesied the destruction of the Temple we need not, I think, question: Mark, evidently, is quite sure that he did (13:1–2).

3. For discussion, see Appendix A.

4. See Appendix B.

5. For discussion of various other theories see Brown, *Death of the Messiah* 1.340–48.

6. J. Blinzler, *The Trial of Jesus* (Westminster, Md.: Newman Press, 1959), 157.

7. See further Brown, *Death of the Messiah*, 1.357–63.

8. Indeed, I have used it myself: see my *Preface to Mark* (New York: Oxford University Press, 1991), 113.

9. Brown, *Death of the Messiah*, 1.520–27.

10. Ibid., 1.520. Luke elsewhere seems unwilling to record directly remarks about or to Jesus that might be perceived as insulting or derogatory (and therefore, from a Christian viewpoint, blasphemous): compare his treatment of Mark 4.38 at Luke 8.24 (see François Bovon, *Luke I*, Christine M. Thomas, trans. [Minneapolis: Fortress Press, 2002], 1.318; Joseph Fitzmyer, *The Gospel according to Luke I–IX* [New York: Doubleday, 1981], 730); compare also Luke's treatment of Mark 8.33, omitted, and of Mark 9.24, also omitted.

11. On the significance of Jesus' "cleansing" of the temple, see page 41. On its connection with Jesus' arrest and arraignment before the Sanhedrin, compare Bond, *Caiaphas*, 67–69.

12. See Appendix B.

13. Brown, *Death of the Messiah*, 1.547; see the whole section, 541–47; also Bond, *Caiaphas*, 68–69.

14. Bond is clear that "there were two clear charges from the Jewish law that could be brought against [Jesus]: leading Israel astray (Deut. 13) and being a false prophet (Deut. 18). The penalty for both was death." She notes that "perhaps Caiaphas regarded Jesus' words and actions against the temple as blasphemous" (*Caiaphas*, 69). My only criticism of this is that Bond appears to interpret "blasphemy" somewhat too narrowly. As I believe I have shown (pages 58–59), Caiaphas would most likely have regarded the whole thing—leading Israel astray, false prophecy, and, in connection with these, Jesus' actions against the temple—as βλασφημία.

15. John's view of *Jewish* law on the matter is made clear later in the narrative, where the representatives of the Sanhedrin say to Pilate, "We have a law, and by that law he ought to die" (John 19.7). See Brown, *Death of the Messiah*, 1.747–49.

16. For discussion, see Appendix C.

17. Schürer revised Vermes, Millar, et al., *History of the Jewish* People, 2.223 and n. 93. Bond (who also regards the question of the Sanhedrin's powers in capital charges as more open than I do) takes more or less the same view of what happened in this case (*Caiaphas*, 69–70).

18. Meier, *Marginal Jew*, 1.66.

19. See further Smallwood, *Jews under Roman Rule*, 156–60.

20. Helen K. Bond, *Pontius Pilate in History and Interpretation*, SNTSMS 100 (Cambridge: Cambridge University Press, 1998), 86. Bond makes the useful suggestion that perhaps something like *m. Shek* 4.2 was in force, allowing for the use of surplus finds for "all the city's needs," but that the building then ran into a cost overrun to which there was objection. As she observes, "building projects are notorious for requiring more money than initially expected" (ibid.). Indeed they are!

21. See Bond, *Pontius Pilate*, 24–48.

22. Compare Brown, *Death of the Messiah*, 1.733–35.

23. Compare Bond, *Pontius Pilate*, 120–37.

24. Compare Bond, *Pontius Pilate* 138–62; Fitzmyer, *The Gospel according to Luke*, 1474.

25. Compare Bond, *Pontius Pilate*, 174–93.

26. Compare Wright, *Jesus and the Victory of God*, 544; Sanders, *Jesus and Judaism*, 329, 294–95.

27. So Horsley notes that Pilate as portrayed in Josephus was "surely not the indecisive figure portrayed in the gospels" (*Jesus and the Spiral of Violence*, 100).

28. Lémonon, *Pilate et le gouvernement de la Judée*, 277–78; similarly B.C. McGing, "Pontius Pilate and the Sources," *CBQ* 53 (1991): 416–38; Bond, *Pontius Pilate*, xvi. These are evidently the most important and useful studies of Pilate to appear in the past three decades. Their interpretations of the Roman governor, though varying in detail (McGing is inclined to be rather kinder to Pilate than Lémonon or Bond), are nonetheless broadly in agreement and largely underpin my own conclusions.

29. Lémonon, *Pilate et le gouvernement*, 273, 274–75.

30. Bond, *Caiaphas*, 54–55. Mason's observation that, according to Josephus, Pilate had "appropriated" the funds (*Josephus and the New Testament*, 167) appears to go beyond Josephus' meaning, for if the governor had taken the funds by force, Josephus would surely have said something about violation of the temple's sanctity. As it is, he merely accuses Pilate of ἐξαναλίσκων ("using up," "spending entirely") the funds for his project (Bond, *Pontius Pilate*, 86). See above n. 20.

31. The theory has been put forward, largely on the basis of some non-Jewish symbols on Pilate's coinage, that Pilate was part of an anti-Jewish plot linked with Sejanus, the supposedly anti-Semitic (so Philo, *Embassy*, 159–60, *In Flaccum*) commander of the Praetorian Guard, a man who, prior to his fall, exercised great influence over Tiberius; this could, indeed, account for the different "Pilates" portrayed by Josephus and Philo, as opposed to the gospels. The former represent the earlier, anti-Jewish, pro-Sejanus Pilate; the latter, a later, more accommodating Pilate post-Sejanus (so Edward Stauffer, *Jerusalem und Rom im Zeitalter Jesu Christi* [Bern: Dalp-Daschbücher 331, Franke, 1957], 16–18; also Smallwood, *Jews under Roman Rule*, 165–67). But Philo may have exaggerated his portrait of Sejanus in order to contrast it with Tiberius' leniency (see Lémonon, *Pilate et le gouvernement*, 224–25). In any case, non-Jewish symbols had been used on Roman coins before, and there is no real evidence in Pilate's coinage either of a desire to provoke the Jews (such as we might infer from the image of a pagan god or of the Emperor, neither of which appear) or a connection with Sejanus (see further Lémonon, *Pilate et le gouvernement*, 276; Bond, *Pontius Pilate*, 21–23).

32. It is *not* clear, despite common assumptions to the contrary, that Pilate retired in disgrace or even that Vitellius, who referred him to Rome after a complaint against him by the Samaritans, thought he was to blame: see the sensible discussion in Bond, *Pontius Pilate*, 92–93.

33. Brown sees as most likely years for the crucifixion either 30 or 33: see *Death of the Messiah*, 2.1373–76.

34. In general, see Smallwood, *Jews under Roman Rule*, 146–47. But, at this period, Syria's governor appears to have been resident at Rome, which could have led to communication problems should the Judean prefect have needed speedy assistance: see Bond, *Pontius Pilate*, 13–15.

35. See Bond, 13, and literature there cited.

36. Brown, *Death of the Messiah*, 1.383–86.

APPENDIX A TO CHAPTER 4

1. See Christopher Bryan, *A Preface to Mark: Notes on the Gospel in Its Literary and Cultural Settings* (Oxford: Oxford University Press, 1993), 67–160.

2. I would have said that the passion narrative is the church's "myth," in the sense of a guiding narrative that functions to provide one's view of the universe: save that I fear the prejudice that associates "myth" with "falsehood" (see, briefly, Christopher Bryan, *And God Spoke* [Cambridge, Massachusetts: Cowley, 2002], 37–39).

3. Thus—to pick virtually at random—the last supper narrative speaks of Jesus' "blood of the covenant" (Mark 14.22-26//), so associating him with traditions of the Exodus (Exod. 24.4–8) and Jeremiah's prophecy of God's coming redemption (Jer. 31.31–34); false witnesses stand up against Jesus at his trial (Mark 14.56–59//), so setting him with the righteous sufferer of the psalms (Ps. 27, 109); Jesus is silent when accused (Mark 14.60–61, 15:44-5//; Luke 23.9), as is the Lord's Servant (Isa. 53:7); he is condemned to shameful death, as is the "just one" (Wisd. 2:12–20); he is struck and spat upon (Mark 28:65//, 15:7–20//; John 18:22), as is the Servant (Isa. 50:6); soldiers cast lots for his garment (Mark 15:24//; John 19:24), passers-by mock him (Mark 15:27–32//); and when he thirsts, bystanders offer him vinegar (John 19:28–29), all again identifying him with the righteous sufferer (Ps. 22:7–8, 18; 69:3, 21; 109:25; Wisd. 3.18). For the use of Scripture by Mark in particular, see Bryan, *Preface to Mark*, 146–50.

4. Hans Conzelmann, *1 Corinthians*, James W. Leitch, trans. (Philadelphia: Fortress, 1975), 255; Raymond Collins, *First Corinthians* Sacra Pagina 7 (Collegeville, Minn.: Liturgical Press, 1999), 534. Ellen Bradshaw Aitken is surely correct when she points also to resonances with Moses and Israel's wilderness tradition (*Jesus' Death in Early Christian Memory: The Poetics of the Passion* [Göttingen: Vandehoeck & Ruprecht / Fribourg: Academic Press, 2004], 32); in Baltzer's view these connections were basic to Deutero-Isaiah's own understanding of the Servant (see *Deutero-Isaiah*, 20–22, and esp. 408–14), and, as Baltzer points out, such connections were certainly present in the later rabbinic tradition (e.g. *b. Sota* 14a, cited ibid., 20 n. 108)

5. Christopher Bryan, *Preface to Romans* (Oxford: Oxford University Press, 2000), 54; see the entire section, 50–54.

6. Of course, Christians did sometimes make that kind of enquiry into Scripture, and it is obviously reflected in passages such as those in which an evangelist tells us that certain things happened in order that such and such a scripture might be fulfilled (e.g. Matt. 2.17–18, 5.14–16, John 19.24, 20.36–37); but that does not affect the main point.

7. Compare Bryan, *Preface to Mark*, 150.

8. John Dominic Crossan, *The Historical Jesus: The Life of a Mediterranean Jewish Peasant* (HarperSanFrancisco, 1991), 387, cf. 375–76; *The Cross that Spoke: The Origins of the Passion Narrative* (San Francisco: Harper and Row, 1988), 405; similarly Helmut Koester: "One can assume that the only historical information about Jesus' suffering, crucifixion, and death was that he was condemned to death by Plate and crucified. The details and the individual scenes of the narrative do not rest on historical memory, but were developed on the basis of the allegorical interpretation of Scripture" (*Ancient Christian Gospels: Their History and Development* [London: SCM /Philadelphia: Trinity Press International, 1990], 224).

9. Crossan, *Historical Jesus*, 375.

10. Ibid.

11. E.g. Pliny the Younger: "Scribit exitus illustrium virorum, in his quorumdam mihi carissimorum." (He writes about the deaths of famous men—among them, somewho were very dear to me.) (*Letters* 8.12.4). See Richard A. Burridge, *What are the Gospels? A Comparison with Graeco-Roman Biography* SNTSMS 70 (Cambridge: Cambridge University Press, 1992), 77, 164–66, 179–80, 208–9.

12. Duane Reed Stuart, *Epochs of Greek and Roman Biography* (Berkeley: University of California Press, 1928), 245; see 243–46.

13. Ibid., 246. See again, Pliny the Younger, *Letters* 8.12.4–5.

APPENDIX B TO CHAPTER 4

1. For discussion see Schürer rev. Vermes, *History of the Jewish People*, 1.430–41; Bond, *Caiaphas*, 61–62; Brown, *Death of the Messiah*, 1.373–78; Crossan, *Historical Jesus*, 373–74; Meier, *Marginal Jew*, 1. 59–69.

2. Schürer rev. Vermes, *History of the Jewish People*, 1.437.

3. Brown, *Death of the Messiah*, 1.373, n. 103.

4. Meier, *Marginal Jew*, 1.61; Crossan, *Historical Jesus*, 373–74.

5. Schürer rev. Vermes, *History of the Jewish People*, 1.437.

6. So Graham N. Stanton, "Jesus of Nazareth: A Magician and a False Prophet Who Deceived God's People?" in *Jesus of Nazareth: Lord and Christ*, Joel B. Green and Max Turner, eds. (Carlisle: Paternoster/Grand Rapids, Mich.: Eerdmans, 1994), 169–71; tentatively accepted by Wright, *Jesus and the Victory of God*, 439.

7. A second passage speaks of Jesus as a sorcerer and false prophet: "Jesus the Nazarene practised magic and led Israel astray" (*b. Sanh.* 106b). It is, however, so full of difficulties (not least that it appears to make Jesus the contemporary of Alexander Jannaeus [103–76 BC]) that it is hard to make much of it. For discussion see, however, *SederNezikin* 3 *Sanhedrin*, Jacob Schachter and H. Freedman, trans. (London: Soncino Press, 1935), 736, n. 2, and literature there cited.

8. Schachter and Freedman, *SederNezikin* 3 *Sanhedrin*, 3.281.

9. See further Otto Betz, "Probleme des Prozesses Jesu," *ANRW* 2.25.1 (1982): 565–647, esp. 570–80.

10. See Louis Ginzberg, *Midrash and Haggadah: Geniza Studies in Memory of Doctor Solomon Schechter*, 1 (New York: Jewish Theological Seminary of America, 1928), nos. 34 and 35.

11. William Horbury, "The Trial of Jesus in Jewish Tradition," in *The Trial of Jesus: Cambridge Studies in Honour of C. F. D. Moule*, Ernst Bammel, ed., SBT 13, 2nd ser. (London: SCM, 1970), 115.

APPENDIX C TO CHAPTER 4

1. Smallwood, *Jews under Roman Rule* 149. Vermes regards the arguments as evenly balanced: see Schürer rev. Vermes, *History of the Jewish People*, 2.218–23.

2. So Jean Juster, *Les Juifs dans l'Empire romaine: leur condition juridique, économiquw et sociale* (Paris: P. Geuthner, 1914). Perhaps the most important response to Juster is that by A. N. Sherwin-White, *Roman Society and Roman Law in the New Testament* (Oxford: Clarendon, 1963), 35–43.

3. So Paul Winter, *On the Trial of Jesus*, 2nd ed. Studia Judaica 1 (Berlin: de Gruyper, 1974).

4. Borne out by an inscription stating that any foreigner found in the Temple "will himself be to blame if his death ensues." See further P. Segal, "The Penalty of the Warning Inscription from the Temple of Jerusalem," IEJ 39 (1989): 79–84.

5. Smallwood, *Jews under Roman Rule*, 150.

6. Sherwin-White, *Roman Society and Roman Law*, 36–37.

7. See V. Ehrenberg and A. H. M. Jones, *Documents Illustrating the Reigns of Augustus and Tiberius*, 2nd ed. (Oxford: Clarendon Press, 1955), # 311; see further F. de Visscher, *Les édits d'Auguste découverts à Cyrene* (Louvain, 1940), 44–49. (These edicts were discovered only in 1927 and were therefore not available to Juster.)

8. The *baraita* says that the right of pronouncing in capital cases was taken from Israel forty years before the destruction of the Temple. There is some argument as to whether this should be taken literally, meaning that it happened in AD 30, or whether (as I would argue) "forty" is here being used in its well-established biblical sense to represent a period of divine testing and retribution and the change actually came with the establishment of direct Roman rule over Judea in AD 6. In either case, the essential fact remains, that *in rabbinic understanding, Roman rule meant that the Jewish courts had lost capital jurisdiction* (see Brown, *Death of the Messiah*, 1.365–66).

9. The evidence really does not allow for much more precision than this: see Bond, *Caiaphas*, 77, 181–82; also C. K. Barrett, *The Acts of the Apostles*, vol. 1, ICC (Edinburgh: T. & T. Clark, 1994), 381–82.

10. So Brown, *Death of the Messiah*, 1.365–66.

11. Bond, *Caiaphas*, 78. Compare David Catchpole who, following Blinzler, suggests that "the trial was interrupted and ended without sentence, and the accused summarily lynched" ("The Historicity of the Sanhedrin Trial," in *The Trial of Jesus: Cambridge Studies in Honour of C. F. D. Moule*, Ernst Bammel, ed., SBT 13, 2nd ser. [London: SCM, 1970], 63; Blinzler, *Trial of Jesus*, 162.

12. Marta Sordi, *The Christians and the Roman Empire*, Annabel Bedini, trans. (London: Croom Helm, 1983), 12–13; similarly, Joachim Jeremias insists on the legality of the proceedings: see "Zur Geschichtlichkeit der Verhörs Jesu vor dem Hohen Rat," ZNW 53 (1950–51): 145–50; cited in Brown, *Death of the Messiah*, 1.370, n. 93.

13. So Bond, *Caiaphas*, 86, 87; Sordi, *Christians and the Roman Empire*, 13.

14. Jeremias, "Geschichtlichkeit," 146–47.

15. There is also, as happens, some confusion about just how many visits Vitellius paid to Jerusalem (compare *Antiquities* 18.120–26). Lémonon speculates that there were as many as three, one in 36 and two in 37: see *Pilate et le gouvernement*, 242–44).

16. So, for example, John Dominic Crossan, *Who Killed Jesus? Exposing the Roots of Anti-Semitism in the Gospel Story of the Death of Jesus* (San Francisco: HarperSanFrancisco, 1996), 148.

17. Bond, *Caiaphas*, 87.

18. Ibid., 87.

19. So Sordi, *Christians and the Roman Empire*, 13.

20. Galatians 1.15–24 appears to put Paul's meeting with the apostles in Jerusalem in 36, that is, fourteen years before 49 CE (including the two years in the reckoning), and three years after the death of Stephen and Paul's conversion.

21. Sordi, *Christians and the Roman Empire*, 15.

22. Smallwood, *Jews under Roman Rule*, 150.

23. See, for example, Rudolph Schnackenburg, *The Gospel according to St. John*, David Smith and G. A. Kon, trans.(New York: Crossroad, 1987 [1975]), 258, also 245; C. K. Barrett, *The Gospel according to St. John*, 2nd ed. (London: S.P.C.K, 1978), 531; Raymond Brown, *The Gospel according to John XII to XIX* (New York: Doubleday, 1970), 877.

24. See J. D. M. Derrett, "Law in the New Testament: The Story of the Woman Taken in Adultery," *NTS* 10 [1963–64], esp. 10–16; Sherwin-White, *Roman Society and Roman Law*, 42; also Barrett, *John*, 590, 592.

25. Sherwin-White, *Roman Society and Roman Law*, 36.

CHAPTER 5

1. Fitzmyer, *The Gospel according to Luke*, 800; Luke Timothy Johnson, *The Gospel of Luke*, Sacra Pagina 3 (Collegeville, Minn.: Liturgical Press, 1991), 153, 156; Bovon, *Luke 1*, 376.

2. As will be clear from what follows, I perceive a natural progression from 11 to 12, and between 12 and 13.1–7, and I see the last passage as particularly appropriate to the Roman situation: see further my *Preface to Romans* (Oxford: Oxford University Press, 2000), 194–208; also N. T. Wright, "The Letter to the Romans," in NIB 10 (Nashville: Abingdon Press, 2002), 718; Anthony J. Guerra, *Romans and the Apostolic Tradition: The Purpose, Genre, and Audience of Paul's Letter*, SNTSMS 81 (Cambridge: Cambridge University Press, 1995), 160–64. Other commentators, however, find the relationship of 13.1–7 to Romans as a whole problematic: see, for example, Ernst Käsemann, *Commentary on Romans*, Geoffrey W. Bromiley trans. (Grand Rapids, Mich.: Eerdmans, 1980), 352; Luke Timothy Johnson, *Reading through Romans* (New York: Crossroad, 1997), 185–91.

3. A number of scholars in the twentieth century, most notably Oscar Cullmann in *The State in the New Testament* (New York: Scribner's, 1956), suggested that by "au-

thorities" (*exousiai*) Paul intended to refer to supernatural and angelic powers that he understood to stand behind empirical states, or else that he intended a reference both to the empirical state and to the supernatural powers. Here let it suffice to say that, in company with most recent exegetes of Romans, I consider this interpretation to be mistaken: see further my *Preface to Romans*, 208–209. Equally mistaken is the suggestion that Paul is referring to the "governing authorities" of the Roman synagogues (Mark Nanos, *The Mystery of Romans: The Jewish Context of Paul's Letter* [Minneapolis: Fortress Press, 1996], 289–336). Fatal to this are, first, Paul's reference to authorities that "bear the sword," which, though not (as commonly assumed) a reference to the *ius gladii* (see earlier discussion) would surely (despite Nanos's ingenious attempt at an alternative explanation) have been understood as referring to the general life-and-death power that was a mark of Roman *imperium*; and, second, Paul's references to φόρος (NRSV "tribute"—probably direct taxes, such as property or poll tax) and τέλος (NRSV "tax"—probably indirect taxes, such as customs and sales tax) (13.7), which (again, despite Nanos's ingenious attempts to find other referents) find their natural place in the context of day-to-day relationships with the Roman authorities (see BDAG φόρος, and τέλος 5).

4. On civil authorities as "instituted by God, see further Bryan, *Preface to Romans*, 209–10.

5. N. Collins, *Diakonia: Interpreting the Ancient Sources* (New York: Oxford University Press, 1990), 335; for usage in Romans, see my *Preface to Romans*, 184–85.

6. Sherwin-White, *Roman Society and Roman Law*, 8–11.

7. Cited, with other relevant material, in Bruce M. Winter, *Seek the Welfare of the City: Christians as Benefactors and Citizens: First Century Christians in the Graeco-Roman World* (Carlisle: Paternoster Press/Grand Rapids, Mich.: Erdmans, 1994), 35.

8. On *leitourgos*, that is, one who performs a public service, see Ceslas Spicq, *Theological Lexicon of the New Testament*, James D. Ernest, trans. (Peabody, Mass.: Hendrickson, 1994), 2.378–84.

9. See above page 45, and footnote 33.

10. In Wilhelm Dittenberger, *Orientis Graeci Inscriptiones Selectae: Supplementum Sylloges Inscriptionum Graecarum* (Hildesheim: George Olms Verlag, 1970 [Leipzig: Hirzel, 1903–5]), 2.458.

11. Cited in Spicq, *Theological Lexicon of the New Testament*, 3.54; see 3.53–55 for numerous other illustrations.

12. Jean Rouffiac, *Recherches sur les caractères du grec dans le Nouveau Testament d'après les Inscriptions de Priène* (Paris: Ernest Leroux, 1911), 73–74. For citation and discussion of some earlier approaches to the phenomenon, see Peter Oakes, *Philippians: From People to Letter*, SNTSMS 110 (Cambridge: Cambridge University, 2001), 129–38.

13. Horsley, *Jesus and Empire*, 134; similarly, Wright, "Romans," 719; John Dominic Crossan and Jonathan L. Reed, *In Search of Paul: How Jesus's Apostle Opposed Rome's Empire with God's Kingdom* (New York: HarperSanFrancisco, 2004), 10–11.

14. The unity of Philippians continues to be debated. This is not the place to enter that debate. Suffice it to say that I personally incline to accept that Philippians is a

unity. See in particular Paul A. Holloway, *Consolation in Philippians: Philosophical Sources and Rhetorical Strategy*, SNTSMS 112 (Cambridge: Cambridge University, 2001), 7–33.

15. This is the only use of this word in the NT: see BDAG πολίτευμα.

16. Though this word occurs in reference to Christ quite frequently in the Pastoral Letters, and once at Ephesians 5.23, this is its only occurrence in the undisputed Pauline letters: see BDAG σωτήρ.

17. Historians differ as to the significance of this account. Some think the difficulties were real and the emperor's assistance genuine: so Peter Salway, *Roman Britain* (Oxford: Clarendon Press, 1981), 85–87. Others (to whose view I personally incline) argue that Aulus Plautius (who seems to have been a perfectly competent soldier) already had the military situation well under control, so that Claudius' coming was merely a successfully stage-managed project that gave military glory to a most unmilitary emperor: so Colin Wells, *The Roman Empire* (Cambridge, Mass.: Harvard University Press, 1984), 111; similarly, R. G. Collingwood and J. N. L. Myers, *Roman Britain and the Early Settlements*, 2nd ed. (Oxford: Clarendon, 1937), 83–85. In either case, the "mythology," which is all that concerns us here, is the same. (Aulus Plautius is, incidentally, interesting to us for another reason: there is every reason to believe that his wife, Pomponia Graecina, was a Christian: see Tacitus, *Annals*, 13.32.3, and comments in Sordi, *Christians and the Roman Empire*, 26–29.)

18. Peter Oakes has demonstrated that while veterans may have been influential in the conduct of affairs at Philippi, their actual number, and hence the number of them who might have been members of the Church, was probably smaller than some commentators seem to imply: see Oakes, *Philippians*, 50–54, 71; contrast, for example, Gerald F. Hawthrone, *Philippians* WBC 43 (Waco, Texas: Word, 1983), xxxiii–xxxiv. On the composition of the Philippian church, see further note 19.

19. Oakes estimates that the membership of the Philippian church was 36 percent Romans and 64 percent Greeks (*Philippians*, 76). Of the latter group, very few would have possessed citizenship (*Philippians*, 72). All, however, would in their varying ways and from their different points of view have been conscious of the significance of Roman control and Roman order in Philippi: see Oakes, *Philippians*, 70–76.

20. Oakes, *Philippians*, 73. Peter Garnsey cites various examples of citizens receiving "a milder penalty than aliens for the same offence" and also, unlike aliens, having "the right of appeal (*provocatio*) against magistrates" (in other words, unlike aliens, citizens were not subect to Roman magisterial coercion [*coercitio*]). In sum, "Discrimination in favour of citizens as opposed to aliens was thus a permanent feature of the Roman judicial system. It was practised in all spheres of the law where aliens were technically excluded, as from the *ius civile*, and where they were not, as in criminal law as administered by the *cognitio* procedure" (*Social Status and Legal Privilege in the Roman Empire* [Oxford: Clarendon Press, 1970], 261, 262). In the particular context of Philippians, it is also worth noting that "Octavian's edict about veterans includes immunities from tribute, local taxes, public duties, and corvées, including the billeting of Roman officials" (Andrew Lintott, *Imperium Romanum: Politics and Administration* [London: Routledge, 1993], 164, citing V. Ehhrenberg and A. H. M.

Jones, *Documents Illustrating the Reigns of Augustus and Tiberius* [Oxford: Oxford University, 1975], 301).

21. Also evidenced by his appeal to his "true yoke fellow" to help them in their reconciliation. It is evident that Euodia and Syntache, "who have struggled beside me in the work of the gospel, together with Clement and the rest of my co-workers, whose names are in the book of life" (Phil. 4.3), were persons who had been of direct personal assistance to Paul in his work. It is possible that one of them is Lydia ("the Lydian woman") of Acts 16.14–15, though that, of course, is only a conjecture (Gerald F. Hawthorne, *Philippians* WBC 43 [Texas: Waco, 1983] 179). Nils A. Dahls has made the interesting suggestion that Euodia's and Syntache's quarrel was actually the presenting symptom that caused Paul to write to the Philippians as he did: see "Euodia and Syntache and Paul's Letter to the Philippians" in *The Social World of the First Christians: Essays in Honor of Wayne Meeks*, L. Michael White and O. Larry Yarborough, eds. (Philadelphia: Fortress Press, 1995), 3–15.

22. See above, page 46.

23. Oakes, *Philippians*, 138–47.

24. Ibid., 138.

25. On metaphor, see Sandra M. Schneiders, *The Revelatory Text: Interpreting the New Testament as Sacred Scripture*, 2nd ed. (Collegeville, Minn.: Liturgical Press, 1999), esp. 27–40. For a brief, more popular introduction to the question, see my *And God Spoke: The Authority of Scripture for the Church Today* (Cambridge, Mass.: Cowley, 2002), 51–56. On analogy generally (of which metaphor is a particular and very powerful form), see above, page 144, note 36.

26. Oakes, *Philippians*, 147–74.

27. Ibid., 149.

28. Richard Bauckham, "The Worship of Jesus," in *Where Christology Began: Essays on Philippians 2*, Ralph P. Martin and Brian Dodds, eds. (Louisville, Ken.: Westminster John Knox, 1998),133–34; Bauckham, *God Crucified: Monotheism and Christology in the New Testament* (Grand Rapids, Mich./ Cambridge: Eerdmans, 1999), 51–53, 56–61. Bauckham is, of course, building on earlier important discussions, notably Ernst Lohmeyer, *Kurios Jesus: Eine Untersuchung zu Phil, 2,5–11* (Heidelberg: Carl Winter, 1928, 1961²), 33–36, and Lucien Cerfaux, "L'hymne au Christ-Serviteur de Dieu (Phil., II, 6–11 = Isa., LII, 13–LIII, 12)," in *Miscellanea historica in honorem Alberti de Meyer* (Louvain: Bibliothèque de L'Université/Bruxelles: Le Pennon, 1946), 1.117–130. "Le contraste entre l'humiliation et l'exaltation du Christ, qui fournit le suget de l'hymne, est inspiré du chant du Serviteur de Dieu (*Is.*, LII, 13–LIII, 12) (The contrast between the exaltation and the humiliation of Christ, which furnishes the subject matter of the hymn, is inspired by the Song of the Servant of God [Isa. 52.13–53.12])" (ibid., 118). Oakes cites Bauckham and concedes that Phil. 2.5–11 "presumably does carry an idea of worship" (*Philippians*, 169) but considers his own focus on "Christ not the Emperor" as "the true figure of authority" (*Philippians*, 170) to be better directed toward the main thrust of the passage. (A survey of studies of the Philippians hymn in the twentieth century is to be found in Ralph P. Martin, *A Hymn of Christ: Philippians 2:5–11 in Recent Interpretation & in the Setting of Early Christian Worship*

[Downers Grove, Ill.: InterVarsity Press, 1997], 24–95. The range of interpretations that has been offered is wide, and I should perhaps admit that in my main text I have limited myself to discussing those that I personally consider to have a degree of credibility.)

29. Oakes, *Philippians*, 168.

30. BDAG ὑπερυψόω; but the point was noticed by J. B. Lightfoot, *Saint Paul's Epistle to the Philippians* (London: Macmillan, 1885 [1868]), 113.

31. Oakes, *Philippians*, 151; see 151–60.

32. Bauckham, *God Crucified*, 58–61.

33. For example, G. B. Caird, *Paul's Letters from Prison* (Oxford: Oxford University Press, 1976), 118–24; N. T. Wright, *The Climax of the Covenant: Christ and the Law in Pauline Theology* (Edinburgh: T & T Clark, 1991), 57–62; Charles B. Cousar, *Reading Galatians, Philippians, and 1 Thessalonians: A Literary and Theological Commentary* (Macon, Ga.: Smyth & Helwys, 2001), 154.

34. Compare Bauckham, *God Crucified*, 57. The notion that language can or should only mean one thing at a time is an entirely post-Enlightenment phenomenon and certainly would not have occurred to Paul or his hearers. Much ancient literary interpretation proceeds, indeed, on the assumption that language—and especially the best language, the language of poets and prophets—will naturally mean more than one thing at once: see Christopher Bryan, *Preface to Romans* (Oxford: Oxford University Press, 2000), 71–72.

35. See Bryan, *Preface to Romans*, 77–83, 124–29; Hans Conzelmann, *1 Corinthians*, James W. Leitch, trans. (Philadelphia: Fortress Press, 1975), 267–69.

36. Wright, *Resurrection of the Son of God*, 228.

37. J. B. Lightfoot, *Saint Paul's Epistle to the Philippians* (London: Macmillan, 1868), 110; F. W. Beare, *A Commentary on the Epistle to the Philippians* (London: Adam & Charles Black, 1959), 75–76; Ernst Käsemann, "A Critical Analysis of Philippians 2: 5–11," in *God and Christ: Existence and Providence*, Robert W. Funk, ed. (New York: Harper, 1968), 45–88; Ralph P. Martin, *Philippians* (Grand Rapids, Mich.: Eerdmans, 1976), 91–93; Hawthorne, *Philippians*, 80–81; Larry H. Hurtado, "Jesus as Lordly Example in Philippians 2:5–11," in *From Jesus to Paul*, Peter Richardson and John C. Hurd, eds. (Waterloo, Belgium: Wilfred Lauieer, 1984), 113–126; Stephen Fowl, *The Story of Christ in the Ethics of Paul: An Analysis of the Function of the Hymnic Material in the Pauline Corpus* JSNTSup. (Sheffield: JSOT, 1990), 77–101; Holloway, *Consolation in Philippians*, 121–23.

38. For example, Käsemann, "Critical Analysis," 83–88; Martin, *Hymn of Christ*, 71–74, 84–88; Cousar, *Galatians, Philippians, and 1 Thessalonians*, 155; but contrast G. N. Stanton, *Jesus of Nazareth in New Testament Preaching*, SNTSMS 27 (Cambridge: Cambridge Univerity Press, 1974), 99–103; Hawthorne, *Philippians*, 79–80; Holloway, *Consolation in Philippians*, 23, 121–23.

39. Cousar, *Galatians, Philippians, and 1 Thessalonians*, 155. Paul seems to use exactly the same kind of argument at 2 Cor. 8.6–9: there, too, Christ's actions are both warrant and paradigm for the actions to which Paul summons his hearers.

40. See page 84 and note 21.

41. "All these things he [Paul] says for the consolation (*paramuthia*) of the Phi-

lippians" (Chrysostom, *In Epist. ad Phil.* [*PL* 30.842.C]); cited in Holloway, *Consolation in Philippians*, 46. On letters of consolation (*paramuthētikai*) generally, see Stanley K. Stowers, *Letter Writing in Greco-Roman Antiquity* (Philadelphia: Westminster, 1986), 142–51. On Philippians as a letter of consolation, see Holloway, *Consolation in Philippians*, especially 34–83.

42. Richard J. Cassidy, *Christians and Roman Rule in the New Testament: New Perspectives* (New York: Crossroad, 2001); Cassidy, *Paul in Chains: Roman Imprisonment and the Letters of St. Paul* (New York: Crossroad, 2001).

43. Cassidy, *Paul in Chains*, 191–92.

44. Hooker, "Philippians," in NIB vol. 11 (Nashville: Abingdon, 1996), 475–76; Cousar, *Galatians, Philippians, and 1 Thessalonians*, 125–27.

45. See Bryan, *Preface to Romans*, 231–32; N. T. Wright, "Romans," 764–65.

46. Cassidy, *Paul in Chains*, 144–62.

47. See the useful comments in Chris Mearns, "The Identity of Paul's Opponents at Philippi," *NTS* 33 (1987): 198–99; also Beare, *Philippians*, 104–105; Hawthorne, *Philippians*, 123; Cousar, *Galatians, Philippians, and 1 Thessalonians*, 126.

48. So Ben Witherington III, *Friendship and Finances in Philippi: The Letter of Paul to the Philippians* (Valley Forge, Pa.: Trinity Press International), 53; Hawthorne, *Philippians*, 58.

49. Hooker, "Philippians," 496–97; similarly Cousar, *Galatians, Philippians and 1 Thessalonians* 147.

50. Oakes, *Philippians*, 99; see 72–99. Impressive here is Oakes's imaginative reconstruction of how a family of craft workers—likely to have been the most numerous group in the Philippian church—might have experienced hardship as a result of their becoming Christians: see *Philippians*, 89–91. While Oakes focuses on economic problems as a cause of the Philippians' distress, Holloway focuses on Paul's imprisonment (*Consolation in Philippians*, 45–47). There seems to be no reason why both elements should not have played their part, reinforcing each other in causing the kinds of pressure that would have led the Philippian Christian community to disintegrate in precisely the ways that Paul perceived.

51. Thomas Jefferson's first draft of the Virginia Constitution asserted against George III that "he has waged cruel war against human nature itself, violating its most sacred rights of life & liberty in the persons of a distant people who never offended him, captivating & carrying them into slavery in another hemisphere, or to incur miserable death in their transportation thither. this piratical warfare, the opprobrium of *infidel* powers is the warfare of the *Christian* king of Great Britain. determining to keep open a market where MEN should be bought & sold, he has prostituted his negative for suppressing every legislative attempt to prohibit or to restrain this execrable commerce" (cited in Pauline Maier, *American Scripture: Making the Declaration of Independence* [New York: Knopf, 1997] 120). If that paragraph, or something like it, had survived into the final Declaration of Independence of the United States, it would surely have committed the new nation to an irrevocable opposition to slavery. Unfortunately, Congress removed the paragraph before adopting the Declaration—according to Jefferson's notes, "in complaisance to South Carolina & Georgia," and with the consent of "Northern brethren" who had few slaves themselves but were "pretty

considerable carriers of them to others" (Maier, *American Scripture*, 146). So the opportunity was lost. In John Adams's view, the Congress had "obliterated some of the best of it [the Declaration], and left all that was exceptionable, if anything in it was. I have long wondered that the original draft had not been published. I suppose the reason is the vehement philippic against Negro slavery" (*The Works of John Adams, Second President of the United States*, Charles Francis Adams, ed., vol. 2, *The Diary* [Boston: Little, Brown, 1850]). Certainly that deletion left a deadly ambiguity about the Constitution's attitude toward Negro slavery and the racism that went with it, an ambiguity that was exploited by slaveholders for a century. One irony of this story is that Jefferson, who could write insightfully—indeed, prophetically—about the evils of slavery (see his *Notes on the State of Virginia* [1781–85] Query 18), could not bring himself to part with his own slaves and remained a slaveholder until his death (see Dumas Malone, *Jefferson and His Time*, vol. 6: *The Sage of Monticello* [Boston: Little, Brown, 1981], 318, 488–89, 513, and—for comment that is a good deal more pungent—Michael Lind, *The Next American Nation: The New Nationalism and the Fourth American Revolution* [New York: Free Press, 1995], 369–71, 375–76). Another irony is that, in the end, the British abolished slavery before the Americans did. The British Parliament passed the Slavery Abolition Act, which gave all slaves in the British Empire their freedom, in 1833. More than thirty years later, on 1 February 1865, President Lincoln approved Amendment 13 to the U.S. Constitution, which did the same for the United States. See Hugh Thomas, *The Slave Trade: History of the Atlantic Slave Trade, 1440–1870* (New York: Simon & Schuster, 1997), 459–785.

52. "And so even though we face the difficulties of today and tomorrow, I still have a dream. It is a dream deeply rooted in the American dream. I have a dream that one day this nation will rise up and live out the true meaning of its creed: 'We hold these truths to be self-evident, that all men are created equal.' . . . I have a dream that my four little children will one day live in a nation where they will not be judged by the color of their skin but by the content of their character" (Martin Luther King, speaking in Washington, D.C., August 28, 1963).

53. I use the phrase "various forms of imperial cult" advisedly. As Mary Beard, John North, and Simon Price have reminded us, there was in fact "no such thing as '*the* imperial cult.'" That phrase is simply a convenient way in which "to group together some rather different practices which in a variety of ways across the empire related the emperor to the gods" (*Religions of Rome*, vol. 1, *A History* [Cambridge: Cambridge University Press, 1998], 348; see further 140–49, 206–10, and [esp.] 348–63); compare Ittai Gradel, *Emperor Worship and Roman Religion* (Oxford and New York: Clarendon Press, 2002), 7–8.

54. Samuel Sandmel, "Parallelomania," *JBL* 81 (1962). Sandmel was discussing those who appealed to rabbinic "parallels" to the New Testament regardless of their date and regardless of the content and context of the passages in which the alleged "parallels" occurred. Evidently, the caution that Sandmel required in that area of study is required, *mutatis mutandis*, in our appeal to classical and imperial parallels also.

55. Crossan and Reed, *In Search of Paul*, 11.

56. Gradel, *Emperor Worship and Roman Religion*, 263; see 262–76.

57. See J. J. Collins, *Scepter and the Star: The Messiahs of the Dead Sea Scrolls and*

Other Ancient Literature (New York: Doubleday, 1995) 154–72; Joachim Schaper, *The Eschatology of the Greek Psalter.* WUNT 2/71 (Tübingen: Mohr-Siebeck, 1995) 138–44.

58. See N. T. Wright, *Climax of the Covenant: Christ and the Law in Pauline Theology* (Edinburgh: T. & T. Clark, 1991), 30, 43–44; Larry W. Hurtado, *Lord Jesus Christ: Devotion to Jesus in Earliest Christianity* (Grand Rapids, Mich.: Eerdmans, 2003), 101–108.

59. See e.g. Stephen J. Friesen's stunning description of the relationship of the gods and the emperors as presented by the Temple of the Sebastoi at Ephesus (*Twice Neokoros: Ephesus, Asia, and the Cult of the Flavian Imperial Family* [Religions in the Graeco-Roman World 116; Leiden: E. J. Brill, 1993], 74–75)

60. For discussion see Sordi, *Christians and the Roman Empire*, 17–20.

61. See below, pages 115–19.

62. Oakes, *Philippians*, 149.

63. Ibid., 170.

CHAPTER 6

1. I use the name "Luke" as a convenience. For discussion, see Fitzmyer, *Luke I–IX*, 35–53; Johnson, *Luke*, 2–3; Bovon, *Luke 1*, 8–12. Personally, I agree with Fitzmyer that "some of the modern objections to the traditional identification are not all that cogent," although it actually "makes little difference to the interpretation" (53).

2. Jacob Jervell, *The Theology of the Acts of the Apostles* (Cambridge: Cambridge University Press, 1996) 11–17; Luke Timothy Johnson, *The Acts of the Apostles.* SP (Collegeville, Minn.: Liturgical Press, 1992), 7–9. Johnson, in contrast to Jervell, sees Luke's intended audience as chiefly gentile.

3. C. K. Barrett, *A Critical and Exegetical Commentary on the Acts of the Apostles.* Vol. 2. *Introduction and Commentary on Acts XV–XXVIII.* ICC (Edinburgh: T & T Clark, 1998), xlix–liv.

4. Richard J. Cassidy, *Jesus and Politics in the Acts of the Apostles* (Maryknoll, New York: Orbis, 1987) 145–70.

5. Steve Walton, "The State They Were in: Luke's View of the Roman Empire," in *Rome in the Bible and the Early Church* (Carlisle: Paternoster Press/Grand Rapids, Mich.: Baker Academic, 2002), 32–33; Gregory E. Sterling, *Historiography and Self-Definition: Josephos, Luke-Acts and Apologetic Historiography* (Leiden: E. J. Brill, 1992), 382–83.

6. Paul C. Walawskay, *And So We Came to Rome.* SNTSMS 49 (Cambridge: Cambridge University Press, 1983), 15–37; Robert M. Maddox, *The Purpose of Luke-Acts* (Edinburgh: T & T Clark, 1982), 96–97.

7. See Henry J. Cadbury, *The Making of Luke-Acts* (reprint London: SPCK 1958 [1927]), 308–16; Burton Scott Eastman, *Early Christianity: The Purpose of Acts and other Papers* (Greenwich, Conn.: Seabury Press, 1954), 42–57; Hans Conzelmann, *The Theology of St. Luke*, Geoffrey Buswell, trans. (London: Faber and Faber, 1960 [1953]), 137–44, 149; Werner Georg Kümmel, *Introduction to the New Testament*, A. J. Mattill, Jr., trans. (London: SCM Press, 1966 [1965, 14th ed.]), 110–11; Robert F. O'Toole,

"Luke's Position on Politics and Society in Luke-Acts," in *Political Issues in Luke-Acts* (Maryknoll, New York: Orbis, 1983), 1–17; P. F. Esler, *Community and Gospel in Luke-Acts: the Social and Political Motivations of Lucan Theology*, SNTSMS 57 (Cambridge: Cambridge University Press, 1987), 201–19; F. F. Bruce, *The Book of Acts* (Grand Rapids, Mich.: Eerdmans, 1988), 8–13; Harry W. Tajra, *The Trial of St. Paul: A Juridical Exegesis of the Second Half of the Acts of the Apostles*, WUNT 2.35 (Tübingen: J. C. B. Mohr [Paul Siebeck], 1989), 199; Sterling, *Historiography and Self-Definition*, 311–389; Ben Witherington III, *The Acts of the Apostles: A Socio-Rhetorical Commentary* (Carlisle: Paternoster Press/Grand Rapids, Mich.: Eerdmans, 1998), 810–11; Helen K. Bond, *Pontius Pilate in History and Interpretation*, SNTSMS 100 (Cambridge: Cambridge University Press, 1998), 161–62; François Bovon, *Luke 1: A Commentary on the Gospel of Luke 1.1–9.50*. Christine M. Thomas, trans. (Minneapolis, Minn.: Fortress Press, 2002), 9. This (admittedly, in various forms and with at time quite sharply different emphases) may with some justification be described as the "classic" view, since it was presented as early as 1720 by C. A. Heumann, "Dissertio de Theophilo, cui Lucas historiam sacram inscripsit," in *Bibliotheca Historico–philologico-Theologica, Class. IV* (Bremen, 1720), 483–505.

8. Barrett, *Acts*, 2. xlviii. Cadbury did, indeed, attempt an answer to an earlier statement of the same objection, "*de gustibus non disputandum est*" (*The Making of Luke-Acts*, 316), but if course it will not do. With Barrett compare Bruce, *Acts*, 12–13; Kümmel, *Introduction*, 111.

9. Philip F. Esler, *Community and Gospel in Luke-Acts: The Social and Political Motivations of Lucan Theology* (Cambridge: Cambridge University Press, 1987), especially 1–23, 201–219. Esler draws for these concepts (as he makes clear) on the seminal work of P. L. Berger and T. L. Bruckmann, *The Social Construction of Reality: A Treatise in the Sociology of Knowledge* (London: Faber and Faber, 1966; Garden City, New York: Doubleday, 1967); also P. L. Berger, *The Social Reality of Religion* (London: Faber and Faber, 1969).

10. Compare Sterling: "I would like to suggest that Luke-Acts served to help Christians understand their place in the Roman empire . . . Josephos made his case directly to the Hellenistic world; Luke-Acts makes its case *indirectly* by offering examples and precedents to Christians so that they can make their own *apologia*" (*Historiography*, 385, 386).

11. See Beard, North, and Price, *Religions of Rome*, 1.222–23; Gradel, *Emperor Worship and Roman Religion*, 23–24.

12. BDAG οἰκουμένη; see Fitzmyer, *Luke I–IX*, 1.400; Johnson, *Luke*, 49. " 'World,' for Luke, [is] the *imperium Romanum*" (Bovon, *Luke 1* 83).

13. Johnson, *Luke*, 51.

14. Horsley, *Jesus and Empire*, 12; compare Bovon, *Luke 1*, 83.

15. Raymond Brown, *The Birth of the Messiah: A Commentary on the Infancy Narratives in Matthew and Luke* (Garden City, N.Y.: Image Books, 1977), 416–17.

16. So Fitzmyer, *Luke I–IX*, 393–94; Esler, *Community and Gospel in Luke-Acts*, 202–202.

17. Brown, *Birth of the Messiah*, 415–16; Fitzmyer, *Luke I–IX*, 393–94.

18. *Pace* Richard J. Cassidy, *Jesus, Politics, and Society: A Study of Luke's Gospel*

(Maryknoll, N.Y.: Orbis, 1978); for critique of Cassidy's view, see John H. Talbert, "Martyrdom in Luke-Acts and the Lucan Social Ethic" in *Political Issues in Luke-Acts*, Richard J. Cassidy and Philip J. Scharper, eds. (Maryknoll, New York: Orbis, 1983), 106–109; Esler, *Community and Gospel in Luke-Acts*, 207–208.

19. Luke has substituted the more generally used φόρος (tribute) for Mark's and Matthew's Latinism κῆνσος (= Latin *census*), but in the context the word still refers to the Roman poll tax levied on the inhabitants of Judea (Fitzmyer, *Luke X–XXIV* 1296). Luke has also introduced the word "ἡμᾶς (for us)," which, if it has any affect at all on the overall sense, appears to emphasize the practical relevance of the question. For my overall understanding of this pericope, see above pages 42–46.

20. Esler, *Community and Gospel in Luke-Acts*, 218–19; see further A. D. Nock, "The Roman Army and the Roman Religious Year," *HTR* 45 (1952): 187–252.

21. See above, page 12.

22. See Esler, *Community and Gospel in Luke-Acts*, 203.

23. Among some commentators it seems to have become virtually conventional wisdom that Luke's description of Gallio's behavior at Acts 18.12–17 reflects the latter's anti-Semitism (e.g. Ernst Haenchen, *The Acts of the Apostles*, Bernard Noble, Gerard Shinn, and R. McL. Wilson, trans. (Philadephia: Westminster Press, 1971), 536; Johnson, *Acts*, 333; Cassidy, *Christians and Roman Rule*, 59; Witherington, *Acts*, 551–54; Walton, "The State They Were In," 24). Perhaps the historical Gallio was indeed anti-Semitic. Some upper rank Romans evidently were, and it appears that Seneca, Gallio's younger brother, was one of them (Augustine, *City of God* 6.11). On the other hand, some upper rank Romans evidently were not, and elder and younger siblings do not always agree with each other. Indeed, if Gallio were known to be gracious to people whom Seneca despised, then the latter's praise of him gains poignancy and point—"nemo enim mortalium uni tam dulcis est quam hic omnibus" (for no one is so good-natured even with one person as he is with everyone) (*Naturales Quaestiones* 41. *Praefatio* 11). What then of Acts 18.12–17? To begin with, *pace* virtually all the scholars I have just mentioned, nothing whatever of Gallio's attitude can be read into the expression "ὦ Ἰουδαῖοι" (see BD 146; Barrett, *Acts*, 2.874). All Luke actually tells us—and this surely is what is important for him, and why he tells the story at all—is that Gallio considered that plaintiffs who brought charges against Christians before a Roman court were wasting his and the court's time, and so he threw out the case (ἀπήλασεν αὐτοὺς ἀπὸ τοῦ βήματος) (Barrett, *Acts* 2.875). "His final words, κριτὴς ἐγὼ τούτων οὐ βούλομαι εἶναι, are the precise answer of a Roman magistrate refusing to exercise his *arbitrium iudicantis* within a matter *extra ordinem*" (Sherwin-White, *Roman Society and Roman Law in the New Testament*, 102). By that refusal, Gallio in effect found for the defendant, who, from his point of view, was of course just as Ἰουδαῖος as were the plaintiffs. As for Sosthenes' being beaten (18.17), given the antecedent αὐτους (and despite the Western and later ecclesiastical texts, to which we do not normally give credence when they stand over against earlier manuscripts) the most natural way of understanding Luke's Greek is that the πάντες who beat Sosthenes were the Jews themselves (so the text is interpreted in the miniscules 36, 453) (see Tajra, *Trial of St. Paul*, 59). Various motives for such an action, or combinations of motives, might be suggested. As an "official of the synagogue," did the Corinthian

Jews hold Sosthenes responsible for the evidently inadequate presentation of their case? Was Sosthenes actually showing sympathy with the Messianists (was he influenced by Crispus' example? is he the Sosthenes whom Paul later names as co-author of 1 Corinthians?)? Were the Corinthian Jews deliberately challenging Gallio's grounds for dismissal ("You asked for a real crime! Well, here it is! A genuine breach of the peace! What are you going to do about it?")?—in which case, one might argue that Gallio acted both sensibly and humanely in refusing to be provoked (καὶ οὐδὲν τούτων Γαλλίωνι ἔμελεν): a humanity that would, incidentally, accord very well with the "bonitatem publicam (general benevolence)" attributed to him by his elder brother (ibid.). Of course we cannot answer any of these questions, and we should not pretend that we can. More immediately, we should concede that Acts 18.12–17 provides no evidence at all as to whether Gallio was anti-Semitic, or even pro-Semitic, and neither, for that matter, does any other ancient testimony to him.

24. Luke 28.7: the precise sense of this title is not clear (the local magistrate, perhaps?), but epigraphic evidence confirms that Luke is correct in applying it here to a leading personage on the island of Melita (Malta).

25. Cassidy, *Christians and Roman Rule*, 57–58.

26. Ibid., 67.

27. Robert F. O'Toole, S.J., review of Richard J. Cassidy, *Society and Politics in the Acts of the Apostles*, in *Biblica* 70 (1989): 426; compare Barrett, *Acts*, 2.1253.

28. Esler, *Community and Gospel in Luke-Acts*, 210.

29. Tajra, *Trial of St. Paul*, 24–29, 73–76, 81–89.

30. O'Toole, review of Cassidy, *Society and Politics*, 426.

31. Horsley, *Jesus and Empire*, 12.

32. "Paul insists on an official escort, not so much for protection, but as a visible reprobation of the magistrates' illegal conduct. The two apostles wanted this signal gesture of deference so that the rumour would not go about the city that they had escaped from the prison and so that the foes of the Christian mission would not be able to say that the new doctrine was being preached by criminals" (Tajra, *Trial of St. Paul*, 28).

33. See Rapske, *Acts and Paul in Roman Custody*, 288–307.

34. Horsley, *Jesus and Empire*, 12.

35. In his own account of the hardships he has suffered (2 Cor. 11:22–29), Paul speaks of three Roman arrests ("three times . . . beaten with rods"), and six Jewish (five "forty lashes minus one" and once "stoned").

36. "In the chapters devoted to Paul's trial before Roman authorities (21-28), we are not dealing with a political-apologetic aspect, with Roman authorities as addressees, but with the charges directed against Paul from the Jews (21:21, 28; 23:29; 24:5; 25:8, 19; 28:17)" (Jervell, *Theology of Acts*, 15–16). While, as I have indicated, I am not convinced by Jervell's conclusion—that there is *no* political-apologetic aspect to what Luke writes—still, Jervell's analysis of what Luke actually *says* at this point is correct, and indisputable.

37. John Dominic Crossan and Jonathan L. Reed, *In Search of Paul: How Jesus's Apostle Opposed Rome's Empire with God's Kingdom* (New York: HarperSanFrancisco, 2004), 30–32.

38. Esler, *Community and Gospel in Luke-Acts*, 204–205.

39. The apostle Peter was *martyred* under Nero in the 60s, and I use the name "Peter" as a convenience. While definitive decisions as to the authorship and date of 1 Peter are impossible, and while the very lack of anything "identifiably Petrine" in the latter argues for some genuinely historical association with the apostle, still the most likely conclusion on the basis of the evidence we have seems to be that it is the work of an author writing in the apostle's name, at some time round about AD 90, from Rome. See the very careful and detailed discussion in Paul J. Achtemeier, *1 Peter* (Minneapolis, Minn.: Fortress Press, 1996), 1–50; similarly, Donald P. Senior, in Donald P. Senior, C.P., and Daniel J. Harrington, S.J., *1 Peter, Jude, and 2 Peter*, Sacra Pagina 15 (Collegeville, Minn.: Liturgical Press, 2003), 4–8.

40. So, for example, Achtemeier, *1 Peter*, 35–36; Senior, *1 Peter*, 7–8.

41. Achtemeier, *1 Peter*, 188; see 182–88; also Senior, *1 Peter*, 72–73.

42. See above, page 80.

43. Winter, *Seek the Welfare*, 1, 18.

44. Bryan, *Preface to Romans* 206, note 49. The liberationist commentator Pablo Richard states the theological issue precisely: "all power comes from God and hence in itself is good. This power coming from God is given to the Roman empire. When the empire becomes a beast by reason of its idolatrous and criminal character, the beast transforms this power that comes from God into a power that is perverse. Revelation makes a discernment between the power that comes from God and the power that becomes criminal and blasphemous in the hands of the beast. There is no contradiction between Romans 13 and Revelation 13" (*Apocalypse: A People's Commentary on the Book of Revelation* [Maryknoll, New York: Orbis, 1995], 109–10).

45. לְעָבְדָהּ וּלְשָׁמְרָהּ: " 'to till it and keep (or guard) it' . . . Work is regarded here as an essential part of human existence. Life without work would not be worthy of human beings. Just as in Genesis 1:1–2:4a the activity of the creator follows the rhythm of work and rest (as F. Delitzsch has noted), so too God-given human existence follows a pattern of duty. Human existence cannot have meaning or fulfillment without such obligation" (Claus Westermann, *Genesis 1–11*, John J. Scullion S.J., trans. [Minneapolis, Minn.: Augsburg, 1984], 220). It appears to me that Paul's themes and his choice of rhetoric at Romans 1.18–32 indicate that he had in mind *both* the stories of human creation and disobedience in Genesis 1–3, *and* the stories of Israel's disobedience in, for example, LXX Psalm 105 (MT 106) (see further my *Preface to Romans*, 78–79, 82–83), though a number of critics continue to deny the association (e.g. Philip F. Esler, *Conflict and Identity in Romans: The Social Setting of Paul's Letter* [Minneapolis, Minn.: Fortress, 2003], 148–49).

46. Adela Yarbro Collins, *Crisis and Catharsis: The Power of the Apocalypse* (Philadelphia: Westminster, 1984), 73. Similarly Steven J. Friesen is clear that in Ephesus "the imagery, used to articulate the cult of the Sebastoi, was not imposed from Rome. The concept of the neokoros city, the design of the temple, the sculptural figures, and the architectural program all originated in the Greek east. The symbolic systems used in the cult show that the institutions were part of the Asian heritage. As such, the religious imagery reflected local values. The developments in the religious traditions of western Asa Minor . . . were conscious, creative transformations by participants in

those traditions who sought to express a new situation using the received symbolic vocabulary" (*Twice Neokoros: Ephesus, Asia, and the Cult of the Flavian Imperial Family* [Religions in the Graeco-Roman World 116; Leiden: E. J. Brill, 1993], 75). Such affirmation of the imperial in terms of the local, leading to an expression that was (in this case) neither strictly Roman nor strictly Ephesian, is an impressive example of what some postcolonial critics refer to as "hybridity": "The term hybridity has been sometimes misinterpreted as indicating something that denies the traditions from which it springs, or as an alternative and absolute category to which all post-colonial forms inevitably subscribe but, as E. K. Brathwaite's early and influential account of Jamaican creolisation made clear, the 'creole' is not predicated upon the idea of the disappearance of independent cultural traditions but rather on their continual and mutual development. The interleaving of practices will produce new forms even as older forms continue to exist. The degree to which these forms become hybridised varies greatly across practices and between cultures" (*The Post-Colonial Studies Reader*, Bill Ashcroft, Gareth Griffiths, and Helen Tiffin, eds. [London: Routledge, 1995], 184).

47. Yarbo Collins, *Crisis and Catharsis*, 73; see further 99–104.

48. Elizabeth Schüssler Fiorenza, *Revelation: Vision of a Just World* (Minneapolis, Minn.: Fortress, 1991), 126–27.

49. Leonard Thompson, *The Book of Revelation: Apocalypse and Empire* (New York: Oxford University Press, 1990), 166–67.

50. See Thompson, *Book of Revelation*, 193; see 154–58, 174–76.

51. Robert M. Royalty, *The Streets of Heaven: the Ideology of Wealth in the Apocalypse of John* (Macon, Ga.: Mercer University Press, 1998), 34–35.

52. Ibid., 28. "Commentators have generally assumed a situation in which some sort of emperor worship is required in order to participate in commerce." In Royalty's view, however, "the connection between Emperor worship, military power, persecution of Christians, and commerce can only be found in Revelation 13. Just as John tries to associate his three main opponents—the Romans, the Jews, and rival Christian teachers—with Satan in the seven messages, here in Revelation 13 he tries to connect all aspects of social life in a satanic conspiracy theory. Where modern apocalyptic theorists issue alarmist bulletins over shortwave radio, John sent apocalyptic visions by prophetic letter" (ibid., 186).

53. Richard Bauckham, *The Theology of the Book of Revelation*. New Testament Theology (Cambridge: Cambridge University Press, 1993), 38–39.

54. Several studies over the past few decades seem ready to accept Irenaeus' dating virtually without discussion (e.g. Wilfred J. Harrington, *Revelation*, Sacra Pagina 16 [Collegeville, Minn.: Liturgical Press, 1993], 9; M. Eugene Boring, *Revelation* [Louisville, Ken.: John Knox, 1989], 10; G. B. Caird, *The Revelation of St John the Divine* [London: A. & C. Clark, 1966], 6, 14). Yet Irenaeus' dating is not without its problems, nor are there lacking ancient witnesses who offer other suggestions (e.g. Epiphanius, *Haer.* 51.12, 32 [the reign of Claudius]; Tertullian, cited in Jerome, *Adv. Jovin.* 1.26 [the seer's exile was during Nero's reign]). For an intelligent defense of Irenaeus' view see, however, Steven J. Friesen, *Imperial Cults and the Apocalypse of John* (New York: Oxford University Press, 2001), 138–43.

55. In this latter connection, we should note, some interpreters continue to place

far too much weight on Suetonius' assertion that Domitian insisted on being called "our Lord and God" (*dominus et deus noster*) [*Domitian* 8.13.2]—an allegation now agreed by many scholars to be an exaggeration on Suetonius' part, if not an outright fabrication: see Friesen, *Imperial Cults*, 148–50; Pat Southern, *Domitian: Tragic Tyrant* (London: Routledge/Bloomington: Indiana University Press, 1997), 114–15; Brian W. Jones, *The Emperor Domitian* (London and New York: Routledge, 1992), 114–17; Albert A. Bell, "The Date of John's Apocalypse: The Evidence of Some Roman Historians Reconsidered," in *New Testament Studies* 25 (1978–79): 93–102, especially 94–97; Smallwood, *Jews under Roman Rule*, 381–82; L.W. Barnard, "Clement of Rome and the Persecution of Domitian," in *New Testament Studies* 10 (1963–64): 251–60.

56. Royalty, *Streets of Heaven*, 246; compare 177–210.

57. Wilfred J. Harrington, O.P., *Revelation*, Sacra Pagina 16 (Collegeville, Minn.: Liturgical Press, 1993), 234.

58. So Royalty argues, correctly, that the fundamental thrust of Revelation's rhetoric is epideictic (seeking to affect its audience's values or views), rather than deliberative (seeking to persuade its audience to a specific course of action): "the few calls for action in the text are vague; what does it mean to 'hold fast' (3:11), 'rest a little longer,' (6:11), or 'calculate the number of the beast' (13.18)? Rev 13:18 also calls for wisdom; understanding is more important than action. The visions describe 'what is, and what is to take place' (1:19) rather than what the audience should do. While the implied author asserts that events are going to happen in the future, the rhetorical function of these assertions is to change the audience's mind in the present" (*Streets of Heaven* 128; also 199 n. 61).

59. For a proper treatment of various matters that I have presumed merely to file by title in the paragraphs above, see Robert W. Jenson's superb chapter, "The Other Creatures," in his *Systematic Theology* 2.112–32.

60. Eusebius states plainly that, "Vespasian never planned any action against us [Christians]"; he takes, of course, a very different view of Domitian (*Ecclesiastical History*, 3.17).

61. Again, for convenience' sake, I take the normal scholarly view, which regards the Pastorals as pseudonymous and post-Pauline (e.g. Raymond F. Collins, *I & II Timothy and Titus* [Louisville and London: Westminster John Knox, 2002]; Jerome D. Quinn, *The Letter to Titus*, Anchor Bible 35. [New York: Doubleday, 1990]).

62. I believe the theological claim made by John the seer in Revelation was in itself true to the biblical tradition, and therefore has its place as corollary, or coda, to that tradition: namely, that whoever or whatever seriously claims for itself the worship that is owed to God alone, by that fact becomes God's enemy. That granted, let me say plainly that I identify with those who are extremely uncomfortable with the violence of the seer's imagery, and, in particular, with his note of violence toward women. Pablo Richardson suggests that "the hatred and violence found in certain texts of Revelation express the limit of extreme oppression and anguish that the community is undergoing. Revelation reproduces the feelings in order to produce a catharsis (release and purification) in those listening, and thereby transform their hatred into awareness." This goes some way toward addressing the issue, although given our uncertainty over the actual historical situation facing John, it may be that

we should qualify "oppression" as "perceived oppression." Even so, I am not at all sure that Richardson has really addressed the *problem*. Tina Pippin, who (if I understand her correctly) is far more certain than I am about "the evils of Roman imperial policy in the colonies," nonetheless states that problem concisely: "I find the violent destruction of Babylon very cathartic. But when I looked into the face of Babylon, I saw a woman" (*Death and Desire: the Rhetoric of Gender in the Apocalypse of John* [Louisville, Ky.: Westminster/John Knox Press, 1992], 80). Exactly. As Adela Yarbro Collins has said, "[Revelation's] attitudes . . . have a dark side of which interpreters of the Apocalypse must be conscious and whose dangers must be recognized. If Revelation's vision of the future is adopted, it must be in the full realization that it is a partial and imperfect vision. . . . A critical reading also leads to an awareness of how the text is flawed by the darker side of the author's human nature, which we, like all readers, share" (Collins, *Crisis and Catharsis*, 172).

CHAPTER 7

1. Horsley, *Jesus and Empire*, 1, citing Said, *Culture and Imperialism*, 318.

2. When Horsley wrote *Jesus and the Spiral of Violence* (published 1993), he had not, I assume, read *Culture and Imperialism*, also published in 1993. He cites, however, the work of G. Balandier ("The 'Colonial Situation' Concept," in *The Sociology of Black Africa* [New York: Praeger, 1970], 21–56; "The Colonial Situation: A Theoretical Approach," in I. Wallenstein, ed., *Social Change: The Colonial Situation* [London: Wiley, 1966], 34–61), and P. Worsley, *The Third World* [London: Wiedenfeld & Nicolson, 1964]), and applies their discussion "to Palestinian Jewish history from the Babylonian to the Roman empire" (329).

3. Horsley, *Jesus and Empire*, 144. It is only marginally germane to my subject, but for the sake of completeness it should perhaps be pointed out that some observers see this vast consumption by the United States, coupled with enormous debt, as a sign not so much of misused power as of a fundamental weakness. Indeed, in contrast to the views of Horsley and others cited earlier in this study (for example, Horsley, *Jesus and Empire*, 137–49: see above, page 32), such analysts doubt whether the twenty-first-century United States has an "empire" at all, in the sense in which Rome, Britain, and France had empires. See e.g. Arthur J. Schlesinger Jr., "The Making of a Mess," in *The New York Review* 51.14 (2003): 40–43; Emmanuel Todd, *After the Empire: The Breakdown of the American Order*, C. Jon Delogu, trans. (New York: Columbia University Press, 2003), 59–99; Jeremy Rifkin, *The European Dream* (New York: Tarcher/Penguin, 2004), 58–85; for a more popular presentation, see T. R. Reid, *The United States of Europe: The New Superpower and the End of American Supremacy* (New York: Penguin, 2004), 227–43.

4. For general discussion of such values and their significance for our understanding of the period in general and the New Testament in particular, see for example David A.de Silva, *Honor, Patronage, Kinship and Purity: Unlocking New Testament Culture* (Downers Grove, Ill.: InterVarsity Press, 2000); Hanson and Oakman, *Palestine in the Time of Jesus*; also Bruce J. Malina, *The New Testament World: Insights from Cultural Anthropology*, rev. ed. (Louisville, Ky.: Westminster John Knox, 1993) (contains

useful material, although the author's comparisons with contemporary societies should generally be treated with caution); Jerome H. Neyrey, *Honor and Shame in Matthew* (Louisville, Ky: Westminster John Knox, 1998); and Neyrey, *The Social World of Luke—Acts: Models for Interpretation* (Peabody, Mass.: Hendrickson, 1991); on honor and shame, and solidarity, see Christopher Bryan, *A Preface to Romans: Notes on the Letter in its Literary and Cultural Setting* (Oxford: Oxford University Press, 2000), 72–75, 129–33, and literature there cited.

5. Bear, North, and Price, *Religions of Rome*, 1.212; also 75.

6. Mason, *Josephus and the New Testament*, 135.

7. The point is stunningly made in Said's brilliant analysis of the role played by "Antigua" in Jane Austen's *Mansfield Park*, to which I have already referred: see *Imperialism and Culture*, 83–97, and see pages 11–12. In this connection, one ought at least to note that in certain cases, post–Enlightenment colonizers were themselves as much victims of the colonizing system as were the colonized, as in the extraordinary attempt by the British government to export its "criminal classes" to Australia during the late eighteenth and nineteenth centuries. In the event, the experiment produced a successful society, but that success does not alter the fact that the project itself was inhumane and barbaric, both in its attitude toward the original inhabitants of the Australian continent and in its attitude toward those who were transported. See Robert Hughes, *The Fatal Shore: A History of the Transportation of Convicts to Australia, 1787–1868* (London: Collins Harvill, 1987).

8. "Cogita te missum in provinciam Achaiam, illam veram et meram Graeciam, in qua primum humanitas litterae, etiam fruges inventae esse creduntur. . . . Habe ante oculos hanc esse terram, quae nobis miserit iura, quae leges . . . dederit." So when Juvenal cries out, "non possum ferre, Quirites, / Graecam urbem" (Quirites, I can't abide a city [i.e., Rome] that's Greek!) (*Satires* 3.60–61), by the very style and content of his irritation he illustrates what he decries—that there is in fact a great deal of Greek influence and fashion in Rome. Juvenal's spite appears to me to be much closer in spirit to that of a certain kind of American or Englishman who sneers at (and at the same time is clearly somewhat threatened by) French or Italian culture than it is to the same American or Englishman perhaps only vaguely aware that there even *is* such a thing as Native American or African culture.

9. See pages 107–110.

10. The later writings of Tertullian, it is true, urge a practice of Christianity that goes far to debar Christians from participation in the empire (see *De Corona Militum* and *De Idolatria*), but those works, produced at about the years 211–212, are already saturated with Montanism, to which Tertullian would eventually convert.

11. See Robert M. Grant, *Greek Apologists of the Second Century* (Philadelphia: Westminster, 1988), 83–111; also Sordi, *Christians and the Roman Empire*, 72–75.

12. Grant, *Greek Apologists*, 114.

13. Wells, *Roman Empire*, 242–43; on Philippians 1.27–30, see above 89 and notes 50.

14. In Beard, North, and Price, *Religions of Rome*, 2.343–44.

15. Pliny himself does not recount such accusations, but the fact that he speaks of "flagitia cohaerentia nomini" (crimes associated with the name) and considers it

worth reporting to the emperor that the Christians come together only "ad capiendum cibum promiscuum tamen et innoxium" (to take food of an ordinary, harmless kind) (*Letters* 10.96.2,7) suggests that he may have heard something like them. To judge from the way in which some Christians talked about members of rival Christian groups (e.g. Epiphanius of Cyprus, *Panarion*, 26.4–5), there may actually have been something in the rumors: in which case, pagans were hardly to be blamed if they had difficulty distinguishing between one group calling itself Christian and another. See Robert L. Wilken, *The Christians as the Romans Saw Them* (New Haven and London: Yale University Press, 1984), 17–22; Beard, North, and Price, *Religions of Rome*, 225–27, 2.338–43.

16. Beard, North, and Price, *Religions of Rome* 243–44; see also *OLD contumacia* 2 and *coercitio* 2. Although Pliny does not use the word *contumacia* in connection with Christians, it is clear that that is what he is talking about: "neque enim dubitabam, qualecumque esset quod faterentur, pertinaciam certe et inflexibilem obstinationem debere puniri" (for nor did I doubt that, whatever the nature of their admissions, their stubbornness and unshakeable obstinacy surely ought to be punished) (*Letters* 10.96.3). Marcus Aurelius evidently takes for granted the unreasonable stubbornness of Christians (*Meditations* 11.3).

17. Beard, North, and Price, *Religions of Rome*, 243–44. An interesting sidelight on this growth may be evidenced by developments in both the pagan and the Christian calendars. In 274 the Emperor Aurelian established December 25, the day of the winter solstice, as a festival, "the day of the birth of the unconquered sun" (dies natalis solis invicti). Since this involved imagery not unsuited to Christian understanding of the coming of "Sun of Righteousness" (Mal. 4:2; cf. Luke 1:78–79), and since there is no *biblical* evidence as to the date of Christ's nativity, it is possible that the Christian and pagan rites influenced each other. The "history of religions" hypothesis, which is still probably the most widely held view of the origin of Christmas, is that the Christian festival was a deliberate attempt to "Christianize" the associations of the pagan rite (see, for example, John Gunstone, *Christmas and Epiphany* [London: Faith Press, 1967], 11–14, 15–21; Marion J. Hatchett, *Commentary on the American Prayer Book* [New York: Seabury Press, 1980], 39, 86). An alternative to this hypothesis is, however, the "computation hypothesis," first propounded by Louis Duchesne at the beginning of the twentieth century and more recently revived by Thomas Talley. Duchesne, although he did not totally reject the possibility of influence from the coincidence of *Sol novus*, nonetheless regarded as "most satisfactory" the view that "the date for the birth of Christ was fixed from the assumed starting point of His Passion" (see Louis Duchesne, *Christian Worship: Its Origin and Evolution*, M. L. McLure, trans. [London: SPCK, 1903], 261–65; Thomas J. Talley, *The Origins of the Liturgical Year* [New York: Pueblo, 1986], 87–103). In summarizing and evaluating this discussion, J. Neil Alexander makes the intriguing additional suggestion that if pagans and Christians influenced each other over the date of Christmas, the influence might have worked the other way. What if Aurelian's new feast at Rome in 274 were actually an imperial *response* to the increasing size and influence of the Christian movement? See J. Neil Alexander, *Waiting for the Coming: The Liturgical Meaning of Advent, Christmas, Epiphany* (Washington, D.C.: Pastoral Press, 1993), 46–51. Using elements of what is

held to be *superstitio* in the process of guiding people to *religio* has certainly been a factor in Christian mission, but there is no reason to assume that Christians were the only ones who ever thought of it.

18. See Horsley, *Jesus and Empire*, 6–9; O'Donovan, *Desire of the Nations*, 1–12, 243–52.

19. There is now fairly general scholarly agreement as to the Roman rationale for persecuting: see G. E. M. de Ste. Croix, "Why Were the Early Christians Persecuted?" *Past and Present* 26 (1963): 6–38; T. D. Barnes, "Legislation against the Christians," *JRS* 58 (1968): 32–50; Wilken, *Christians as the Romans Saw Them*, 62–67; and Beard, North, and Price, *Religions of Rome*, 1.225–26, 239–44, 361–64. On Roman understanding of *superstitio* (and its companion term *religio*) see especially Beard, North, and Price, *Religions of Rome*, 1.215–27. Texts written in Greek tend simply to call the Christians *atheoi* ("godless"), which came, in effect, to the same thing. Lucian of Samosata is not untypical. He sees Christians as gullible, contemptible, and somewhat absurd. He *accuses* them, however, of one thing only: that their fellowship is established, "ἐπειδὰν ἅπαξ παραβάντες θεοὺς μὲν τοὺς Ἑλληνικοὺς ἀπαρνήσωνται" (*when they have transgressed once and for all and denied the gods of Greece*) (*Peregrinus* 13) (see *Peregrinus* 11–13; also Cassius Dio 67.14; *Martyrdom of Polycarp* 9).

20. Again and again, by the Christians' own accounts, refusal to honor the gods is the reason why Roman authorities punished them—sometimes, it appears, with reluctance, and after repeated attempts at persuasion (for example, *Martyrdom of Polycarp* 9.2–12.2; Justin, *First Apology*, 5–6; *The Acts of Justin and Companions* 5; *The Acts of the Scillitan Martyrs*; *The Acts of Cyprian* 3–4; Eusebius, *Ecclesiastical History* 5.1.53–54, 7.11.7–10; *The Martyrdom of Perpetua and Felicitas* 6; *The Martyrdom of Crispina* 1–3; *The Martyrdom of Pionius* 9.9–13; also relevant are Cyprian, *De lapsis* 8–9; and, from the pagan side, Trajan's response to Pliny in Pliny, *Letters* 10.97.2, and Caecilius' speech against the Christians in Minucius Felix, *Octavius* 6.1, 8.1–4, 9.1).

21. Wilken, *Christians as the Romans Saw Them*, 63; see also Mason, *Josephus and the New Testament*, 56–58. Wilkens's citations are from *Acts of the Scillitan Martyrs* 3, 5.

22. *Pace* Crossan and Reed, *In Search of Paul*, 10.

23. Compare Ittai Gradel, *Emperor Worship and Roman Religion* (Oxford: Clarendon Press, 2002), 3–4, 23–25.

24. Ibid., 1–2; the entire section, 1–4, is important. Gradel's puts forward an overall thesis is that "the man-god divide in the pagan context" reflects "a distinction in *status* between the relative beings, rather than a distinction between their respective natures, or 'species'" (ibid. 26). This view of the situation is certainly not accepted by all students of Greco-Roman religion: see for example Graham Wheeler's review in *Digressus* 3 (2003): esp. 3–4 (at http://www.nottingham.ac.uk/classics/digressus/reviews/r010103.pdf). This debate does not, however, affect Gradel's description of the situation between the church and Rome, which simply reflects the evidence (for which, see note 20). Thus Wheeler (who by no accepts Gradel's view of "the man-god divide") is nonetheless clear that "Roman religion was characteristically more interested in praxis than dogma." Hence, "the Roman world produced no pagan Aquinas; no controversies arose as to whether Jupiter was *factus* or *genitus*; Romandom, as a Gibbon might put it, was never divided by an iota" (ibid., 4).

25. Herbert Musurillo, S.J., ed. and trans., *The Acts of the Christian Martyrs* (Oxford: Clarendon, 1972).

26. "Illis nomen factionis accommodandum est qui in odium bonorum et proborum conspirant, qui adversum sanguinem innocentium conclamant, praetexentes sane ad odii defensionem illam quoque vanitatem, quod existiment omnis publicae cladis, omnis popularis incommodi Christianos esse in causam. Si Tiberis ascendit in moenia, si Nilus non ascendit in arva, si caelum stetit, si terra movit, si fames, si lues, statim Christianos ad leonem! adclamatur." (They deserve the name of faction who conspire to bring hatred upon good and virtuous persons, who cry out against the blood of the innocent, offering as pretext for their hatred the baseless plea that they think that Christians are the cause of every public disaster, of every affliction that the people suffer. If the Tiber rises up to the city walls, if the Nile fails to rise to the fields, if the skies give no rain, or there is an earthquake, if there is a famine, if there is a plague, at once they clamour, 'Christians to the lion!') (Tertullian, *Apology*, 40.1–2.) On the general point, see Beard, North, and Price, *Religions of Rome*, 1.242–43.

27. See Wilken, *Christians as the Romans Saw Them*, 164–205; Henry Chadwick, *The Church in Ancient Society: From Galilee to Gregory the Great* (Oxford: Oxford University Press, 2001), 295–313.

28. W. D. Davies, *Invitation to the New Testament* (London: Darton, Longman, & Todd, 1967), 19. For my point, see e.g. Richard M. Rothaus, *Corinth: The First City of Greece* (Leiden: Brill, 2000), 135–40.

29. Horsley, *Jesus and Empire*, 31.

30. See, for example, Schwartz, *Imperialism and Jewish Society*, 23, 36–44; Hengel, *Judaism and Hellenism*, 1.6–57.

31. Schwartz, *Imperialism and Jewish Society*, 40, n. 55.

32. Horsley, *Jesus and Empire*, 11; cf. Freyne, *Galilee, Jesus, and the Gospels* (Dublin: Gill & Macmillan, 1988), 94–95; Wells, *Roman Empire*, 246–47. Still, even here we must not exaggerate. When Warren Carter says that the Roman system lacked "checks and balances, burdens of proof, and a sense of public accountability" (*Pontius Pilate: Portraits of a Roman Governor* [Collegeville, Minn.: Liturgical Press, 2003], 48), either he is stating the obvious or he is wrong. If he means that the Romans did not have such public accountability in the manner of a modern Western democracy, then he merely states the obvious. No pre-Enlightenment polity had public accountability of that kind. If he means that the Romans had no sense of public accountability at all, then he is wrong. It is a matter of fact that the Romans *did* sometimes put magistrates, provincial governors, and the like on trial at the end of their terms of office, if charges were brought against them (e.g. under Tiberius, a governor of Syria was charged with political and military misdemeanors, as well as with practicing magic and poisoning [see *JRS* 87 (1997), 250–53]). No doubt, with the Romans as with us, there were ways of avoiding all this and (as we say) "getting away with it" (one thinks of President Ford pardoning his predecessor), but that is not the point.

33. Cassidy, *Christians and Roman Rule*, 5–9.

34. Ibid., 9.

35. Carter, *Pontius Pilate*, 35–54.

36. Ibid., 52.

37. *Life of Brian* (Terry Jones, dir., Handmade Films Ltd./Python [Monty] Pictures Ltd., 1979).

38. Said, *Culture and Imperialism*, 9–10. For a powerful fictional portrayal of the kind of thing Said was describing in terms of the British nineteenth-century imperial vision, see R. F. Delderfield, *God Is an Englishman* (London: Hodder & Stoughton, 1970), 14–15; for a fictional view that locates itself with gentle humor in the experiences of the colonized, I have already referred to Smith, *The No. 1 Ladies Detective Agency.*

39. *M. Tulli Ciceronis de imperio Cn. Pompeii ad quirites oratio* (Speech to the Citizens of Rome regarding the Appointment of Gn. Pompeius): the title *On the Manilian Law* has become customary but has no ancient authority.

40. "Reverere conditores deos et nomina deorum, reverere gloriam veterem et hanc ipsam senectutem, quae in homine venerabilis, in urbibus sacra. Sit apud te honor antiquitati, sit ingentibus factis, sit fabulis quoque. Nihil ex cuiusquam dignitate, nihil ex libertate, nihil etiam ex iactatione decerpseris. Habe ante oculos hanc esse terram, quae nobis miserit iura, quae leges non victis sed petentibus dederit, Athenas esse quas adeas Lacedaemonem esse quam regas; quibus reliquam umbram et residuum libertatis nomen eripere durum ferum barbarum est. . . . Recordare quid quaeque civitas fuerit, non ut despicias quod esse desierit; absit superbia asperitas. Nec timueris contemptum. An contemnitur qui imperium qui fasces habet, nisi humilis et sordidus, et qui se primus ipse contemnit? Male vim suam potestas aliorum contumeliis experitur, male terrore veneratio acquiritur, longeque valentior amor ad obtinendum quod velis quam timor. Nam timor abit si recedas, manet amor, ac sicut ille in odium hic in reverentiam vertitur. Te vero etiam atque etiam—repetam enim— meminisse oportet officii tui titulum ac tibi ipsum interpretari, quale quantumque sit ordinare statum liberarum civitatum. Nam quid ordinatione civilius, quid libertate pretiosius?"

41. See Wilken, *Christians as the Romans Saw Them*, 1–30; Betty Radice in *The Letters of the Younger Pliny*, Betty Radice, ed. and trans. (London: Penguin, 1963), 23–29.

42. Smallwood, *Jews under Roman Rule*, 180.

43. Ibid., 174.

44. Here, perhaps, is something of a parallel to the question of how far, from a third-world point of view, is a discipline that is being developed within Western universities not suspect in itself? Could it be one more example of colonization, differing from its predecessors only in subtlety? Although I do not think the criticism really fair, since Said himself was so clear about where he was (as we say) "coming from" (e.g., *Culture and Imperialism*, xxvi–xxvii) still, one is aware that he and other postcolonial intellectuals have been criticized precisely on the grounds that they have been seduced by the Western academy: see Aijaz Ahmad, *In Theory: Classes, Nation, and Literature* (London: Verso, 1992), 195–97.

CHAPTER 8

1. In R. V. C. Bodley, *In Search of Meaning* (London: Hale, 1955), ch. 12.

2. Gillman, *Herodias*, xiii, citing William Barclay, *The Gospel of Luke*, rev. ed. (Philadelphia: Westminster, 1975).

3. Michael Doyle, "Kant, Liberal Legacies, and Foreign Affairs," in *Philosophy and Public Affairs*, 1 and 2, no. 12 (1983): 205–235, 323–353; see also Emmanuel Todd, *After the Empire: The Breakdown of the American Order*, C. Jon Delogu, trans. (New York: Columbia University Press, 2003), especially 10–11, 19–20, 45–57. Doyle's suggestion has been (somewhat notoriously) adapted in Francis Fukuyama's theories about an "end of history" following the collapse of the Soviet Union (Fukuyama, *The End of History and the Last Man* [New York: Free Press, 1992], 262–63).

4. In which connection, we must note the case made by some observers for claiming that within the *forms* of liberal democracy the United States and (in somewhat different ways) France and Great Britain all show signs of moving in the direction of *oligarchy*: see Todd, *After the Empire*, 16–20; also Michael Young, *The Rise of the Meritocracy* (London: Thames and Hudson, 1958); Michael Lind, *The Next American Nation: The New Nationalism and the Fourth American Revolution* (New York: Free Press, 1995), 139–216. Doyle himself, it should be pointed out, sees the "continuing peace" that is "the promise of liberal legacies among liberal regimes" as conditional upon that fact that "republican foundations and commercial sources of interdependence remain firm" ("Kant, Liberal Legacies, and Foreign Affairs," 233–34). In any case, in generally formulating our hopes for world peace and stability, it is evident that other elements than the mere fact of formal "democracy" have to be taken into consideration: see again the stimulating discussion in Todd, *After the Empire*, 45–58.

5. Compare Smith, *Religion of the Landless*, 204–205; Yoder, *Politics of Jesus*, 6.

6. As regards *King Lear*, while the point made in my main text is, I think, enough to sustain my argument, it may be noted that Lear's behavior, particularly in the opening scene, is in Shakespeare's terms actually a good deal *more* culpable than I have stated. Not only does Lear choose to abandon his kingship, he also plans that

> we shall retain
> Th'name, and all th'addition to a king. The sway,
> Revènue, execution of the rest,
> Beloved sons, be yours. (1.137–40)

In other words, Lear wants to continue having the glory; he just can't be bothered to do the work. Added to which, even in the moment of abandoning his responsibility (indeed, as his last act in its exercise) in mere pique he acts with gross injustice toward his liegeman Kent and his daughter Cordelia. In the case of Kent, the only offense committed is, as Gloucester says, "honesty" (1.2.127). In the case of Cordelia, she herself challenges the king to admit that

> It is no vicious blot, murder, or foulness,
> No unchaste action or dishonored step,
> That hath deprived me of your grace and favor;

> But even that for want of which I am richer,
> A still soliciting eye, and such a tongue
> That I am glad I have not. (1.1.229–233)

—all of which, implicitly, Lear *does* admit when, in response, he can accuse her of nothing worse than the incredibly feeble "not t'have pleased me better" (1.1.236).

In the drama that follows, various persons act wickedly—notably Goneril, Regan, Edmond, and Cornwall. But all of them receive space in which to act in this way largely because of the power vacuum that Lear has created. So he has some responsibility for their sins, too. We are left—and presumably are meant to be left—with the uncomfortable feeling that if they had been properly ruled by their king, they would have been free to be better people. At one point Lear accuses Goneril to Regan of having forgotten

> The offices of nature, bond of childhood,
> Effects of courtesy, dues of gratitude. (2.4.181–82)

The irony in the situation is, however, only too obvious, for Lear is complaining that Goneril is behaving in exactly the way he *taught* her to behave, as illustrated by his own treatment of Cordelia and Kent at the beginning of the play.

Possibly there was some contemporary political mileage in all this for Shakespeare. As Dennis Kay says, "when Lear is shown mismanaging and mistreating his family, behaving in a strikingly unjust way, and above all dividing the kingdom, he is the polar opposite of King James" (*Shakespeare: His Life, Work, and Era* [New York: Quill William Morrow, 1992], 317). But in any case, for Shakespeare and his contemporaries, their understanding of Lear's behavior would have remained the same, whatever the current political situation. It is Lear's moral failure to live up to his responsibilities that causes disaster for himself and those around him. So when Northrop Frye claims that "the Gloucester tragedy perhaps can—just—be explained in moral terms, the Lear tragedy cannot" (*Northrop Frye on Shakespeare*, Robert Sadler, ed. [New Haven and London: Yale University Press, 1986], 113), one can only say of this generally perceptive literary critic that in this case he has completely missed the point. It is, incidentally, with much the same understanding of the responsibility of power and office that Dante Alighieri, about four centuries earlier, had condemned Pope Celestine V for "il gran rifiuto" (*the great refusal*)—Celestine having been persuaded to resign the papal office by, as was believed, the man who succeeded him, Boniface VIII. In Dante's view, such dereliction of public duty was "per viltà" (*because of cowardice*) (*Inferno* 3.60) and could earn for its perpetrator nothing but to be with those who are condemned to be forever in the Gate of Hell, persons who lived "sanza 'nfamia e sanza lodo" (*without disgrace and without praise*) (3.36). This is the proper place for those who are guilty of such dereliction, since it involves a refusal to make that free human choice which is God's gift, and as such is as fundamental even to Hell as it is to Purgatory and Paradise. (I am grateful to my friend and colleague Leslie Richardson, Professor of Italian at The University of the South, for drawing my attention to this. The identification is not made explicit, but there can be little doubt that Dante intended it, and that his intention would have been recognized by his contemporaries: see Anna Maria Chiavacci Leonardi, *Dante Alighieri Commedia* 1 *Inferno* [Milan: Arnoldo Mondadori, 1991], 87, 99).

7. *Pace* Smith, *Religion of the Landless*, 204–15.

8. Philip Birnbaum, *The Birnbaum Haggadah* (New York: Hebrew Publishing Company, 1976), 84.

9. Ibid., 84.

10. William J. Danaher, "Pacifism, Just War, and the Limits of Ethics," *STR* 46.3 (2003): 339; see the whole article. Nothing could demonstrate more clearly the need for serious reflection on what may constitute "justifiable war" than the chaotic thinking that led the United States and its allies into the Iraq war.

11. For other prophetic voices during the period of apartheid, see Trevor Huddleston, C.R., *Nought for Your Comfort* (Johannesburg: Hardingham & Donaldson/ London: Collins, 1956), an exposé of the evils of apartheid, as witnessed by Fr. Huddleston during his time as Prior of the Church of Christ the King in the black township of Sophiatown, and Alan Paton, *Cry, the Beloved Country: A Story of Comfort in Desolation* (London: Jonathan Cape, 1948), a novel about life in South Africa under apartheid. Paton himself was also a tireless writer, worker, and witness against apartheid: see Peter F. Alexander, *Alan Paton: A Biography* (Oxford: Oxford University Press, 1994).

12. Anna Elisabeth Rosmus, *Against the Stream: Growing Up Where Hitler Used to Live.* Imogen von Tannenberg, trans. (Columbia, S.C.: University of South Carolina), 3–4.

Index of Holy Scripture

Index of Authors and Sources